DANGEROUS WORDS
Language and Politics in the Pacific

D0060775

Dangerous Words
Language and Politics in the Pacific

edited by

Donald Brenneis

Fred R. Myers

WAVELAND
PRESS, INC.
Prospect Heights, Illinois

For information about this book, write or call:
Waveland Press, Inc.
P.O. Box 400
Prospect Heights, Illinois 60070
(708) 634-0081

Cover: Samoan *matai*. (Photograph by Annette Weiner.)

Dedicated to the Memory of
Michelle Z. Rosaldo

Contents

Preface, 1991   ix

Introduction: Language and Politics in the Pacific
Fred R. Myers and Donald Brenneis   1

I.   Egalitarian Polity: The Production of Contexts of
Understanding   31

   1. "Wrapped Words": Poetry and Politics among the Wana of
Central Sulawesi, Indonesia   *Jane Monnig Atkinson*   33

   2. Straight Talk and Sweet Talk: Political Discourse
in an Occasionally Egalitarian Community
Donald Brenneis   69

   3. Who Speaks Here? Formality and the Politics of Gender in
Mendi, Highland Papua New Guinea   *Rena Lederman*   85

   4. Putting Down Roots: Information in the Language
of Managalase Exchange   *William H. McKellin*   108

II.   Autonomy: Language, Objects, and the Limits of Control   129

   5. Words That Are Moving: The Social Meanings
of Ilongot Verbal Art   *Michelle Z. Rosaldo*   131

   6. From Words to Objects to Magic: "Hard Words" and the
Boundaries of Social Interaction   *Annette B. Weiner*   161

   7. Of Symbolic Anchors and Sago Soup: The Rhetoric
of Exchange among the Chambri of Papua New Guinea
Deborah Gewertz   192

III.   Hierarchy: Speech and the "Taken-for-Granted" Polity   215

   8. *Lāuga* and *Talanoaga:* Two Speech Genres in a
Samoan Political Event   *Alessandro Duranti*   217

9. Three Perspectives on Role Distance in Conversations
between Tongan Nobles and Their "People"
George E. Marcus   243

Bibliography   267
Index   281

Preface, 1991

The initial versions of all but three of these papers were presented at a symposium, "Language and Politics in Oceania: The Social Ecology of Speech Events," held at the 1979 Annual Meetings of the Association for Social Anthropology in Oceania, Galveston, Texas. Both authors' revisions of the original papers and the introductory chapter were guided strongly by discussions during the symposium. Unfortunately, considerations of length and the timetable for the original publication made it impossible to publish all the papers from the symposium; we selected papers on the basis of their coherence as a whole.

As we note in the introductory chapter, this volume argues that talk makes a political difference. Speech is, in effect, social action. Language clearly affords a remarkable resource for individual strategizing and maneuver. Beyond this, however, styles, structures and situations of language use actively shape not only the political contours of daily life in these communities but also broader understandings of and sentiments about the social world.

The ways in which such shaping is effected are rarely straightforward. Reconceptualizing politics from a language-focussed perspective calls into question basic assumptions about the nature and varieties of power, as well as about how it is organized, allocated and used in particular societies. The papers in this volume focus to some extent on language *about* power; all are more concerned, however, with language and language use *as* power. How do the formal and interactional features of talk in particular events — whether ostensibly political or not — reflect the "political" dimension of community life, and how do they allow for its ongoing definition, experience and transformation? What is there in the way such talk is conducted that in itself creates and sustains social life?

It is clear that in writing about talk we are not primarily concerned with "texts." Talk is both process and product. As process, it necessarily involves more than a single speaker, entangling individual performers, their conversational interlocutors, audience members and those who, while not present, will in the future learn all that happened. Political talk is almost always coperformed, and the structures available for participation in themselves are often politically definitive. As product, that is, as what we might record as a transcript, talk displays patterns of stylistic, poetic and linguistic features specific to particular activities. Central to this volume is exploring links between such specifics of verbal performance and the social practices which they help constitute. Since the original publication of *Dangerous Words*, numerous studies pursuing such connections in considerable detail have appeared, most notably Karen Watson-Gegeo and Geoffrey White's (1990) edited volume on conflict discourse in the Pacific and Lawrence Goldman's (1988) detailed accounts of disputing language among the Huli of Papua New Guinea.

Central to this volume and to such subsequent studies is the understanding that language does much more than reflect what is going on elsewhere in sociopolitical life. Language serves a socially constitutive role. These papers argue that often "society" above the level of the coresident family is instantiated only through shared participation in various speech events. Myers' (1986) subsequent work on Pintupi meetings and Helen Schwartzman's (1989) account of the constitutive role of meetings in a large public bureaucracy demonstrate clearly the wide range of settings within which communicative practice creates contexts for social activity and in certain ways defines society itself. Other recent research [for example, the studies in Watson-Gegeo and White (1990) and those by Brenneis (1987, 1990)] link this perspective with aesthetic and ethnopsychological concerns, focussing on how participants conceptualize the social experiences engendered by particular communicative forms, that is, how events "feel" to and acquire a particular experienced reality for those taking part in them.

In short, the papers in this volume are part of a larger conversation concerning relationships between communicative practice and the ongoing construction of social worlds and individual experience. As with any conversation, what has been suggested on our part has been refined, reshaped and extended by our scholarly interlocutors.

Don Brenneis and Fred R. Myers

References Cited

Brenneis, Donald
    1987   "Performing Passions: Aesthetics and Politics in an Occasionally Egalitarian Community." *American Ethnologist* 14: 236-50.
    1990   "Shared and Solitary Sentiments: The Discourse of Friendship, Play and Anger in Bhatgaon." In Catherine A. Lutz and Lila Abu-Lughod, eds. *Language and the Politics of Emotion.* New York: Cambridge University Press.

Goldman, L.R.
    1988   *Premarital Sex Cases among the Huli.* Sydney: Oceania Monographs No. 34.

Myers, F.R.
    1986   "Reflections on a Meeting: Structure, Language and Polity in a Small-Scale Society." *American Ethnologist* 13: 430-447.

Schwartzman, Helen B.
    1989   *The Meeting: Gatherings in Organizations and Communities.* New York: Plenum Press.

Watson-Gegeo, Karen Ann, and Geoffrey M. White, eds.
    1990   *Disentangling: Conflict Discourse in Pacific Societies.* Stanford: Stanford University Press.

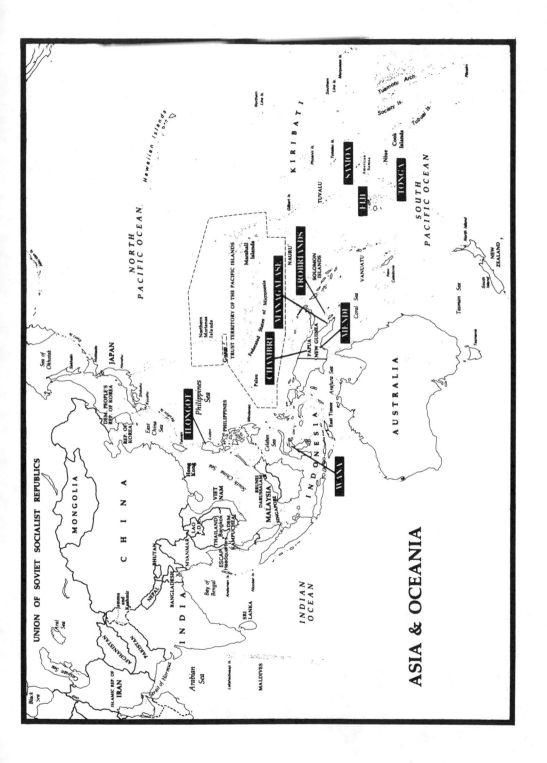

ASIA & OCEANIA

Introduction: Language and Politics in the Pacific

Fred R. Myers
New York University

Donald Brenneis
Pitzer College

... we can see the need for ... a kind of explanation that will link speaking with human history and praxis. To do this is not only to see languages as part of systems of speaking but also to see systems of speaking from the standpoint of the central question of the nature of sociocultural order. (Hymes 1972 : 10)

This collection of writings grew out of a symposium on the subject of "Language and Politics in Oceania," which was held at the February 1980 Annual Meetings of the Association for Social Anthropology in Oceania. Oceania, as a large and diverse culture area, has been a sort of natural laboratory for various kinds of comparative work, and this is an endeavor of that kind.

Comparison in terms of political structure is not new in Oceania, of course, but it deserves renewed interest. While Sahlins (1958) discussed variations in Polynesian political organization in ecological (and redistributive) terms, here we are concerned with the relationship between political organization and language as a form of social action. This focus derives from our view that language, as a sensitive index of social relations as well as an important sort of action with material conse quences, needs more attention from ethnographers. Not only is language of considerable sociological importance in Pacific societies, but the area offers an excellent comparative basis to investigate the relationship between political structure and forms of speaking.

The concerns voiced here reflect a dialectic between ethnography and theoretical formulations. Thus, Maurice Bloch's (1975) attempt to relate oratorical speech form ("formalized language") and function (social control) in "traditional societies" offered the intuition of speaking as a constitutive activity in the social order. Yet, our own fieldwork and informal discussions with other Pacific ethnographers convinced us of the necessity of distinguishing types of sociopolitical structure in order to compare the style and significance of political discourse. His general notion of "formalized language" as a characterization of speech form and the conception of "traditional societies" as a useful category for the analysis of politics are unsatisfactory in this respect. We saw similarities among Pacific societies that were "egalitarian" in regard to the prevailing concern with personal autonomy and corresponding "indirectness" in political language. The form of speech in these societies differs from that in the hierarchical systems of Polynesia, where men of rank could impose regulation and judge disputes. This initial and heuristic differentiation of two ideal types of societies, egalitarian and hierarchical, is intended to raise more fully the questions of *what* political discourse accomplishes and *how* it works. Doing this adequately requires increased concern with the varieties of speech events and their components (form) and reconceptualizing the situation of speech (function).

There is a particular cast to the work in this volume because, in the main, the contributors here are not linguists. They do not take as a given the importance of studying language; nor are their contributions, finally, detailed linguistic analyses. Instead, the focus on language as a form of social action derives from an ethnographic encounter with the uses of speech and a sense of the relationship between language and other features of social life. While much is shared with current sociolinguistic work, the ethnographer's concern to situate acts within a larger social context raises political and economic questions about what speech acts accomplish.

Politics

It is obvious that any attempt to study the effectiveness of speaking in politics depends upon a theory of what sorts of functions speech might serve, a theory of society, and a clear notion of what "politics" is. In this our own intuitions may be deceptive. For example, studies that simply identify politics with our own public domain are unlikely to discern how control, persuasion, and domination occur. It has become evident that "politics" in nonstate societies is not just the adhesive that binds together atomlike domestic units of production (cf. Collier n.d.; Meillassoux 1972). The tendency to identify large meetings—the grand events—with the political and to see such assemblies as equivalent to either legislatures or courts has a basis in our culture, but it has been clear since such work as Kuper's and Richards's (1971) investigation of "institutionalized processes of joint discussion" that the political function of "councils" is a problem for analysis. Council meetings may well not formulate policy at all. Thus, Bloch's work on Merina councils argues that the speeches in meetings "can be seen less as occasions for making decisions about matters at hand than for making decisions about ranking in the community" (1971 : 55). Feminist-inspired studies such as that of women's gossip in Spanish peasant communities (Harding 1975) have also extended our ideas of political activity, of where to look and what to consider. In this volume, Marcus's and Lederman's studies suggest that inappropriate distinctions between "public" and "private" may hinder our understanding of political processes.

Definitions of "politics" often focus on the regulation and maintenance of order and/or the exercise of power, that is, getting other people to do what one wants. Despite its own problems, Fried's (1967) discussion of different sorts of "polity" implies that definitions like these do not attend sufficiently to the content of order or of power. Put briefly, when definitions focus on abstract concepts like "power" and "order," they give us no sense of what politics is for! If understood at the level of structure as well as the level of action (cf. Giddens 1979), Lasswell's conceptualization of politics as "who gets what, when and how" comes much closer to our goal, as it includes a broader range of processes than are usually considered. The deficiencies are apparent when one considers how, for example, the relationship between the domestic sphere and the jural has been ignored, as can be seen in the general failure to analyze "gender relations" as part of the political field. In several chapters "speaking" in a political context does not seem to be a means of coercing others or announcing a decision; where *who* can speak is the primary concern, political discourse may better be analyzed as the reproduction of relations of dominance rather than as the exercise of "power." Since politics is so inherently linked with value, the problem should be approached through the consideration of people's relationships to sources of social value and to the processes that generate it.

As Collier (n.d. : 65) suggests, if the amount of power available to one actor resides in the degree of another's dependence, then our attention should be directed toward the social mechanisms that maintain the dependence of subordinates. In other words, she argues that "remunerative power" depends upon the social processes of stratification, the processes that differentiate actors (Collier n.d. : 89). Such a broadening of what is to be considered political allows us to see that politics is concerned not only with *exercising* power but also with reproducing the mechanisms that make power possible. This view allows us to understand how speech events in many of the societies discussed here do not exercise power so much as they reproduce already existing relations of dominance. Thus, in pronouncing oblique verse forms, senior Wana men do not coerce other social actors so much as they demonstrate their right to be considered "wise" or knowledgeable; they validate their influence and acquire the differential social value it offers (Atkinson, this volume). A similar case is that described by Bloch (1971, 1975) among the Merina where the right to speak — who speaks rather than what is said — is important in reproducing the ranking system by displaying it.

The point of view that the writings presented here suggest, we believe, is that politics is vitally concerned, not just with power in a universal and abstract sense, but also with the reproduction of systems of social relations. Thus, following Turner (1978), we define political processes as those processes involved with the regulation and allocation of social value. This definition does not divorce "polity" from "economy," just as it avoids defining politics through its manifestations in any particular social order. Differences within the class of "egalitarian" societies seem to demand this.

It should be obvious that such an orientation suggests that the rough structural typologies ("egalitarian" and "hierarchical") are unlikely to be very helpful in defining political functions within any society. First, the similarity in terms of "equal numbers of status positions available" (Fried 1967) may disguise significant differences in internal dynamics. Many egalitarian societies turn out to be egalitarian only for certain categories of social actors, such as "senior men." What about the others and their exclusion from the overt political arenas? And how, then, are we to understand these arenas? If we ask what social value the subject of competition and allocation is and, further, how it is produced and extracted, we gain a clearer sense of the *positive* attributes of such systems. Second, there is a variety in the content of the social relations that may be at issue in political action. In no society are all social relations equivalent in content or substance. In a small-scale society where women's role in production is important, for example, a man's relationship with his father-in-law, while undeniably political, is not the same as that between relatively autonomous fathers-in-law.

Language As Action

The failure to attribute much significance to language in the study of politics has its roots in certain attitudes to language. As befits our trade and practice, one of the stubborn convictions of commonsense academic culture is the view of language as essentially a descriptive instrument, an unfortunately clumsy way of making propositional statements about facts of the world. Undoubtedly reinforced by the development of linguistics as a study of texts, the conception of language as essentially propositional — as a passive reflection of reality and an instrument of communication taken up by individuals — has been challenged from time to time (cf. Williams 1977). The challenge by Romantic philosophers like Jean Jacques Rousseau, however, resulted primarily in the conceptual separation of ordinary, referential language from literary and emotive language, the latter being seen as a special category of communication.

That talk might be an important form of action in other ways, a means of affecting "reality," has rarely been appreciated by social scientists in quest of a particular sort of "objectivity" (cf. Cavell 1966). For example, the once prevalent normative approach to sociocultural systems considered language as more or less transparent to its task of communicating information. Essential processes were seen as taking place without any real consideration of language, as all societies had language. Thus, "socialization" and "sanctions" maintained adherence to the norms that sustained structured social life; events were seen only as "instances" of structural form. Language was considered only a way of communicating propositions about the world, as grammar and vocabulary, rather than studied as a constitutive *social* activity. The focus on language as referential was accompanied by a failure to conceptualize language fully as a pragmatic, multifunctional instrument.

The empirically real multifunctionality of utterances has often been obscured by a traditional focus on reference as language's principal end. Change in our understanding of language comes from considering language in use, through a concern with the speech event. In this view, one cannot assume the meaning of linguistic signs to be propositional; that is only one kind of linguistic performance among many (Silverstein 1976 : 18). Thus, Silverstein suggests that numerous characteristics of speech events must be taken into consideration as defining variables and, potentially, media for communicative function (1976 : 13). In several chapters, these features are crucial in constituting the social force of a speech act. Such considerations open the way to expanding our understanding of the significance of language in social life.

One of the notable developments in sociocultural theory in the past decade has been the movement away from the analysis of structures and toward the study of process and now — following a recommendation made long ago by Sapir (1970) — to the study of activity (Geertz 1973; Frake 1977; Kapferer 1976) rather than the products of activity.

Not surprisingly, the elaboration of such an activity perspective has gone hand in hand with work in sociolinguistics (Hymes 1972) and ethnomethodology (Garfinkel 1967; Goffman 1974) that has focused on the importance of individual choice, persuasion, and manipulation of rules and norms in the accomplishment of social action. Such work drew attention to the content of communication as more than proposition. While placing language in the realm of action, the emphasis on subjective strategies in such work has simply posited as "context" or ground rules the rest of the sociocultural system. This is unfortunate from the anthropological point of view (compare Bourdieu's [1976] discussion of "microprocesses"). More generally, Giddens (1979) has discussed the "duality of structure" that leads to the false dichotomization of structural and action theories of social behavior.

In an odd way, the result of the strategy approach is again to cut off such activity, including language, from its part in the larger system. In fact, Borker (1980 : 26) points out that language "provides a means for systematically linking macro- and micro-levels of social process," contending that it may be analyzed as a mechanism for perpetuating social and cultural patterns at the individual and interpersonal level. An example of this sort of work has been Gumperz's (1977) analysis of linguistic miscommunication in the reproduction of ethnic boundaries.

Too frequently, the focus on individual "strategy" has not resolved how the contexts in which it is elicited are themselves generated. Much penetrating criticism has been directed at individualistic priorities of "action" or "transaction" theories of social behavior (cf. Kapferer 1976; Evens 1977; Giddens 1979). In these theories, where the actors are assumed to be trying to maximize some value, social action is seen as the outcome of the externalization of individual intention. Kapferer points out that the notion of maximization "gives little attention to how actors recognize and establish rates of exchange" (Kapferer 1976 : 8), but others maintain that the priority given to the individual as a rational actor is an artifact of our cultural emphases. A coordinate and similar predisposition to posit a notion of self drawn from Western culture — focusing on the actor's transcontextual and continuous intentions as embodied in speech — seems to prevail in speech act theory and to hinder understanding of language as a *social* activity (M. Rosaldo n.d.). Thus, Rosaldo argues

that ways of thinking about language, about human agency and personhood in the world are intimately linked: our theoretical attempts to understand how language works are shaped by those culturally prevalent views about the given nature of those human beings by whom language is used. (M. Rosaldo n.d. : 1)

Rosaldo's contribution to this volume exemplifies this approach, focusing on the relationship between Ilongot oratory and their cultural view of the self in terms of "knowledge" and "anger."

The writings presented here indicate that expansion of our conception of the range of functions offers interesting possibilities in viewing speech as constitutive of the system, as a form of action. As Rosaldo suggests, this "requires much more attention to the ways real human beings use their words to influence and change the world they speak about" (M. Rosaldo n.d. : 2) and to the qualities of the social world within which language takes its place. The *many* functions of language may be of significance in those political processes "defining" the social order — a context of ordering established not only by what is said propositionally but also by who says it, who cannot, the speech situation, and so on. Any of these attributes of a speech act, in relationship to the speech situation, may be the medium for its function.

Form and Function

The recognition of language as constitutive in social life is what has been appealing in Bloch's (1975) work, his sense that the form of speech accomplishes its function. Bloch emphasized the ways in which the nonsemantic, i.e., nonpropositional, functions of "formalized" speech accomplished a *hidden* control, a restriction, on the content of a political event that made disagreement difficult. Thus, much of the basis for social control, he argued, was simply accepted or taken for granted through the particular efficacy of formalized codes. Like Bernstein (1971), from whose distinction of "restricted" and "elaborated" codes Bloch drew his inspiration, Bloch is concerned with power or control that is permeated through social intercourse in a totally unconscious and completely accepted way (1975 : 3). Yet there is some confusion in this argument.

Irvine's (1979) criticism of his conflation of different aspects of form in speech into a single entity that he calls "formalization" points out that Bloch's rather loose usage of "formality" to describe both speech and situation covers a number of distinguishable and potentially varying attributes of a speech event. Citing code structuring, code consistency, focus, and positional identity, Irvine further suggests that these "formal" attributes might be combined variously in the service of different communicative functions. Irvine's approach would require a similar attention to the complexity of functions that might be entailed by different sociocultural systems (cf. Clastres 1974; M. Rosaldo n.d.). In contrast, Bloch's account deduces or infers a function from the posited existence of a form of speech ("formalization"), leaving relatively unanalyzed the situation in which the form occurs, i.e., the total act of communication. Only through this neglect does the category of "traditional society" stand as a proxy for function, despite Bloch's own acknowledgment that the Merina *kabary* occurs in the context of marriage performances as well as in the council meetings he previously discussed (1971). The variation in context and meaning of this genre (Keenan 1975) should make it obvious that the communication takes on the functional character of whichever of Jakobson's six functions (emotive, referential, poetic, phatic, conative, metalingual) dominates (Hawkes 1977 : 85; Jakobson 1960).

While initially Bloch's argument stresses the coercive power of oratory ("In this sort of situation, if you allow someone to speak, you have practically accepted his proposal"; 9), he later indicates (1) that such "formal" speech constrains the speaker's alternatives as well and (2) that such speech cannot be used in arriving at plans or decisions. It appears, then, that an implicit focus on the speaker's intent and manipulation (power as coercion or control) does not clearly specify what is happening. What he has shown is not speech as "coercive" (indeed, Irvine 1979 argues that what happens in speech does not necessarily constrain what happens afterward) but rather that such speech is accomplishing something else. Despite his laudable awareness of "power" as a property of the structure, Bloch continues to discuss it at the level of action, referring to agents' capacities of achieving outcomes (see Giddens 1979 : 88). This view of power makes it difficult to see speech acts as more than individual strategies, as deeply involved in the reproduction of structures of social relations.

By contrasting formalized speech with everyday discourse, Bloch asserts that the resultant code lacks the ability to formulate "meaningful," i.e., representationally informative, utterances. Yet he can accomplish this only by contrast with his unexamined ideal type of "everyday discourse," which he sees as unrestricted and propositional. Contrary to his implications, however, all linguistic communication imposes some restrictions on language. Formalization can also be characterized in other than negative terms, as Atkinson and McKellin suggest in Chapters 1 and 4, respectively. Restriction, repetition, and other such features may highlight the choices that have been made, focusing on the fact of selection as the significant content. Thus, he cites the inability of formalized speech to "communicate messages concerning particular events" (Bloch 1975 : 15) because the limited proverbial stock of illustrations makes all events appear alike, merged into "an eternal and fixed order" (ibid.). He sees this as moving communication to a level where disagreement is ruled out, since one cannot disagree with the right order. Possibly, however, the "conservatism" of speech is *not* to be found at the action level of "persuasion" or "coercion" — as accomplishing policy. The analysis of policy does not exhaust the political significance of formalized speech; the acceptance of the eternal and fixed framework may contain — implicitly — acceptance of existing relations of dominance as "natural."

Formalization, characterized by the impossibility of contradiction or replacement by alternatives ("what is being said is the right thing ... because it has become the only thing"; 22) might well be seen as a constructive characteristic of language, a mechanism to create a universe of discourse, a context or polity within which certain meanings are taken as axiomatic. This is one means of accomplishing a framework in terms of which the event and action is to be understood. While, as Bloch says, the formal features of such speech may rule out disagreement with the framework, nothing rules out disagreement with specific plans. Furthermore, as Bloch increasingly admits through this piece, formalized speech is not the whole of political discourse, nor are these events the only situations in which political action occurs.

"Formalization" does not simply encapsulate a speaker's intentions, a distinction Hymes (1972) captured as that between the speaker's goal and the audience's function. In attacking a rival within such terms, an actor may reproduce the system however much he may change the position of actors within it.

Political Discourse among Apparent Equals

As a group, the chapters in this volume focus on forms of speech in relation to political function, thereby establishing comparatively a richer and deeper conception of the varying concerns of politics in these societies. Besides sorting out the different qualities of elaboration speech might have, these writings show how the effects of speech are related to the nature of political relations overall and to the content of the social relations in question in any particular event. To understand the illocutionary force — the work they do — we must identify speech forms and place them precisely within the social relations of their use.

Speech events in situations where egalitarian relations prevail seem strikingly concerned with the construction and maintenance of a polity, with the constitution of a *context* within which interaction can occur (e.g., Brenneis, this volume). What characterizes "egalitarian relations" is the relative political autonomy of actors (Myers 1979); no defined relations of subordination or superordination are present. When one examines the evidence of these types of situations, one is struck by the extent to which a political arena is an *achievement*, rather than a category of analysis to be taken for granted. A theme uniting these writings is the contribution of actors' linguistic work in creating and maintaining the political arenas in which they contend. From this point of view, it appears that a polity is as much the creation of meaning as of sanctions or coercion. Thus, what are obviously political events among Fiji Indians (Brenneis), Wana (Atkinson), and Mendi (Lederman) are less concerned with coercion or collective decisions by which participants would be bound than with arriving, however tentatively, at a rubric within which an understanding is possible for equals.

Viewing politics simply as decision making or as coercion does not catch the experience of events as these writings do. Emphasizing the relative weakness of constraints on individual autonomy, for example, Atkinson writes that the "wrapped words" verse form (*kiyori*) used by the Wana to express the general condition is not an instrument of political control. Indeed, where collective social life is fragile, the indirectness of these verses represents part of a larger pattern in the society of avoiding confrontation and conflict. While attached to a speaker, its structured form detaches it from the appearance of coercion or imposition of will: people take it or leave it.

Instead of being instruments of control, the verses have implications for political status; they display one's value. Like other sources of political status in Wana society, the use of "wrapped words" provides a means by which persons of influence identify and negotiate threats to the collectivity; part of their effectiveness lies in the cultural premium the Wana place on "hidden" meanings. In other words, the illocutionary force of the formal features of obliqueness and verse structure (1) draws upon the structure of a wider cultural logic (i.e., hidden/overt), which draws attention to the speaker as an expert and portrays the listeners as dependent upon him and his skills; and (2) produces a controlled set of images many stages removed from the passions that may lurk on all sides, allowing for a political forum that does not threaten the fragility of association.

A central issue is who gets to be heard rather than who coerces, who is worth hearing. The message defines a general condition, a context shared by all, but the verses also display their speakers. While "wrapped words" are not the sole medium of Wana political life, their circulation does seem to be the substance of a larger polity not organized by social structure. Given the mobility of Wana social life, Atkinson writes, the Wana polity is "an elusive notion brought into focus only when juxtaposed with threats to its existence." These threats exist socially through their articulation in "wrapped words." Perhaps the extreme in this quality of political life is the Hadza case of "minimal politics" described by Woodburn (1979), in which a combination of economic and social factors provides few occasions or conditions "which set clear and important constraints on individual autonomy" (253) and few occasions that can "appropriately be described as policy-making or as the administration of public affairs" (253). In the millenarian milieu of the Wana world, "wrapped words," taken as expressions of the composers' concerns, are rather cautious phrasings of a polity defined through suggestions of a shared situation. They are nonprovoking proposals for how to understand an ambiguous world and how to respond to it.

The maintenance of a polity as a rubric for understanding is also a central concern for Fiji Indian disputants. Brenneis discusses political action surrounding disputes among equals. While the political order is "egalitarian," the relative immobility of village life and the necessity of cooperation in some agricultural tasks as well as the external threat of other ethnic groups give the Fiji Indian village polity a heavier functional load than that of the Wana, if less than that of the Mendi subclan. Within the context of such a community, without courts or formal offices, ostensibly religious speeches (parbacan) provide a means of discourse in which parties to a dispute can employ an elegant variety of Hindi and overtly religious themes in addressing veiled accusations against their opponents. The indirectness of such attack fends off retaliation from the antagonist, while its very obliqueness is a mechanism for recruiting the interest of others who feel they must comprehend the hidden meanings. While such a speech can diminish the reputation of an enemy, it can also provoke community involvement in settling a dispute. When a legitimate, established formal authority does not simply exist, the use of indirect and oblique speech is a means to create a polity, to entrap a third party. It should be seen as part of the process in which individual matters are accorded public and political significance but differing in form from politics embodied in an office or a title. In contrast to Lederman's essay, this sort of strategy prevails only among status equals, i.e., adult males, and denies women and adolescents the stature of political citizenship. (cf. Brenneis 1979, 1980).

It should be clear from the Fiji Indian case that there is no question of a particular genre constituting the whole of political discourse. The discussion of the symbiosis of genres shows how "straight talk" is involved in the community arbitration sessions (pancayat) that follow if the religious speech has been successful. Under sanction of oaths, witnesses are required to speak unambiguously in these sessions. What is intriguing and significant is (1) that directness is the marked case for speech, something achieved through an interrogative format that helps all participants avoid the onus of individual responsibility for the public account created — a vital theme where egalitarian relations prevail; and (2) that there is no summing up and no decision at the end of such an event; this is not consensus building. What is accomplished is an authoritative, cooperative account of a disputed event (cf. Frake 1963). Henceforth, only this definitive account can be drawn upon in public talk. Whereas previously, when knowledge of that dispute came only through private and partisan lines, villagers feared that discussion might draw them into the conflict, after the public account the case no longer constitutes such a threat to the idle talk that is the web and content of village social relations. Finally, the joint participation of the disputants signals a change in their relations, away from avoidance toward "talk." As is often the case in egalitarian societies, no one is declared "winner" or "loser," and no one's autonomy is impinged upon.

As both Brenneis and Atkinson describe, in egalitarian situations, open disagreement and expressed confrontation or coercion are avoided through oblique and "indirect" speech—a form of speech that maintains the overall context sustaining civil relations within which difference or disagreement is being resolved or expressed (cf. Read 1959; M. Rosaldo 1973; A. Strathern 1975b). While demonstrating that the collective arena does not simply exist but must be achieved and sustained by actors' work, these accounts also show that the goal of political discourse may be neither a decision nor coercion but rather the sustaining of an appearance of autonomy while at the same time constituting or reconstituting a polity. They seem largely the product of negotiating acceptable interpretations, both of the event and of the relationship of the parties. Brenneis, like Rosaldo and Strathern, gives attention to indirectness in egalitarian political discourse as a means of bringing conflict to the group arena without sacrificing autonomy. Brenneis is concerned with *how* the speaker keys the audience to hidden meanings, but Rosaldo — because Ilongot oratory is a negoti- ation — emphasizes the use of ambiguity to *allow* for settlement. In

Rosaldo's case, disputants can "discover" each other's meaning in the process of negotiating an acceptable construction of the case without either losing face.

Consequently, where a central feature of social relations is the autonomy of actors, there is always a tension with relations of "polity." What characterizes speaking situations of this sort is not only that "one cannot force others to act" (Borker 1980) but also that there is no preexisting and continually available context for interaction. To speak the literal "truth" assertively under such circumstances, one supposes, might often threaten the basis of any extended polity or community. Without enduring, legitimate political offices, what is political is always to be negotiated, a process of interpretation that is less regularized than where the polity has its own representatives.

Nowhere is this clearer than in the phenomenon of "indirection," one of the most striking features of public political talk in many of the communities represented in this volume. To say that a particular bit of discourse is "indirect" is to comment on its referential character, that is, to claim that it "means" more — or other — than it appears to say. Thus, indirection has to do with the relative opacity of messages and its potential for multiple interpretations. Therefore, the signification of such indirect discourse encompasses not only whatever literal meaning there might be but a variety of interactions between textual and contextual components of the event as well (cf. Jakobson 1957 : 3 for the crucial distinction between a "narrated event" and the "speech event" in which narration takes place).[1] Indirection calls attention to context, both to semantic frames and to metalinguistic ones.

If indirection is defined by the relative opacity of the relationship between narrated event and speech event, it does not necessarily follow that the text itself is obscure. Two of the studies in this volume (Atkinson, Weiner), as well as most of the accounts of indirect political language in the ethnographic literature focus on imagistic, metaphoric, and unclear texts, those where semantic puzzles are evident and ready for the disentangling (e.g., A. Strathern 1975b; M. Rosaldo 1973). This strategy of indirection depends primarily upon tropes, those "figures of speech that operate on the meaning (the 'signified') rather than the form (the 'signifier') of words" (J.D. Sapir 1977 : 3). Another strategy (analyzed by both Brenneis and McKellin, this volume) is akin to that of parables, in which a story is told that, complete in itself, can be interpreted as it is. However, through various keying devices, the listener is made aware that there is a second, parallel interpretation to which he or she should be attending; an analogical relationship between the narrated text as a whole and some features of the speech event and its broader context is proposed. Central to this strategy are the devices by which listeners are guided to the alternative meanings, the "keys," which may be stylistic features. Important as these strategies are, not all "indirection" concerns this sort of referential function, as (for example) in the utterance "I am hungry" as a request for food. It seems vital to consider these "everyday" uses as part of the broader category of speech forms that "veil" the links between "narrated event" and "speech event."

"Indirection" generates questions about the relationship of message and context, concerning both intention and reference: listeners are "keyed" (guided or alerted) to relations between speech and context through generic and other formal features. One must make an effort to work out meanings. This sort of referential character can serve a variety of functions at the same time. It may allow for (1) the deniability of a meaning; (2) leaving the ultimate interpretation up to the listener; (3) by its very opacity, compelling listener involvement or engagement in a case; (4) providing a possibility for a shared, corporate understanding. There has been an emphasis on the formal features of metaphor and other tropes in much of the literature and especially on their semantic properties (see Crocker 1977), but the use of these features is not invariably a matter of indirection. Metaphors are not always "opaque." Nor are these features, as we have seen, the only means through which indirection is accomplished. It is the relationship of such devices to metalinguistic context that is of greatest importance here.

In situations where actors sense their own parts in the construction and sustaining of a political arena as a context for interaction, there often is a cultural respect for the illocutionary power of words to affect or reorganize reality rather than simply to reflect it propositionally. We would expect that the organization of speech and linguistic ideology will reflect the situational and cultural constraints on language use, a notion discussed in recent studies by Rosaldo (n.d.) and Weiner (this volume).

According to Weiner (this volume), Trobriand Islanders regard language as dangerous and powerful. For Trobrianders, speech contains the possibility and therefore the inherent power to provoke disruptive and destructive events. This would be instanced in the public revelation of well-known facts, in the transformation of private feelings into public knowledge, and in accusations that create or alter social realities. Where all social relationships are seen as problematic and requiring work to maintain and create, one should avoid "hard words" — irreversible public facts. One should disguise one's thoughts in ambiguous speech or employ specialized codes such as exchange objects in making public one's desires and intentions in contexts of uncertainty, in the political and sexual contexts in which autonomy is particularly at issue (Weiner, this volume).

This suggests, as well, that knowing "what is going on" (i.e., function) in a context is necessary to interpret the communication of a speech form and to understand how it accomplishes its function. This is yet another argument against inferring function from form. For example, Rosaldo reports that, in Ilongot oratorical contexts where disputes and group relations are at issue, speakers' discussions of events are less concerned with the factual detail they apparently report than with who withholds or reveals a knowledge of well-bruited fact (M. Rosaldo n.d.: 25); it is not like a trial or a hearing. Like Bateson's account of the message "It's raining" (Bateson 1972 : 132), the apparent propositional form is only part of a larger communication. In the context of oratory, Ilongot "assertives" (after Searle 1969) are "less a matter of reporting facts about the world in words than of articulating relationships and claims within the context of a history that is already known" (M. Rosaldo n.d. : 28).

Information often must be communicated; yet, as we have indicated, an important concern of autonomous actors is to keep their options open. In this light McKellin's (this volume) discussion of Managalase allegorical political communication focuses on the linguistic means for accomplishing political functions in precarious situations. Certain formal features, i.e., overlay and linkage, are essential to the interpretation of the speaker's message to a selected audience. They are structuring mechanisms that focus or highlight through repetition of the parts of the allegory crucial to the interpretation of its message — its links with the present situation. The ambiguity of this form of political discourse is motivated by its function, allowing a speaker to restrict the audience for his message to those who are directly involved with the problematic situation at issue. Its indirectness is a mechanism to exclude others or to achieve a degree of privacy in arranging sensitive matters; for example, how to respond to a deviant marriage that threatens existing alliances. The form also reflects a caution appropriate to fragile political relationships. Thus, McKellin notes that it is a means of testing the opinions of one's allies before committing oneself to a stand. In a decentralized polity, maintained through networks of exchange relationships constantly being renegotiated, this is a means of arriving at a shared policy without exposing weakness or demeaning the autonomy of one's allies.

A number of the accounts in Bloch (1975), particularly those of Parkin, Comaroff, and Salmond, stress that formal codes are only part of the range of political discourse. Many of the accounts stress the use of formal codes and ideology to sustain or create a polity, a basis of moral community. Thus, Comaroff shows how criticism of the chief's performance in more or less "straight talk" follows upon an earlier part of the speech in a more formal code wherein the "office" of chiefship itself is set forth as a legitimate, real context to which all historical events must be compared. These suggest that a transcontextual frame is important to political activity, that disputes and events are usually placed in a larger context, and that certain features of speech have important roles in accomplishing this.

One problem not addressed in Bloch is whether there are differences in how this is accomplished according to qualities of the social system involved. A somewhat similar position is implied by Rosaldo (1973 : 218) and this volume, who argues that the stylistic features of Ilongot debate oratory create a context in which interaction can occur and define what might be appropriate resolutions. In the creation of this context, actors invoke shared norms and public understandings while rendering the situation meaningful by arriving at an acceptable interpretation (cf. Brenneis, this volume). This procedure — what Garfinkel terms "accountability" — thereby elaborates the devices by which, in ordinary social life, people and events are treated as instances of and understandable in terms of these general categories (M. Rosaldo 1973 :

209). In other words, in the process of resolving a difficulty, actors reproduce the categories and resources through using them, although their value and relationship may be altered. These devices, which are used in rendering some other event or situation meaningful, are rarely themselves the object of scrutiny. They are, it seems, tools to resolve difficulties that are the objects of concern and are therefore a kind of shadow projected by the problem at hand. Nevertheless, for all their practical use in resolving and making accountable a situation, by providing a context for its encompassment they have a further significance, as Bloch seems to have perceived. In the process of accountability these forms themselves are reproduced as usable, real, even universal and necessarily true. They are reproduced as the axioms of the moral and social universe of the actors, everything that "goes without saying" or is "taken for granted," the transcontextual basis of the polity. Thus, the public identities taken up by parties in resolving a dispute are reproduced in the process of resolving the dispute as real, natural, and in some sense what the world is really made of. As Giddens (1979) suggests, then, the process of rendering accountability may be part of the process whereby the structure of social systems is reproduced. The situation resulting from this process stands over and against the actors as an objective reality alienated from their control. This perspective allows us to consider the final part of that problem of the actor's or speaker's intent. We are not saying that actors are trying to reproduce the relations of dominance but that, in the act of accomplishing something they do intend, such as resolving a dispute or winning a debate, the meaning of their acts and utterances may come to be more, or other than, what was the simple intent.[2]

There are, then, two levels of action in much of the political discourse presented here; a context for understanding provides a basis for actors to converse, but it also creates an axiomatic universe of meanings that may have implications for future situations. While obviously it is always true that people need to know "what this talk we are doing now means," the process of contextualization is an important device, particularly in political discourse. The examples in this volume imply that speech events among egalitarian actors often contain a metamessage or broader frame about the relationship and identities of the parties that allows the message itself to be interpreted. Sometimes, of course, the correct interpretation of the message is intended to imply the meta-message. That is, the actor may use an utterance or an event to constitute a wider system of meaning.

This ability to shift levels in discourse, in fact, seems to be the basis for the exchange of objects to carry meanings about the context of which it is part, i.e., the relationships of the parties (see Weiner, this volume). Participants in such systems of discourse are often conscious of the ways in which the interpretation of the context implied may limit their ability to define the meaning of their actions. Gewertz (this volume) shows how a Chambri politician's exchange attempts to cast a particular meaning of dominance on a current situation. Because the meaning, like a metamessage, is only implied, it cannot be imputed or actively denied, only ignored.

What we are suggesting is that the broader frame, the meaning or context established, is the polity in egalitarian orders, defining actors as political persons and specifying the sorts of relations that should obtain among them. It is essential to understand how the implications of its accomplishment often go unquestioned. Rather than focusing on legislation as an implicit model for the political, these examples suggest that various two-party processes may be appropriate—e.g., diplomatic negotiations or courtship. These are situations, it should be noted, at which talk is important because it constitutes the social relations while it transforms them. Participants are conscious of the fragility of these occasions.

This is illustrated by Lederman's description of the meeting of the Mendi subclan, ostensibly to decide when to have their parade. In this event, she reports, a prominent big-man opposed marching with a rival but allied subclan. His speeches did not result in a decision about what actions were to take place; as it happened, many men from his subclan joined in the parade. While the meeting did not have the power to determine what action people took, it did shape public understanding about the group meaning of these actions; the actions of those who marched were seen as private, individual decisions. What was at issue was "how any of the actions were going to be publicly construed and understood." Concluding that "during formal, public discussions, attention is focused on the group significance of events," Lederman considers *how* the organization of the speech event conveyed this context.

Unlike the situation of Strathern's well-known analysis of "veiled speech" between members of equal but opposed groups (1975b), this Mendi event was intragroup. And, unlike Brenneis's case, this is not a dispute. While respect for the autonomy of the other actors remains significant, discourse seems not to have to bridge a precarious gulf of political individuality such as that described by Strathern. In Mendi, comembership in the subclan constitutes the context in which the event has meaning, specifying and constituting certain aspects of the participants' social identities as relevant, in essence making the tribe a social fact. Lederman's study emphasizes that in egalitarian orders coercion is not necessarily the substance of politics and that, while one may be unable to coerce others, this is not the only value at stake in political relations. The solution to this problem is suggested by Lederman in the following definition:

"political" relations refer not only to the way access to a given set of culturally valued resources is restricted for certain people (or "statuses") and not others, or the way in which a particular given social order is maintained and enforced; they also refer to the way in which this social order and these valuations are themselves created and reproduced or are denied and transformed. (Lederman, this volume)

From this point of view, the process by which order gets defined is an essential part of politics, and, further, we are directed toward the place of politics in the process of social reproduction. In Lederman's account we see how the definition of broader order (in gender relations) is accomplished almost by fiat, in the creation of the context of understanding among men. Thus, political activity is to be seen not only in occasions of persuasion and manipulation but also in the processes whereby relations of dominance are reproduced — a central issue posed by Lederman's analysis of the way Mendi formal occasions and their exclusion of women create gender asymmetries. In this analysis she shows how formal features accomplish a taken-for-granted order of male dominance through their compelling redundancy. The form of the event accomplishes the dominance of the group meanings of actions over those of individual networks, but it devalues both "femaleness" and the individual network transactions of both men and women. Obviously, women lose more than men in this definition of order. Thus, Lederman shows how talk concerning clans is reinforced by features of formalization that focus attention on men, who actively constitute the groups that their maleness represents, an effect difficult to challenge precisely because it is never explicitly articulated. Since it is through the maintenance of such tribal units and their identification with them that men are able to appropriate glory and prominence to themselves, the reproduction of these units is the reproduction of the social relations that assure their dominance.

Political Discourse in Hierarchies

Much of the argument we have been making applies, as well, in situations where hierarchical relations prevail, although the strategies of participants seem different. In discussion, for example, Duranti stress how ranked Samoan orators felt that speaking forced them to risk power they already had. In much of Polynesia, those with political status try to avoid exposing it in situations of potential criticism by using representatives or hired orators to speak (cf. Salmond 1975; Arno n.d.). This should make us aware, again, of the different sorts of political functions embodied by speech when political relations vary.

In a paper presented at the symposium, Nancy Lutkehaus (n.d.) made a point very similar to Lederman's in discussing Manam Island, Papua New Guinea. She showed how the "rubric of understanding" created by speech events — in this case, the social meaning of the *miting* — could place significance on planned or proposed actions that constrain individuals. This is what she referred to as the "constricting web of tradition." The young leader in her case is not so much "persuaded" by the speaker's oratory as he is captured by the universe of meanings applied to his proposal to withdraw from a cooperative venture and strike out on his own. Lutkehaus described how the speeches opposing the young leader's withdrawal impose his identity as hereditary leader on the situation. They allude to familiar myths and employ figures of speech that depict the leader's responsibility to help his group and the disastrous consequences of his failure to do so. As in Comaroff's (1975) analysis of Tswana political discourse, political critics constrain a leader by calling upon the very qualities on which his office is based. By drawing out these understandings of the leader's importance and value, they insure that he will undertake his responsibility as *tanepoa* to behave correctly; otherwise, he will be seen as the cause of any further misfortunes. A construction of failure will be imposed on him and, one presumes, his position as leader diminished.

Therefore, the *miting*, set off from other social events by certain formal features, provides an effective forum for his opponents to broach these issues. Speaking in this context necessarily juxtaposes his action with the values embodied in the scene; the "cargo" ambience of the *miting* and the sense of great import the context conveys metonymically help to portray this event as more than just a business discussion, as a problem in the morality on which the society is based. In this sense, the assimilation of the leader's proposed action to his position and to the deepest structures of social life is accomplished in a way he cannot really deny. Speakers do not assume their personal identities as affines or relatives; instead, by invoking their positional identities through forms of address, they emphasize the *tanepoa's* position as leader and the obligations associated with it. The choice of speakers also conveys part of the message: as affines they communicate that the context is not one of opposition but of conciliatory alliance.

Rhetorically, then, the speeches set up an opposition between "inside man/outside man" in such a way that the leader is forced to choose between the uncertain value system of individual entrepreneurship and that of traditional cooperative social activity in which his position as leader is embedded, the very values upon which his status is based. However, while the strategy retains his support, binding him as leader to the values of his position, his opponents reproduce the relations from which his dominance emerges. What we see in this case is how a polity already constituted and embodied in the *tanepoa's* office is drawn upon and used to constrain the occupant of the position. But, having constrained the potential deserter, his opponents also reproduce as meaningful and relevant the context invoked — the dependence of the village on cooperative submission to the leader. In a sense, contrary to some theories of speaking that view it as communicating the speaker's intentions, here we see that context and its control may determine a speaker's meaning and limit options. As Bloch (1975) noted, institutionalized control of context may be an important political resource in reproducing the social relations of dominance.

An interesting feature of the essays in this volume was how those based on research in societies with centralized, formal political authority took the "polity" for granted, apparently following the focus of their informants. Nonetheless, these essays demonstrate that maintenance of a political arena required linguistic work, although it seems not always to be everyone's concern, or a mandatory part of every performance. In other words, identifiable genres might be analyzed as performing those functions at appropriate points in the political process, although the trajectory of those processes may vary according to the nature of political relations.

In Chapter 8, Duranti discusses a particular Samoan speech genre (*lāuga*) in relation to *fono*, meetings called to discuss important matters that could upset the social equilibrium of the community. He shows how the same genre, what Bloch saw as the speech form, can be used as part of different speech events in which it accomplishes different functions. Duranti further demonstrates how features of a speaker's performance tell the audience how they should interpret his words; they establish a frame. Thus, within a *fono*, varieties of speech performances are distinguished by variation in such features as topic choice, sequential ordering, turn-taking, and lexical selection. For example, a *lāuga* occurs at the beginning of a *fono* meeting, and, while the agenda may be mentioned, the rules of this genre prevent speakers from expressing their opinions. This is not the point at which political argument occurs. Duranti maintains that the *lāuga* in this event is a sort of transition point, but it is also clear that it establishes or invokes a moral context without difference of opinion, a framework of meaning within which antagonistic interaction can take place. While Duranti's own emphasis is the way in which an event can be seen as a frame for interpretation, the reverse is also true. We can examine how the speech act accomplishes its function in the event through these distinctive features. Similar features applied in the performance of the same genre (*lāuga*) in a ceremonial event are used publicly to represent an agreement of some sort already reached by parties, to announce a new social reality. The ceremonial *lāuga*, Duranti writes, goes back to the eternal values of the community, iconically reinforcing those enduring values with the sophistication of verbal art displayed. An interesting question is whether the *fono lāuga* draws some of its illocutionary force from the ceremonial context.

The taken-for-granted nature of the polity in hierarchical societies was striking in several other papers presented. For Black (1982), Arno (n.d.), and Marcus (this volume), the discussion of their research started with a political system, while for many of us this was precisely the problematic issue.

Far from arising from theoretical differences, we think it likely that both the essays dealing with egalitarian societies and those concerned with hierarchical ones retain a close touch with their informants' intuitions and representations. We are in the presence of Fijian logic, Tongan logic, and so on. Thus, titles, ranks, and structure exist in some of the social systems. However, the view of the polity as a separate, self-existing structure is, as Bloch (1975) suggested, an *achievement* of the system, one that Marcus (this volume) identifies appropriately as a "mystification." Arno's (n.d.) distinction between persuasive and impressive speech in Fiji maintains that the latter, depending upon previously embodied authority, is a means for those with such authority to avoid depending upon the will or judgment of subordinates. Oratorical performances that depend on authority previously embodied may mystify the actual source of dominance. The assumption that political influence is inherently unproblematic may lead one to accept the local logic too readily. Obviously, we still need to know what the content of political relations is.

This concern for the content of political relations motivated our earlier discussion of politics and the allocation of social value. If we do not identify politics with political structure, but rather consider these structures as part of a larger system of relations, we can grapple more suitably with the question of what political organization accomplishes and how language contributes. As Marcus implies, traditional political organization in these societies was composed of mechanisms for reproducing the social relations of dominance from which those of "rank," as symbolic representatives of their estate residents, appropriated the social value produced by those of lower rank (see T. Turner 1979, 1980 for the theory of value on which this is based); their noble "value" is of course made possible by those who appear in the system as their dependents. Herein is the basis of the logic Arno describes: to speak persuasively to inferiors would imply that such individuals have or could have judgment, endangering the very basis of the dominance of nobles or chiefs. Thus, those of rank avoid public persuasion and appeal to individual motives. Hierarchy assumes as a precondition the superordinate authority embodied in a title and seeks to validate it. Because nobles validate their positions through the display of appropriate qualities, such occasions may also provide the danger of exposing themselves to risk. The logic of political action in this sort of system, then, is to conserve the social process already constituted that regularly manufactures social value for superordinates. As Collier (n.d.) noted, the remunerative power superordinates have derives from these processes, and the polity preserves these relations.

Language enters into these processes in quite specific ways, and different modes of discourse take on specific functions. Consequently, among status equals, as Arno (n.d.) describes, "impressive" talk has no place. It is clear, however, that "impressive" talk is *not* a mechanism for decision making. Like Wolof village political meetings, it appears that in Fiji such speaking is used for "announcing decisions made from above and answering questions about them" (Irvine 1979 : 781). As the decision of those of rank, what is proclaimed has legitimacy, and the focus of the event is to convey that basis. This sort of political event is a kind of self-presentation of the social system, as anthropologists have noted. Concern with order of speaking, consistency of codes, and the like should be understood in this light — as presenting an image of the legitimate order that produced the decision. Thus, the Fijian genre *sevu sevu* (Arno n.d.) is effectively comparable to the Samoan *lāuga* and formalized speech as described by Bloch in emphasizing unanimity and common values. *How* this is accomplished — that is, how an axiomatic, unquestioned universe of meanings is established — is only hinted at in some of the chapters. Some recent structuralist work, such as Rosaldo's (1975) discussion of "semantic focusing" in Ilongot magical spells and Turner's (1977) analysis of deeply embedded "temporizers" and "precipitators" in mythopoetic narratives, suggests, in the manner of Jakobson's (1960) poetics, linguistic means for inscribing certain values and forms as eternal, necessary, or basic. The *sevu sevu* provides a framework, the basis for political order. This Fijian genre is, similarly, employed to acknowledge and constitute the authority of a village leader, placing a current event in a broader context; and an elaborated form is also used in chiefly installation, to stress the propriety and justice of the new relationship. While much negotiation may have occurred offstage, that does not render the presentation as without political consequences; who speaks is of vital concern. We propose that such events be seen as part of the process through which relations of domination are reproduced and justified.

Marcus's study illustrates the importance of placing the Polynesian polity in a larger systematic perspective. In it he describes the "idle talk" at informal kava sessions as a process through which contemporary Tongan nobles try to convert the resources of their titles into leverage on new sources of value. As in other Polynesian systems, formal public occasions are marked by protocol and impressive displays of status and polity. However, this account shows that the mystification of persons of rank, while an essential foundation of their position, is an obstacle to obtaining instrumental support for other projects. The isolation from speaking that is common to Polynesian nobility creates difficulties in achieving the trust based on knowledge of one's personal qualities necessary to organizing estate residents for other purposes. Therefore, while discomfort with status inferiors usually leads to avoidance of situations of proximity, contemporary nobles who are without strong claims to chiefly substance must do some public relations work on their own. As Marcus elucidates the situation, Tongan nobles face something of a double bind, which they attempt to resolve on culturally unmarked occasions by taking up "idle talk," a role distancing that allows some of their personal qualities to appear without the usual mystification. The knowledge gained of "their noble" enables the subordinates to build some expectations of his behavior, while their relaxation in his presence may provide him with information useful for his political activities.

Conclusion

The essays in this volume have a number of implications, both methodological and substantive. First, it is clear that things are rarely as straightforward as one might hope. Such typological notions as "hierarchical," "egalitarian," and "formal" are valuable as initial guides to an understanding of language and politics, but any synthetic attempt that stops with these distinctions will necessarily miss or distort the complex relations between the two. An overeager equation of linguistic form with function or too set an a priori notion of what "politics" is can provoke serious misapprehensions. A failure to consider the diversity of political performances within a particular speech community would be similarly misleading. Focusing on the character of social relations and of specific speech situations in a community can help provide less predetermined interpretations.

Given these caveats, it is clear from these writings that public political discourse has a different flavor in those communities where the maintenance of individual autonomy is a concern from that which it has in those where relations of dominance/subordination are crucial. In the first case, the polity is constituted through speech and those events in which it takes place; social order is an achievement and a performance. In the latter case, a political order seemed to be taken for granted. There was considerable concern for public political performance, but the more problematic area was that of relations in private, especially with those who were not clearly one's subordinates.

Finally, talk makes a political difference in all these communities. In some situations the crucial factor is that talk can occur at all; the creation and maintenance of communicative contexts is the creation, however fleeting, of a political order. Such contexts also provide for public understandings, both of specific events and of more general assumptions about the social world. At a more specific level, particular rhetorical strategies draw upon contextual, stylistic, and ideological resources quite effectively, whether to engage audience concern or to ensnare a reluctant chief. Political talk goes beyond persuasion and display. At the heart, it compels specific visions of the social world through its own organization. Individual issues may be debated, but the understandings implicit in the conduct of political discourse are rarely addressed and even less frequently challenged.

Notes

In addition to our fellow participants in the symposium, "Language and Politics in Oceania," (1980 Annual Meetings of the Association for Social Anthropology in Oceania) we would like to thank Bette Clark, the late Michelle Z. Rosaldo, Daniel Maltz, and Ruth

Borker for their comments on earlier drafts; Jane M. Atkinson also provided particularly helpful discussion, criticism, and suggestions.

1. When Jakobson talks about a "narrated event," he does not necessarily mean a story, but rather a proposition of any kind.

2. This is a response to a debate among those concerned with utterances as meaning what speakers intend; for example, Grice, and those preoccupied with the interpretation of texts who maintain that what speakers mean to say is irrelevant to elucidating the meaning, that is, that context determines the meaning of an utterance (Giddens 1979 : 82 – 83). Nonetheless, it is important not to see "accountability" as only an intellectual process, because "power is expressed in the capabilities of actors to make certain 'accounts count' and to enact or resist sanctioning processes, but these capabilities draw upon modes of domination structured into social systems" (Giddens 1979 : 83).

I. Egalitarian Polity: The Production of Contexts of Understanding

1. "Wrapped Words": Poetry and Politics among the Wana of Central Sulawesi, Indonesia

Jane Monnig Atkinson
Lewis and Clark College

In his introduction to *Negara: The Theatre State in Nineteenth-Century Bali*, Clifford Geertz (1980 : 3 – 4) makes the following assertion:

one of the most important institutions (perhaps *the* most important) in shaping the basic character of Indonesian civilization is, for all intents and purposes, absent, vanished with a completeness that, in a perverse way, attests its historical centrality — the *negara*, the classical state of precolonial Indonesia.

Geertz's claim makes intuitive sense for the crowded islands of Java and Bali, formerly sites of royal centers. It rings true as well for Indonesia's coastal peoples who have been linked together by trading principalities for centuries. That the claim might apply also to the hinterlands of islands like Sulawesi and Borneo challenges the image of isolated hill tribes as primitive survivals barely touched by historical currents in the wider world.[1]

This chapter offers an analysis of a poetic form used by the Wana, a population of swidden farmers in eastern Central Sulawesi, Indonesia. The poetic form, known as *kiyori*, typically takes as a theme Wana relations to external political orders — not only the *negara*, but subsequent colonial and nationalist regimes as well. At first glance, this fact is somewhat curious. Owing in part to the remoteness and ruggedness of their mountainous interior homeland, sectors of the Wana population have managed to maintain a high degree of political autonomy into the last quarter of the twentieth century. But, as I shall demonstrate, years of political marginality to centers of power have had a profound effect, not only on external dealings with coastal populations, but on the constitution of political authority and dependence within Wana communities as well.

My discussion will bring out the importance of two dominant features of the *kiyori* form — verbal disguise and the theme of Wana relations to coastal authority. I shall explore how a premium on concealment and reference to external political orders serve to build political authority in Wana communities. The analysis to be developed here has direct bearing on the study of politics and language in so-called egalitarian societies.

That a speech form might be a key to understanding political process is an important recognition in recent anthropology. Maurice Bloch (1975) called attention to a relation between language and politics by proposing that what he termed "formalized language" might have coercive uses in traditional political orders. Critics of Bloch, drawing on speech act theory, have pointed out that Bloch's formulation presumes that oratory is simply a reflection of power, not a means to create it. They argue that political speech must be seen as political action, or as Paine (1981 : 9) puts it, "saying" can be "doing." Political forms of language, then, are not simply expressive; they are constitutive as well. Thus, the activity of speaking politically is not simply a means of displaying power; instead, it is a means of establishing and sustaining it (cf. Williams 1977).

If political language is constitutive, the next question concerns the kinds of political relationships that are its "condition and consequence" (Giddens 1976 : 157). At the Galveston conference, a contrast between egalitarian and hierarchical political systems served as a useful, if somewhat crude, shorthand for distinguishing the cases under examination. As Myers and Brenneis explain in the Introduction to this volume, the egalitarian/hierarchical dichotomy is a heuristic, not an inflexible or ultimate typology. Of the cases treated in this volume, the Wana clearly fall at the more egalitarian end of the spectrum, but there are clearly problems with that characterization. First, in general, does "egalitarian" apply to the society in general or just to particular social settings or relationships within the society? Certainly there are settings in hierarchical social systems where interaction among equals is appropriate. And in none of the societies examined in this collection are vertical relationships entirely absent. Then, too, there is danger of assigning linguistic traits to specific societal types as though one social form had a premium on features like indirection or metaphor. One can easily locate instances of each in oratorical styles associated with both egalitarian and hierarchical interactions.

The appropriateness of the term "egalitarian" can be further qualified for the Wana case in particular. Through partial integration into stratified states, the Wana have been acquainted for generations with social hierarchy. Dealings with sultans, colonialists, and Indonesian government officials — or, more correctly, with their representatives — have generated models of autocratic rule. These models are not easily implemented in Wana communities but are familiar just the same. In addition, Wana values accord authority and respect to seniority. Finally, the conditional authority of experts who manage health, agriculture, and marriage is an important dimension of social life. But authority is sharply constrained in a number of ways. It tends to be context-specific and difficult to generalize across all social contexts. What is more, it lacks a firm grounding in the control of productive resources that could facilitate its perpetuation. There are no effective forms of coercive sanctions to back its use. Finally, those who claim a measure of political authority cannot assume a fixed constituency but must continually work to establish a community dependent upon their services. For these reasons, Wana politics resembled more the processes described for hunting-and-gathering peoples and simple horticultural populations (cf. Collier and Rosaldo [1981], Leacock and Lee [1982], Lee [1979], Myers [1979], M. Rosaldo [1980]) than the politics of the stratified societies that border on the Wana region.

As Myers (personal communication) has noted before me, political speech in the kind of societies he and Brenneis provisionally label egalitarian often tends to be "all talk and no action." Time and again in my fieldwork among the Wana I was personally distressed as well as analytically perplexed when after engaging in weighty discussions of vexing problems my companions would later "fail" to act on what I took to be their resolve. But then talk *is* action, and the accomplishment of these discussions had more to do with creating and sustaining relationships among participants than with taking direct and concerted action regarding the ostensible topic of the talk.

How and why the *kiyori* form serves an appropriate resource for constructing relations of authority and dependence is the focus of this chapter. The puzzle I specifically wish to solve concerns a link between the premium placed on metaphoric disguise and a thematic preoccupation with external political orders. The solution is to be found, I suspect, in some inherent constraints of egalitarian political systems and in some distinctive aspects of Wana social values and history. My investigation will unfold in the following way: after a brief introduction to the Wana, the *kiyori* form will be discussed in some detail. A series of *kiyori* will be translated and interpreted in order to illustrate the properties of the form. Then the political dimensions of *kiyori* will be explored in relation to historical, social, and cultural dimensions of Wana experience. Finally, some implications of the Wana case will be drawn for the study of politics in comparable societies.

The Ethnographic Setting

The Wana are the "country cousins" of the Pamona speakers of the Poso area, whom Adriani and Kruyt (1950) called the Bare'e-speaking Toraja. Numbering some 5,000, they inhabit a mountainous interior region of eastern Central Sulawesi through which winds the great Bongka River. The Wana have had attentuated connections to coastal governments for at least a century and a half.[2] Formerly, sectors of the population paid tribute to the Islamic sultanates of Bungku and Tojo, one to the southwest and the other to the north of the Wana territory. In the first decade of the twentieth century, Dutch colonial authorities assumed direct administration of the Wana region. Since Indonesian independence after World War II, the Republic of Indonesia has held sovereignty over the region. But outside control of the Wana area has always been partial. Incentives to surmount the difficulties of travel and communication over rugged terrain have not been great enough to date for government or private interests to establish a lasting presence in the interior.[3] Compromising Wana autonomy, however, is an economic dependence upon coastal sources of salt, cloth, and metal — goods for which Wana trade rice, resin, and recently, rattan.

Wana settlements are thinly scattered across hills that flank an extensive network of rivers and streams. They are composed of households (ranging in number from several to ten or more) that build their dwellings in conjoining swidden fields. Households typically include a married couple and their dependents, both young and old. Both sexes cooperate in farming and gathering. Men hunt, using spears, dogs, and blowguns. There are economic differences among Wana, although in this subsistence-based economy these differences may fluctuate year by year, depending upon success or failure of the annual rice crop. Households that are well off have rice supplies to feed them for the year with enough extra to pay others for farm labor (which bodes well for future harvests) and to sell for salt, cloth, and a few other luxuries at coastal markets. Members of less fortunate households must work for others to obtain rice and cloth, a fact that may mean that their own farms suffer, thus guaranteeing the same situation for the following year. Some households are known for consistent successes or failures. Most see fatter and leaner years.

There is little in the way of explicit social structure beyond the personal networks of mutual cooperation that obtain among households in Wana communities. These networks receive ritual emphasis through the practice of shamanism, through an annual cycle of agricultural ceremonies, and through the management of marriages and disputes in the framework of a law code. Shamans, farming leaders, and legal experts control the special secret knowledge on which these activities depend. In some communities, a single person controls all three forms of expertise; in others, a number of different individuals manage one or more. There is a tendency for households to cluster around kinsmen who possess expertise in one or more of these areas. While recognition is accorded influential individuals on the basis of their expertise, such individuals hold no absolute power or authority. They maintain their influence only so long as they remain helpful and congenial neighbors. Should they prove selfish or autocratic, others may become dissatisfied and move away.

Wana society has been markedly transformed through relations with wider political orders. Formulation of a millenarian world view has been one important Wana response to the fact of being peripheral (and subordinate) to distant centers of power. Throughout this century and perhaps earlier there have been periodic millenarian movements in the Wana area as people anticipate the overthrow of the current order and the establishment of a new one. Like other forms of leadership in Wana society, millenarian authority derives from special knowledge to which the majority of people lack direct access.

This section has briefly sketched the forms of conditional authority at work in Wana communities. The next step is to examine the *kiyori* form and to consider its use for creating and sustaining authority in ongoing social life.

Kiyori: Form and Performance

A *kiyori* is a two-line stanza, each line of which is broken into two half lines consisting of eight syllables each.[4] The final two vowels of each half line are rhymed assonantally with the final two vowels of the other three half lines. When formally delivered in *kiyori* style, the stanza is spoken slowly and emphatically with a fixed pitch contour. The pitch rises on the third or fourth syllable of the first line, then is lowered in even intervals with each syllable through the first verse. A verse is delivered on a single breath. The speaker than pauses for a second breath and delivers the second line in the same manner as the first. There may well be distinctive personal and regional styles of delivery — something I did not investigate in the field.

The vocabulary used in *kiyori* ranges from everyday words to the more elegant terms of stories sung of the magical past, shaman's chants, and legal speech. Whether the words used are ordinary or elegant, ideally all should lend meaning to the verse (instead of simply filling in to fit requirements of meter and rhyme). In addition, the meanings contained in the stanza should be expressed metaphorically. Rarely is the sense of a *kiyori* conveyed directly. Instead, it is "wrapped," and the verse itself may be called a "metaphor" (*ligi*).

Admired on aesthetic grounds, *kiyori* also serve rhetorical ends as they encapsulate a state of affairs in a fitting image, express opinions or sentiments, pose questions, or propose a course of action. They may be aphoristic or they may go pointedly to the heart of an issue involving the speaker and his audience. Some *kiyori* contain no allusion to the situation they depict. Others make veiled or unveiled reference to a political theme. Interpretation requires knowledge of context, discussants, and motives, as examples in the next section will demonstrate.

Kiyori derive from two sources — human and spirit. A *kiyori* may be composed by a human, usually an adult man. In this case, it is taken as a reflection of its composer's thinking on a particular subject. A well-received *kiyori* is a testimony to its creator's cleverness and insight. It carries no implication of superhuman prophesy or divine inspiration.

Kiyori may also come from spirit sources, generally through a dream. Dreaming a *kiyori* does not lend any special status to the dreamer except insofar as he or she has something novel to reveal to family and neighbors the next day. The dreamer of a *kiyori* receives no special credit or respect as a medium. If a ghost is the giver of a *kiyori*, the verse is commonly interpreted as the opinion or sentiment of the dead person. Sometimes the being who delivers the *kiyori* is not recognized. I have heard such dreams interpreted as a message from the "great darkness" (*wuri bae*) dividing earth from heaven. *Kiyori* of this kind may be regarded as prophecies, but once again, no special status is accorded the dreamer. By contrast, people who dream spells, medicines, and other esoteric knowledge may gain reputations as healers, even shamans, by indicating that they have obtained special knowledge from spirits and by putting that knowledge to use. Unlike *kiyori*, such knowledge is not revealed by the dreamer.

While women rarely if ever invent *kiyori* in waking life, women occasionally report dreaming them. Furthermore, while living creators of *kiyori* are both adult and male, it seems that sex roles among ghosts are by no means so dichotomized. Ghost reciters — were the form a literary one, they would be ghost writers — include both sexes and all ages.

Occasions that commonly provoke *kiyori* include sociable gatherings of men.[5] These may be as casual as a visit by one neighbor to another or as structured as a shamanic performance, a marriage, a funeral, a farming festival, or a legal discussion. *Kiyori* may be created or repeated in the company of friends and neighbors; oftentimes a bottle of wine shared among men prompts a spate of verses. A visitor from another community if he is clever at *kiyori* will generally pose at least one verse to his hosts, and if the latter are also skilled at the art of versifying, the visitor will receive *kiyori* to ponder as well.

Whether the occasion is a quiet meeting of two or more men or a large and noisy group of celebrants, the mode of delivery is the same. No matter what the size of the audience, a *kiyori* is addressed by one man to another. A *kiyori* is delivered by catching the attention of the man one wishes to address, then reciting one's poem. The recitation need not be letter perfect the first time. Commonly, a few false starts precede a complete delivery. The verse is then repeated several times so that the receiver may grasp its meaning and remember its words. The receiver may repeat the verse out loud in order to memorize it. The listener usually nods in agreement and responds as though he understands the verse, often saying *kono*, "correct," "on the mark." As for the others present, the loud and distinctive delivery alerts them to the fact that a *kiyori* is being spoken. The false starts and repetitions allow people to quiet down, pay attention, and hear the lines, should they care to. General silence is not mandatory. If the speaker can sustain the attention of one listener, he will continue his poem.

What portion of the group attends to the performance depends upon the size of the gathering and general interest in the speaker and what he has to say. Prominent and influential men can be more sure of a general hearing than the young, the weak, and the unskilled. When a prominent man delivers a *kiyori* in a large group, his comrades may urge others to quiet down so the words may be heard. The larger the gathering, the more important one's social prominence is for attracting general attention. While a person with little influence may make himself heard in a small gathering of friends, in a larger company he will be drowned out.

Sometimes a single *kiyori* is delivered and ordinary speech continues. Other times, if the receiver is also a skilled versifier, an exchange of *kiyori* will follow. Often succeeding *kiyori* pick up the phrase or theme from the *kiyori* that came before. Sometimes exchangers of *kiyori* confirm the opinions expressed by their partners. Other times they disagree or change the emphasis, but through the use of the refined verse form, dissension may remain implicit rather than being drawn out in extended and explicit debate.

Because of its fixed, brief form that allows it to be easily memorized, a *kiyori* possesses a quality lacking in most forms of political oratory. That is, it can be repeated verbatim over time in a variety of contexts.

Full analysis of *kiyori*, then, ideally would consider its usage, not only at its inception and first telling, but also as it may be repeated, discussed, and interpreted in different settings.

Kiyori and Commentary

While critics of Ricoeur (1971) might raise objections to treating texts apart from context, there are advantages to be gained here by presenting a series of texts to illustrate the *kiyori* form. In part, the presentation reflects the nature of my data. *Kiyori* delivery tends to be spontaneous and proved difficult for me to anticipate and record. My best examples of the form came from retellings held sometimes for my benefit and sometimes for small groups wanting to discuss what a particular *kiyori* had meant. The mode of presentation used here reflects as well my desire to draw attention to features of the poems themselves that relate to issues of political authority to Wana society.

Elegant Disguise

As opposed to "straight speech," the *kiyori* offers a way to disguise meaning, to say something indirectly in an elegant way. Pantenggel, a favorite character of Wana tales, was a man who always spoke in *kiyori*, never in "straight speech." Pantenggel's associates enjoyed frustrating him, just to hear his complaints delivered in *kiyori* style. For example, they would signal the start of a shamanic performance by beating the drum and gongs. But, as soon as Pantenggel approached, they would hide their instruments to provoke him to express his dismay in verse. Similarly, if he performed a day's work in their fields, they would present him with only a tiny portion of food in order to hear his well-phrased response (Kruyt 1930 : 614 cites Pantenggel's classic *kiyori* on this occasion). Pantenggel's elegant verses concern topics as mundane as smoking bees from their hives in pursuit of honey, noting excrement nearby while one is chewing sugarcane, and the fluttering of a butterfly's wings. Humor lies in the discrepancy between style and subject, between Pantenggel's elaborate imagery and the homely themes expressed.

Whereas Pantenggel would speak elegantly and indirectly about little matters, the following *kiyori* speaks plainly and directly about an important one, and in its deviance highlights the characteristics of the form. By breaking the rules with his explicitness, the speaker underscores his statement and in doing so helps to clarify what more typical *kiyori* can accomplish. The *kiyori* dates back a half century or more. It belongs to a man named Towuwa known for his bravery and his resistance to the Dutch. Till his death, Towuwa, refused to accede to Dutch demands that Wana register as members of officially recognized villages and carry documentation of their membership, known as *sura kampung*. His poetic expression of defiance has been remembered over a wide area for several generations. I first heard the *kiyori* in a Muslim village at the coast from a non-Wana. Later I checked in the interior and found that the verse was well known there as well.

1. tako to'oka pai tua   Go tell the gentleman,
     ma'i patuu nTowuwa   here is the message of Towuwa:
     meta buya pada ngkura   black white the bottom of a pot,
     bungku pei mantima sura   [he'll be] hunchback before [he'll]
                                 receive a letter.

This message sent to Tua Petor, a Dutchman in Kolonodale, is phrased in no uncertain terms — the black bottom of a kettle will turn white and Towuwa himself will be a cripple before he will register with the Dutch authorities. Another version of the *kiyori* has as its last halfline *bo'onya mantima sura*, "he refuses to receive a letter." Either way, the declaration is direct and unambiguous. It is significant to note that expressions like "I refuse" and "I'll be crippled before doing that" invoke violent retribution from a vengeful thunder spirit, if for any reason one's resolve is broken. By speaking so forcefully, Towuwa is risking not only the anger of the Dutch but also sickness or even death.

Informants credited Towuwa's bluntness to his bravery: "He was not afraid even if people were angry." The suggestion implicit here is that people hide their meanings because they are not "brave" and are afraid if people are angered by their words. Comments about Towuwa's unusual *kiyori* reinforce my sense that the use of *kiyori* is in keeping with a cultural avoidance of confrontation and open conflict. While not wishing to undercut Towuwa's reputation for bravery, one might note that his strong words were not delivered directly to the Dutch official but, so the verse says, to another Wana to pass along.

The lack of subtlety contained in Towuwa's *kiyori* may be contrasted to the oblique message of his son, Pai L., who composed the following *kiyori* to express his refusal to vote in the national elections as the government was calling upon the Wana to do. The election was then and is today a source of concern and anxiety among the Wana.

2. rani kupansoe witi   I want to swing my feet
    ri pana nu eo mpili   in the rays of the afternoon sun.
    ndate tondosi nruring   Up at the perch of the *ruring* bird
    pasi ngoyu taa nairi   even the wind does not chill.

The expression *eo mpili* refers to the late afternoon sun that is still bright and yellow, as an informant noted, but no longer hot. Pai L. is envisioning a place that is neither too hot nor too cold, one in which neither sun nor wind is a problem. Freedom from heat and cold represents freedom from the dangers posed by the elections and the Indonesian government. *Eo mpili* may also be a play on the Indonesian word *pemilihan*, "election," referring to the different "choice" Pai L. is making. As for the proposed refuge "up at the perch of the *ruring*," the *ruring* is a mythic bird that inhabited the Wana land in the magical age of the past. The word *ndate*, which means "up there," implies *ndate Wana*, "up in Wana" rather than *lo'u tasi*, "down at the sea," from which elections and government come. In effect, then, the creator of the *kiyori* is saying that he prefers the traditional order up in Wana to the new order with its feared election down at the coast. But, unlike Towuwa, Pai L. does not come out and directly state his message. Only those familiar with the speaker, the circumstances, and current concerns could discern the implication of the verse.

The *kiyori* form offers a way of speaking with great caution. Carefully chosen words can hint at a meaning without confronting others directly. The following *kiyori* is attributed to a man who speaks eloquently if cautiously in dire circumstances. Whether in fact the words were spoken in the circumstances described I cannot say, but in any case, the story as told to me reveals how my informants in the 1970s envisioned the incident.

Pai Oti, brother of Towuwa, was peacefully cooking sweet potatoes when twelve Dutch soldiers arrived in search of the millenarian leader Pai Monso, who was at that time in hiding with his followers. Pai Oti had not even visited their congregation. Thus, he was an innocent man. Realizing the presence of the soldiers, hapless Pai Oti fled his house and dived over an embankment to hide. But the troops had divided, and he was cut off by a wing of them on his path to escape. Poor Pai Oti was struck with a rifle that split his pate. With blood and brains spilling forth, Pai Oti was asked by his captors if he was "still going to fight." Pai Oti, resigned and cautious Wana that he was, replied in verse:

3. wetumo to la'u sala   It's like that for the one down on the path,
   yore ri tutua maya   sleeping on the barkcloth pounding board.
   re'ewa nabi ngkuasa   There is still a spirit of power,
   mantoru i pue ala   Lord Allah protects.

As one informant summarized, Pai Oti is saying that there is still protection from God, because he was not dead from the blow. The expression *yore ri tutua maya* is a coded reference to "runaways living in the forest," that is, Wana who resist the government's control. Barkcloth is a badge of identity for the Wana as a people. Once used universally for clothing, barkcloth is still used today by those who are too poor or too afraid to obtain cloth from coastal markets. It represents Wana autonomy and Wana poverty. My informant stressed the *kiyori* as it speaks to the general state of the Wana. Looking back at the verse, it is apparent that Pai Oti is also making a sly reference to himself as the one down on the path, sleeping on the pounding board, in other words, beaten nearly senseless by the soldiers.

In the second verse of the poem, both halflines use Wana concepts expressed in borrowings from coastal Islamic culture. *Nabi ngkuasa* is a spirit of magical power associated with Pue, the creator and Lord of the world. Pue is often qualified as *pue ala*, from the Islamic term Allah. It should be noted that both expressions have meaning for traditional Wana and do not connote an acceptance of a world religion (cf. Atkinson 1983).

Persuasive Strategies

Men may deliver *kiyori* to cement their friendships, to offer friendly advice or stringent criticism, or simply to express an opinion. All these motives will be illustrated in the following examples, which demonstrate as well the high degree of complexity these short verses can possess.

The following *kiyori* is an old one, delivered by one influential community leader to another as an expression of friendship and shared interest:

4. embangku lale mangura	My friend, the handsome young one,
madaroi kita dua	let us love, the two of us.
rasepaka kumbo buya	White *tabang* leaves overlapped,
toru taamo mpea uja	a hat that no longer awaits the rain.

The first two lines are highly romantic, employing quaint terms characteristic of traditional stories and shamans' chants (*emba, madaroi*). Lale Mangura is the name of a spirit familiar who figures in the much-admired *molawo*, an esoteric shamanic performance prized for its intricacy and beauty. The speaker is flattering his companion by likening him to a charmed spirit familiar, quite likely with persuasive intent.

The second verse has *tabang* leaves being overlapped as in the construction of a sleeping mat. *Tabang* is a plant important to the *molawo* performance and the traditional spirit familiars of which Lale Mangura is one. In the last line it seems that the overlapping leaves have gone into the construction of a broad-rimmed Wana rain hat. Most rain hats are made of *naso* leaves, but *tabang* here invokes the magical protection offered by shamanic spirit familiars (such as Lale Mangura). The implication of the poem, then, is that the two men in friendship should guard against impending rain, in other words, hardship.

The interpretation I received was that the verse calls for the speaker and his listener to be "mutually supportive" (*masintuwu*) vis-à-vis the government (the rain); that is, the two leaders of their respective communities should stand together in dealing with the Dutch. I do not know the specific issues confronting the two men at the time nor the stance each in fact took on that occasion toward the government. What can be gleaned from the *kiyori*, though, is a playfully romantic enticement to ally, one with the other.

Occasionally the advice contained in *kiyori* can be quite pointed. The following *kiyori* was sent by a third party to Apa R., a highly intelligent and cautious man with grave worries about the government's intentions regarding the Wana. Apa R. had converted once to

Christianity, and then to Islam, fearing dire consequences from the government if he did not. When I met him he had begun to eat pork again as a traditional Wana. The following *kiyori* is one of two sent to him by a Muslim acquaintance disturbed by the news that Apa R. was reverting to his old ways. Apa R. was so upset by the ominous overtones of the *kiyori* that he could not sleep. After all, in his mind they did not come from a man as powerless as himself. Instead, they came from one allied with an authoritarian and outside presence in the Wana land, and hinted at actual retaliation for Apa R.'s decision.

5. kodi la'u kupomawo   I mourn a little down inside
    panjau rawonsekamo   for the stitching that has been shed.
    mabalimo ntano rando   Changed have been the stripes
    ri tonga mbalo ntolalo   on the bamboo shaft of the *tolalo.*

Two metaphors are juxtaposed here. One is an image of discarded clothing, representing an Islamic faith that has been cast aside. The other is the design carved on a *tolalo*, a tuning fork made of bamboo, a traditional musical instrument. The suggestion is that the convert, like the *tolalo*, has changed his "design," that is, his intent or conviction. To answer his critic, one might say that the old man has returned to his traditional ornamentation, neither of the world religions, but the *agama ruyu*, "the early religion," as the Wana term their ways.

The next example, like the verse delivered to Apa R., also expresses a difference of opinion between the speaker and the "you" addressed in the verse:

6. koni konimo la'u komi   Eat, eat, you down there
    bolu sole ri indoli   cookies fried in coconut oil.
    kami totonsi majoli   We are the swift bird
    piyokonya mokoli   whose flight turns back.

If one knew nothing of the circumstances surrounding this poem, one could detect that its creator is choosing a different course of action from the person or persons he addresses in the first line. What is being said is roughly "you partake of something supposedly pleasant while we flee." One familiar with Wana imagery would also note the fact that the speaker is identifying himself with *totonsi majoli*, the harbinger of news in heroic tales of a magical past (*katuntu*). It is *totonsi majoli* who reveals important information first, before it is known in other ways. It would seem, then, that the speaker — besides saying I am going to flee speedily from what it is you are enjoying — is also indicating that he may in fact have some foreknowledge about the true outcome of the avoided event. An astute reader of *kiyori* might also observe that the treat that does not tempt the speaker is a foreign one associated with the coast where confections fried in coconut oil abound.

So far I have outlined what an interpreter of *kiyori* might glean from the verse itself. The circumstances of its composition make plain its meaning. The speaker had been summoned, as had all the Wana, to greet the governor of the province on his visit to the district capital of Morowo on the north coast of the Wana area. The meeting was to take place at the site of a planned resettlement project where Wana could expect to be given gifts and the opportunity to sample all manner of coastal delicacies, like cookies fried in oil, a treat unfamiliar in their homeland. The speaker and his associates refused to be so lured, fearing that the implications of participating (like resettlement to the coast) might not be so sweet.

The *kiyori* is a challenge to the party addressed in its first line. Most likely, however, its composer presented the poem, not directly to that party, but rather to others who chose not to attend the meeting with the governor. Like most *kiyori* that treat controversial topics, the poem was passed along to communities that accepted the government's invitation. It was in one of these communities that it was told to me.

As for the following poem, I do not know if it was delivered directly to its target — a missionizing minister — or simply shared with others of like mind. The latter would be more in keeping with the avoidance of direct confrontation that characterizes most Wana interactions.

7. pokunde papa saemba   Go upstream father, friend,
    mojuyu pai malaeka   in the company of angels.
    kambaraka boru tenda   Spread out a tentlike mat.
    longko aku mou seja   Far away I am sheltered too.

Words like *papa* and *tenda* are Indonesian words that indicate the alien quality of the minister. (I am not sure how much Wana associate the word *malaeka* [*malaikat* in Bahasa Indonesia] with coastal culture. Other Islamic borrowings such as *nabi, saruga, do'a* are regarded as indigenous Wana concepts.) The verse expresses the conviction of unconverted Wana that their traditional ways have merit also. This is expressed in the image of the minister and the speaker each camping at a distance from one another (in an ideological as well as physical sense) yet both enjoying shelter from the rain. By mentioning himself only in the last line, the speaker develops a picture of the minister going about his business with conviction, then finding out perhaps with surprise that the speaker is faring equally well without that *boru tenda*, i.e., the foreign doctrine the minister wishes to deliver.

Specificity and Context

Kiyori vary in their degree of specificity. Some are general aphorisms; others pertain to very specific situations. The more specific the verse, the more essential are circumstantial details to its interpretation. The next two verses both make statements about the pathetic conditions of Wana life; one remains at a general level; the other poses a specific strategy.

8. masiasimo wotua Poor is the slave
   yore la'u ara njuya sleeping down beneath the floor.
   kale ngkaju rapa ntu'a The root of a tree, the top of a stump,
   etu semo rapoyuna exactly that serves as his pillow.

To grasp the portrait of pathos expressed in these lines one need know little except Wana familiarity with an earlier regional practice of debt slavery. The other important piece of information to know is that the speaker is not making a dispassionate reference to the condition of slaves in times gone by but, rather, is identifying himself and the Wana in general with that condition, although the verse itself contains no direct reference, pronominally or otherwise, to the speaker or his society. As mentioned in the preceding section, *kiyori* are taken as expressions of their composer's concerns. This *kiyori* does not pose a political strategy. This might well reflect the fact that its composer was a meek and unassuming man, covered with ringworm — neither prepossessing nor influential. He delivered this *kiyori* while drinking with an in-law and myself.

In contrast to the general statement of woe expressed in the verse above, the following *kiyori* is more complex:

9. ilumoe ewa katuntu   Orphaned as in the old stories,
   kedo nu manu pituwu   in the manner of a laying hen,
   naliwu kaju sanjuyu   following a line of trees,
   da napodonda manguru   preparing to roost on the row.

This *kiyori* expresses a more calculated position in a social field. Like the *kiyori* above, it begins by portraying a person in a pitiable state. Once again the poor individual represents the composer. In this case, the sufferer is not a slave but an orphan, a typical protagonist in stories sung of the magical past. But, rather than dwelling on his own poverty, the speaker outlines a strategy. He indicates that, like a chicken looking for a place to roost, he will follow an established path. As the verse was explained to me, he is saying where the many go, he will follow; he will abide by group consensus. The *kiyori* itself outlines a course of action whereby the speaker yields to the decision of others. To know why he would do so and exactly what he was agreeing to requires further information that I am lacking. (As I understand the history of this *kiyori*, it referred to a government edict.) This *kiyori* reveals more complexity than the one before, and its greater specificity suggests a pointed use.

A third *kiyori* opening with the same general theme also proposes a particular strategy and requires some knowledge of details external to the verse itself in order to comprehend its meaning.

10. katuwuku masiasi   My life is poor,
    kupodungku tumangi   I hunch over weeping.
    pulasimo parajanji   Once the promised date has passed, then
    pone nja'u salamati   peace will arise.

Once again the speaker opens with a general statement of poverty and pathos. In contrast to the two *kiyori* above, he emphasizes the fact he is referring to himself by using first person pronouns twice in the first line. But he is also predicting that hope lies in a promise that, once past, will bring safety, presumably for the speaker and for the Wana land. There is no clue in the verse as to what the promise concerns. This verse was delivered by a visitor from another settlement. After its author had left, the local elder who had been present interpreted the *kiyori* for the rest of us as meaning that the Wana are poor, the government keeps adding to their woes, but people should expect safety after the national election (scheduled to occur some six months later). His reading interprets the promise alluded to in the verse as the pending elections. This topic had come up during the visitor's stay. The elder, then, was bringing to bear his own worries and prior conversations to lend specific meaning to a *kiyori* that internally contains only a very general prediction.

Shifting Meanings

Kiyori, as the reader surely recognizes, possess a high potential for ambiguity, or — if that word seems too negative for what is clearly an important stylistic device — multiple meaning (cf. Abrams: 1957: 4).

That interpretation of a *kiyori* may differ according to the concerns of the interpreters may be illustrated by the following verse:

11. kutuntuka siko Ede   I stretch you, Ede,
    matao mansoe ende   take care as you swing and dance.
    masae pampolengke   Long is the search
    jaya ri kuno mareme   for the path in the bright clouds.

This *kiyori* was told in a dream by a dead man, Game, to his nephew Ede. Game had been *mandor*, an official messenger appointed by the government in a village that included Christian converts. While he was never baptized, he did attend church on account of his official status.

This *kiyori* was explained to me by three adherents of *agama ruyu*, that is, Wana who prefer not to convert to Christianity or Islam. As they understood the *kiyori*, Game's ghost was counseling Ede to be careful about how he conducts himself; that he, Game, took a long time to die because he could not see the path for his soul to travel. The idea behind this is that one who has been consistent in religious practice should have a speedy death and a direct passage to the afterlife, whereas one who has wavered in confusion will not. The *kiyori* reflects two important Wana concerns about existence and emotions. First, punishment for wrongdoing comes in life, not after it, in the form of sickness or slow and painful death. Second, ambivalence is unseemly, dangerous, and something to be avoided.

There is nothing in the verse itself to determine whether Game is advising Ede to convert to Christianity or to maintain the *ada ruyu*. My informants took the *kiyori* as Game's statement that wavering toward Christianity had made his trip to heaven longer, the suggestion being that remaining faithful to Wana tradition would have saved him some agony. While I never questioned a Christian Wana about the matter, I suspect it might be possible to make a case for Game's long search for the route to heaven reflecting the suffering of one who had not fully accepted the new faith. Nothing in the *kiyori* itself favors one reading over another. The sense is left up to the context and the interpreters.

In addition to various possible interpretations for the same *kiyori*, sometimes the verses themselves are changed as they pass from person to person. I have claimed elsewhere that the fixed poetic style makes a man's words eminently quotable. Still, through a series of retellings, chances for *kiyori* to change both words and meanings are great. The following case illustrates such a change occurring over a period of about a year during my field stay. When millenarian activity began near the northern coast of the Wana area during 1975, an elder living in the center of the Wana region sent the following *kiyori* to his son-in-law in the north:

12. buyu ntana nu linjaki   The ridge of land that is walked
    bukunya rani nunsani   his book requires understanding.
    aku taa kukalingangi   I do not forget
    oyu oyu ngkaramati   the earlier royal power.

The first line speaks of land to be covered, a book to be known. Evidently there is something hidden that requires understanding. The second line is a declaration that the teller has not forgotten the previous *karamat*, a word borrowed from Indonesian in which it means holy or sacred, and identified by the Wana with the *raja*. The allusion is to Pua Pansu or Tanjumbulu, the last *raja* of Todjo, who was executed on spy charges by the Japanese in 1942. Wana sense some responsibility for his death, for he had gone to disperse a millenarian gathering and had met the Dutch, approaching from another direction. On that occasion, some Wana feel that individuals betrayed the *raja* by signing documents that led to their ruler's arrest months later by the Japanese. It seems clear to me that the events were unrelated, but many Wana share a sense of collective guilt and apprehension that derives from their efforts to make sense of a series of bewildering incidents beyond their control. Millenarian endeavors are a means for anticipating and coping with further consequences of the ruler's death.

The composer of the *kiyori* is seeking advice from a relative concerning the latest millenarian outbreak. He establishes with his allusion to *karamat* that he has not forgotten the promised return of the dead *raja*, but indicates with his first line that he wants to know his son-in-law's estimation of the millennial prospects. In effect he is saying, "I'm interested, but I want to know more." As it turned out, the relative and his family moved back to live in the old man's community, convinced that what was happening in the north was a sham.

The *kiyori* of that influential elder continued to be repeated. A year or so later another version was brought from the southern reaches of the Wana area by a visitor. The following words were attributed to the same elder:

13. buyu ntana rakama'i   The stretch of the land is approached
    maka maliwu gambari   in a search a picture.
    wimba nsa nu kalingangi   How is it perhaps forgotten,
    parajanji ngkaramati   the promise of royal power.

This version transforms the poem from an inquiry into a declaration about a millenarian claim. It is as though the composer of the *kiyori* knows something important about the promise of royal power and is testing the receiver. Significant in this *kiyori* is the reference to a "picture." My husband Effort spent much of his stay in Wana painting pictures. The allusion to a picture here raises the issue — a popular one during our stay in Wana — that our arrival might have something to do with the anticipated millennium. Should the creator of the original *kiyori*, who was our host, have hinted at such a possibility, his intimation would have been highly provocative. In fact, as the original *kiyori* is stated, there is no such suggestion.

Exchange of Kiyori

The following case illustrates the way in which men trade *kiyori* at a large social gathering. These verses were delivered by two first cousins from different communities on the night of a wedding feast I attended, just before a shamanic performance. Apa D. began with the following verse:

14. kita ne'e mata mata   Let us not be careless
    sangka ratilaka ana   in dividing belongings among the children.
    pea raponsai naka   Wait till it has been swept,
    liano toru ngkiama   the crop, survivors of the destruction.

The *kiyori* anticipates a world disaster and possibly a partial destruction of people. The word for such catastrophe is a borrowing from Indonesian *kiamat*, and no doubt Wana visions of the end of the world have been influenced by the ideas of their Muslim and Christian neighbors. *Liano* is a traditional metaphor for the Wana as "God's crop." The suggestion is that certain plans, represented here as the division of possessions among heirs, should be delayed until after it is known who has survived the destruction. On other occasions the speaker expressed concern about certain Wana who may have somehow betrayed their *raja* (see *kiyori* no. 12). These individuals are expected to receive retribution in the final days. Perhaps he is alluding to such a sorting out when he composed this *kiyori*.

His cousin answered the *kiyori* with his own verse:

15. ane silamo munimo   When it is safe once again,
    mayamo da rapotiro   it will be possible to see
    ane Meki ore indo   if Meki remembers mother
    ungka nja'u mowengimo   from over there where it has darkened.

The verse indicates that only when the present turmoil has subsided can some determination be made. The issue concerns a person called Meki who is the child of B., a dead leader with associations to the executed *raja*. Like the *raja*, B. is expected to return someday to Wana. *Ungka nja'u* is a phrase that commonly alludes to something from the world beyond the present, an afterlife. The reference to darkness calls to mind the "great darkness" said to separate heaven from earth. Prophetic dreams are often said to come from this "great darkness." The final half line may indicate that truth regarding the dead leaders is obscured, unknown. The suffix *-mo* identifies a completed act and appears to suggest that the outcome of the current confusion is still in doubt.

Like many *kiyori* delivered in response to others, this one picks up a theme from the preceding verse, then brings out another aspect of it. The second *kiyori* makes explicit the issue of the royal line's return.

It also extends the general allusion to children in the first *kiyori* to a specific child, Meki. Yet the specificity is deceptive. It is not Meki's recognition of a kinsman but recognition by the Wana of their leader that is significant here.

If, as my understanding of the verse suggests, the allusion in half-line three is to a man, B., then why is he referred to as "mother" rather than "father," particularly when his actual progeny, Meki, is mentioned? It is not uncommon in Wana metaphor for a leader to be referred to as mother. The same image is noted in *kiyori* no. 17. Occasionally, the relation between a leader and his dependents is phrased as that of a mother hen protecting her brood.

I cannot go much further in my analysis of these two *kiyori*. What I wish to point out is the style of interchange they involve. The expression of ideas is indirect and rests on innuendo. The creator of a verse may allude broadly or specifically, openly or subtly, to his concern. In the exchange of verse cited here, neither speaker challenges the other, although their viewpoints on matters such as the one treated here are not the same. Instead, the second speaker takes the general theme introduced by the first and highlights a different facet of it. This is not a face-off but a change in emphasis. Thus, a company of men might give voice to their thoughts, each offering a different insight or confirming another's but never confronting their differences directly or spelling out their positions in detail. The effect of an evening spent drinking and exchanging *kiyori* is often solidarity, seldom divisiveness.

Commentary in the Realm of Dreams

All but one of the *kiyori* discussed thus far have been verses invented by living men. The next two come from dreams and reveal some uses to which dreams are put. Significantly, both were reported by men who for different reasons were not highly influential men in their community. For those who hesitate to deliver authoritative commentary on profound matters, reporting a dream may be a more comfortable way to express an opinion.

The following verse was dreamed by a crippled man with little influence in the community. He rarely offers a *kiyori* of his own creation in public discussion, but he occasionally is known to dream highly significant poems imparted to him by spirits and ghosts. Thus, he does not take the role of *kiyori* creator, but occasionally he recounts a message from a spirit for the community to ponder. Doing so gives him no power as a community leader and no status as a visionary or a shaman. But it does allow him to contribute in noteworthy fashion to community discussions. The following words were told to him in a dream by his dead aunt:

16. yowu da rapsinjuyu   The hole that is to be shared.
    liu ri jampu kamumu   Passing beyond the purple veil of invisibility,
    sangkodi taamo kululu   I almost no longer followed
    jaya ri wali ngkatuntu   the path of the magical story.

As it was explained to me by the dreamer and others, the dead woman's husband, Apa E.—worried about government insistence that Wana adopt either Christianity or Islam—was considering conversion out of fear. He pressed his relative and co-elder Apa I. to join him and convert. Apa I. said essentially, "fine, go ahead, but I won't." Apa E. then decided that he would not either. As the dreamer explained, had Apa E. persisted with his initial resolve to convert, his wife, who was dying or dead at the time, would not have received a traditional Wana funeral. The *kiyori*, then, is the dead woman's observance that she almost missed following a Wana route to heaven. The hole she speaks of could be the grave or the new religion that her husband wanted to share with others. *Jampu kamumu* is the invisibility that sets this world off from heaven. The *jaya ri wali ngkatuntu* refers to the paths and vehicles of heroes in magical stories sung of the past (*katuntu*). If a *katuntu* is chanted in the period following a death and preceding a funeral, the soul of the dead will be conveyed to heaven in the manner of the story's hero. The dead woman's fear was that, if her husband had converted during the period of mourning, she would have been sent to the afterlife in the manner of other ethnic groups, not her own. As I noted earlier, living women rarely compose *kiyori*. But that does not mean that their ghosts cannot deliver clever *kiyori* on topics of such general importance as Wana conversion.

The final *kiyori* to be discussed here is not only one that has political and predictive significance but is also one that reflects on the dreamer in a way unlike the *kiyori* mentioned up to now. Like the invalid who dreamed verse no. 16, the young man E. who dreamed the following verse was not used to presenting *kiyori* of his own creation in large public gatherings. He may very well feel more confident delivering verses as products of dreams rather than presuming to deliver personal commentary on current events in the manner of his elders.

17. soba yau pei potiro   Try going out and inspecting
     kamaju nsoyo marimbo   the course of the powerful rapids.
     wetumo nsa nene indo   That's how it is for dear mother,
     ndende jo koro ngkalio   happy only she herself.

This *kiyori* was dreamed during the period when the speaker's community was under great pressure to join a millenarian endeavor built around a government-sponsored resettlement project for the Wana at the coast. The organizer of the movement, N. — the widower of the dreamer's first cousin — had been involved in a millenarian retreat with the dreamer's community once before, when the dreamer was still a boy. Now N. was urging others to go along with the coastal resettlement plans, claiming that they were linked to the end of the present world order, the return of the dead *raja*, and direct transport to heaven. Others suspected that he might be receiving bribes for inducing fellow Wana to go along with the relocation. Tensions had been high in E.'s settlement when the *kiyori* was dreamed. As he tells it, the dream involved an argument in which the dreamer and the organizer debated the possibilities of the latter's plan, then began to pit their esoteric knowledge about God's secret names in the kind of contest in which only shamans and sorcerers with powerful spells and spirit associates dare engage. The dreamer defeated his opponent with secret knowledge he would not publicly reveal when recounting the dream. The E.'s *own* dream agent (*tanuana*, the representation of the dreamer who enacts the dream) delivered the *kiyori* cited above. This is unusual. As seen in the cases examined previously, typically the dreamer's double only receives a *kiyori*. Here, the dreamer's soul is responsible for composing it.

To interpret the significance of this dream, one needs to know that the dreamer is a a junior shaman. The active part his dream agent played in struggling with the spirit of a man known for his control of esoteric knowledge testifies to the dreamer's shamanic potential. Like a shaman on a vision quest, the dreamer is dealing in arcane and powerful knowledge. He is not the simple receiver of a spirit's verse. Instead, his own dream agent creates the poem. Unlike most accounts of *kiyori* dreams, there is secret knowledge being withheld by the dreamer from his audience in the telling of the dream. The dreamer will not let his audience in on the secrets that his dream agent has revealed. (To let these secrets become public would be to dissipate their magical efficacy.) By recounting the dream and withholding the secret knowledge, the dreamer makes a bid for public recognition of his shamanic claims.

Now, how was the *kiyori* itself interpreted? This *kiyori* came to make more sense in retrospect, months after its initial telling. I did not become really aware of the *kiyori* until news came of the organizer's sudden death. Then people recalled the *kiyori*, and its full sense was reconstructed. The reference to "mother" was said to be the dead man himself, the organizer of the millenarian endeavor. The swift rapids were interpreted as the tumultuous goings-on associated with the movement he led. And, in the end, the only one to achieve heaven (a goal of Wana millenarian movements) was the organizer himself, "dear mother happy only she herself." That is, instead of helping his followers to escape earthly sufferings and attain paradise en masse, the organizer alone reached heaven, but only by dying first.

The *kiyori* is a bitterly harsh and critical one, pointedly attacking the organizer as a fraud. Significantly, the angry exchange of the dreamer and the organizer occurred in a dream and not in person. Wana are on the whole extremely timid about confronting each other directly in an antagonistic manner. Inviting another's anger is something most people prefer to avoid. *Kiyori* as acerbic as this one are more likely to be dreamed or told to others of like mind than posed to the antagonist himself.

Constituting Political Authority

It should be evident from the examples that have been presented that *kiyori* is an expressive form well suited for speaking in oblique and clever ways. A thematic preoccupation with Wana relations to a wider political order should be obvious as well. In this section I wish to consider why elegant indirection should be a prized mode of expression associated with respected older men and why allusions to external political structures should figure prominently in such speech. It is my intention to show how both verbal disguise and exogenous powers "work" in the constitution of political authority in Wana society. I shall do so first by considering Maurice Bloch's (1975) treatment of political language to show what Wana political talk is *not*. Then I shall attempt a more positive characterization of what *kiyori* are doing in the Wana case.

If one accepts Bloch's argument about the function of oratory in traditional societies, the reason for the link between verbal disguise and political authority in the Wana case should be patently clear. Wana *kiyori* meet the criteria of "formalized language" set out by Bloch. Requirements of meter, assonance, pitch, contour, and the premium placed on metaphor make *kiyori* a highly structured code. As a formalized code, Bloch's reasoning goes, *kiyori* should restrict "the very potential for communication" (15) between speaker and audience and limit the political options of both as well.

Let us consider each of these claims in turn. By asserting that formalized language restricts communication, Bloch challenges the classic (and elitist) assumption that formal styles represent the fullest possibilities for expression in a culture by calling attention to the confines in which formal styles must operate. One could counter that limitations of form need not necessarily imply impoverishment of expression. Consider the case of poetry. Indeed, it may be due precisely to its formal rules that a poetic form offers the expressive possibilities it does.[6] (A similar argument has been made for Northwest Coast Indian art: by straining against a complex set of formal restrictions, the tradition achieves its dramatic dynamism.) I would go further and argue that, in the case of *kiyori*, it may sometimes be possible to communicate more through a poem than through exposition, not because of the formal characteristics of each, but because of a shared sense on the part of actors that Wana social relations are fragile and easily upset by direct and fractious speech. In other words, there are occasions when certain issues will be framed in *kiyori* or not at all.

As for Bloch's claim that formal language functions to restrict political options, it fails to illuminate the workings of *kiyori* in Wana political discourse. The *kiyori* form does limit a speaker's choices for the duration of thirty-two syllables (i.e., if the speaker chooses to engage in it at all — unlike many forms of political oratory, *kiyori* is an optional style used to *embellish* ordinary speech, not to displace it). After that, the speaker is free from the constraints of the form and can exercise the options of ordinary speech. As for the receiver of a *kiyori*, he has the choice of responding in *kiyori*, in conversational style, or in silence. He may pursue the theme of the *kiyori*, or he may redirect the discussion to another topic (see *kiyori* nos. 14 and 15). *Kiyori*, then, place no serious restrictions on subsequent behavior. What is more, no binding commitments regarding future courses of action are established through the use of *kiyori* (cf. Irvine 1979: 784 for a discussion of oratory and political decision making).

So, if *kiyori* are expressive, not coercive, and if they have no necessary effect on subsequent action, what is political about them? I shall argue that these features themselves typify politics in systems like the Wana where in fact people possess few means — linguistic or otherwise — to coerce, control, or dominate their companions. It is suggestive in this light to note that *kiyori* is closely related to another Wana verse form, *tende bomba*, which is itself a Wana version of a pan-Indonesian verse form called *pantun*, a genre associated with courtship among the Wana as well as other Indonesian populations. What differentiates a *kiyori* from a love poem is primarily its weighty theme and its sonorous style of delivery. Why should an instrument of flirtation be a hallmark of Wana political authority? Because, like lovers, influential Wana men seek to charm others, to attract peers and dependents with displays of wit and wisdom. (Example no. 4 is a fine example of these points.)

The appropriateness of seductive rather than coercive tactics becomes apparent when the realities of Wana social life are considered. Given the shifting nature of Wana households and settlements, political authorities can presume no enduring constituency, let alone the conditions to exercise coercive control. Swidden technology and a lack of land pressure place few limits on residential mobility. Individuals may farm in any settlement where they have relatives or friends. A customary system of exchange whereby people perform farm labor in return for rice means that some households move between and during farming seasons to settlements where there is enough food to support them. Each year it is an open question as to which households will farm together in the year to come.

In addition to these internal factors, external factors also contribute to the centrifugal nature of Wana settlements. In the historical memory of my informants, headhunting raids by neighboring populations that had pushed some Wana settlements eastward were succeeded by colonial efforts first to resettle all Wana at the coast, then to organize them into permanent villages. World War II and the presence of Japanese soldiers in the area caused further dislocations. Since Indonesian independence, government policies regarding village membership, taxation, religious conversion, and coastal resettlement have promoted further residential instability and social dis-ease. One response to fears of persecution from outside authorities is millenarian activity that typically involves flight to hidden sanctuaries in the forest. These factors clearly make it difficult for Wana political leaders to establish or maintain stable constituencies.

If our model of politics is the exercise of coercive power in state societies, then there is no politics in Wana society. But if politics is construed as the production and reproduction of relations of dominance and dependence (Myers and Brenneis, this volume), we can find politics in the efforts of influential men to create and sustain followings by managing certain forms of knowledge on behalf of their supporters. Politics in this case depends on attraction, not coercion. Thus, the idiom of Wana politics is appropriately courtship, not realpolitik.

The place of verbal disguise in *kiyori* can now be brought into focus. Ambiguity is a premium in *kiyori* use because it serves as a means to avoid opposition and conflict, while at the same time conveying an impression of cleverness and profound insight. Even in situations where the potential for divisiveness exists between speaker and audience, direct confrontation can be avoided through elliptical speech. In contrast to other highly metaphoric speech styles like Ilongot *purung* (Rosaldo 1973, 1980, this volume) or Wana legal oratory that creates two opposing sides, *kiyori* do not generate divisions among parties to a discussion; instead, they unite participants through the presumption of shared understandings. *Kiyori* that express social division typically draw a line of opposition, not between speaker and audience, but between those present and an absent "other."

The strategy of uniting one's audience rather than dividing it offers a clue to the thematic preoccupation with external political orders. By defining an "other," *kiyori* speakers bring into focus the common interests of the "we." By alluding to the coastal government, they conjure a sense of a Wana polity in opposition to the external and foreign state. In this way they seek to transcend the centrifugal tendencies in Wana society and to create common grounds for understanding and unity among seemingly autonomous households and communities. It could be argued that the process of creating solidarity through contrast to external political authority is responsible for the construction of Wana self-identity. Proximity to a succession of coastal states has provided the political conditions for the emergence of a shared sense of ethnic identity among the scattered communities in the Wana hills.

The opposition of Wana and coastal polities is more than a formal one. "They" are commonly represented as an ominous presence that threatens the very existence of an "us."[7] By positing external threats to a Wana way of life, speakers underscore the need for solidarity in the face of a shared danger. The case illustrates Douglas's (1983) claim that weakly integrated social groups are characterized by ideologies that emphasize danger from without. This is not to say that in fact Wana culture is not endangered by coastal hegemony. Rather, it is to say that cultural emphasis upon that danger serves to unite Wana communities.

Giddens (1979) noted that the conclusions reached by social analysts are not always very far from the conscious understandings of social actors. Some of my informants observed that the only way that Indonesian officials could even mobilize Wana to follow development plans would be to bribe influential Wana to stage a millenarian movement that covertly involved cooperation with governmental directives.[8] Their reasoning was that Wana will unite for large-scale collective action only when faced with imminent threats from outsiders, a recognition consistent with my own.

So far I have argued that metaphoric concealment and reference to external political orders are used to construct a sense of unity and solidarity among members of *kiyori* audiences. In effect, *kiyori* are a means of identifying a constituency by conjuring an image of polity. But concealment and allusion to coastal regimes serve to establish differences as well between political authorities and their dependents in Wana communities. This point can be demonstrated by considering the nature of power in Wana society. As Myers and Brenneis (this volume) point cut, anthropological investigations of politics cannot proceed by assuming the content of "power" to be self-evident. The nature of power or powers must be spelled out for the social system under examination. This can be done by examining cultural notions of power as they take shape through social action.

In cultural terms, the word *pangansani*, "knowledge," comes closest to what can be called a powerful resource in Wana life. "Knowledge" here does not mean commonsense or empirical knowhow. It means control of magical formulas (*do'a*) that derive ultimately from spirits. Spirits, in turn, are hidden agents that inhabit the forest beyond Wana settlements. Notable success in any endeavor is considered possible only when augmented by powerful magic that originates with these external agents. The sense that knowledge is limited and derives from beyond the community is fundamentally important to the construction of political authority in Wana society. Shamanism, farming expertise, legal authority, and millenarian leadership all presuppose access to restricted forms of exogenous knowledge. Shamans gain their power from spirit alliances. Farming specialists use magic passed down from former generations. Legal authority is based on a code allegedly carried to the Wana land from the distant sultanate of Bungku at some point in the historical past. And prophets of a millennium are presumed to be following directives from hidden and external agents. In all cases, the powerful knowledge possessed by influential people is thought to derive from magical sources removed by space or time from Wana communities.[9] Thus, in the Wana view, authority is predicated, not upon social differences within communities, but rather upon differential access to external forms of knowledge.

Just as authority is grounded in exogenous resources, so too it relies on secrecy to be upheld. Were powerful knowledge common knowledge, there would be no basis on which to establish authority. Thus, magical spells retain their potency only when kept secret. And the styles of discourse associated with the implementation of powerful knowledge all involve verbal disguise. Shamans use a highly metaphoric speech style when they perform to demonstrate their secret knowledge, while at the same time concealing it. Like shamans, the specialists who perform agricultural ritual murmur secret spells and complex oratorical addresses as they mediate with spirits on behalf of their communities. Legal experts settle cases in stylized oratory that attests to their control of the legal code at the same time as it elevates the discussion beyond ordinary exchange. And millenarian leaders, claiming to know the future, speak elliptically, sometimes in *kiyori*, to convince others to follow them. In all cases these special uses of verbal disguise are expressive — that is, they signal a speaker's claim to powerful knowledge. At the same time, they are constitutive — they are efforts to establish, through their very performance, the authority of the speaker.

The place of *kiyori* in the construction of political authority can now be clarified. *Kiyori* verses themselves are not regarded as potent magical formulas, although effective composers of *kiyori* are presumed to use spells to make their performances clever and persuasive. What is more, *kiyori* composers do not claim to control the external powers of the state to which they allude in their poems. But, through metaphorical language and references to a wider political order, they create an impression of a deep understanding of the Wana condition that exceeds the limits of people's everyday lives.

Authority presumes a division between those who hold it and those who do not. *Kiyori* performance tacitly brings those differences to light. A *kiyori* is always delivered to another party. The act of delivering a *kiyori* to someone else is a recognition of a fundamental likeness between giver and receiver. It is a statement that they are people who comprehend hidden meanings and dealing with far-reaching concerns. By phrasing questions about Wana relations to external political structures, it also suggests that they possess the authority to articulate for others their common condition. *Kiyori* are not delivered by or to women (this ethnographer was an exception).[10] Nor does an influential older man banter in *kiyori* with younger men. Instead, a respected elder may recite a *kiyori* to a young visitor with instructions to convey the message words to the "old man of his place," that is, to the influential elder with whom the youth is affiliated, thereby keeping lines of generational authority clear.[11]

Kiyori exchanges, then, constitute relations of authority and dependence in Wana society. But it would be incorrect to assume that they do so automatically. Firth (1975: 42) helpfully identified an experimental aspect to political language use. Delivering *kiyori* does not guarantee political success. Some speakers are little noticed. Some are ridiculed for their compositions and pretensions behind their backs. Certain influential individuals are not skilled in the form. Some gifted composers are little heeded in contexts other than *kiyori* performance. In the end, the construction of political authority through *kiyori*, like the authority possible through shamanistic performance, rice ritual, legal debate, and millenarian activity, is only partial. Effective performance in these contexts, while it may augment one's stature as an influential person, can never be consolidated into political dominance that holds across all areas of Wana life.

In tracing the link between metaphoric language and the theme of Wana ties to a wider political order, I have highlighted here the relations of mature elders to their peers and dependents. I have done so by using an interpretive approach that relates cultural forms to ongoing political processes . It should be stressed that relating these forms to political processes is not a matter of reducing them to the same; instead, it involves catching the interplay of cultural forms and social experience. Thus, I have argued that, far from simply ratifying political relations, *kiyori* create them. Put more strongly, there is no "Wana polity" that exists in terms of an articulated social structure. Instead, Wana polity is an elusive notion brought into focus only when juxtaposed with threats to its existence. By identifying external threats to a Wana way of life, *kiyori* serve as one means of conjuring a sense of polity in a context of political ambiguity and confusion.

If the hegemony of the Indonesian nation-state is problematic, so too are interpersonal ties among Wana. The premium placed on ambiguity and indirection in *kiyori* is consistent with other key features of Wana culture that identify danger in disagreement. Prominent examples include a dreaded disease sanction that threatens those who would make strong resolutions, then reverse them, and the pessimistic expectation that animosity finds expression in sorcery. Cultural notions that identify danger in verbal offense were matched in my experience by expressions of personal anxiety over conflict and confrontation.

Indeed, one could speculate that *kiyori* derive potential effectiveness from the fact that a *kiyori* composer who presumes to comment on general conditions of Wana existence must do so carefully in a way that does not offend the collectivity he addresses. The delicacy of his poem expresses the tenuous nature of social ties in the Wana hills as well as in the wider political context. Highly prized as an aesthetic form, *kiyori* encapsulate the fragility of political relations within, between, and beyond Wana communities.

Conclusion

My analysis has demonstrated how verbal disguise and exogenous resources play a part in the constitution of authority in Wana society. Wana define themselves as weak in contrast to powerful beings beyond their own communities. Spirits and the state are both conceived as powerful entities and thereby serve to define relations of authority within Wana communities. It is worth considering the contrast Wana draw between themselves and these exogenous orders in light of the structuralist opposition of culture (or society) and nature. The nature/culture dichotomy has come under recent critical fire, in part because of the problem of reading the varied Western connotations of each term into the conceptual categories of non-Western peoples (see McCormack 1980). Bloch and Bloch (1980) propose that rather than searching for equivalences of meaning, procrustean style, between Western and non-Western categories, anthropologists should investigate the way "nature/culturelike" oppositions serve in "ideological discourse" to legitimate and to oppose "domination." They explore the ideological dimensions of the nature/culture dichotomy in eighteenth-century French Enlightenment thought in order to demonstrate its polemic uses for upholding or challenging existing social orders. The Wana, as we might expect, have no explicit categories that match the Western categories of nature and culture. They do, however, formulate contrasts between their farming communities and the surrounding forests and between the upland Wana region and the coast. In the one case, they are posing an opposition between humans and spirits; in the other, between Wana and Indonesian society. What is significant in light of Bloch and Bloch's work is that the oppositions in both cases involve a discourse about authority. As shamans, farming experts, legal specialists, and millenarian leaders, influential people in Wana society build authority by calling on external powers at the same time that they identify dangers deriving from those sources.[12]

Reliance on exogenous powers is a characteristic of small-scale, relatively undifferentiated nonindustrial societies (T. Turner 1980) (although invocation of external powers is certainly not unique to such systems). If the Wana case can serve as an example, it is quite evident why authority is phrased in terms of exogenous powers rather than internal societal ones. Power implies differentials. By building on powers exogenous to the social system, internal social differences are not identified as the basis of authority and dependence. As my analysis has made clear, in a system like that of the Wana, where constituencies are fragile, implications of difference can be socially divisive.[13] Authority is leveraged primarily in terms of personal access to extrasocietal resources.

When societies of this sort are encompassed by larger political orders —whether preindustrial kingdoms like the Indonesian *negara*, or colonial or postcolonial states — extrasocietal resources must be redefined.[14] What we see in the Wana case is a partial merger of powers of the wild and powers of the state. Exogenous resources for the Wana today include not only hidden spirits in forest haunts but vanished *negara* and the modern Indonesian nation as well. Influential leaders have the wisdom to exploit them all.[15]

Notes

The research on which this paper is based was carried out in Indonesia from July 1974 till December 1976 under the auspices of the Lembaga Ilmu Pengetahuan Indonesia, the Indonesian Research Institute. Support was provided by the Gertrude Slaughter Award from Byrn Mawr College, a National Science Foundation predoctoral fellowship, and a

National Institute of General Medical Studies training grant administered by Stanford University.

I am deeply grateful to Fred Myers and Anna Lowenhaupt Tsing for their extensive editorial advice and support during a major overhaul of my analysis. I am indebted also to the following individuals for helpful comments on the material presented here: Greg Acciaioli, Don Brenneis, Jane Fajans, Karl Heider, Morton Jacobs, Susan Kirschner, the late Michelle Rosaldo, Terence Turner, and Annette Weiner.

1. Anna Lowenhaupt Tsing (n.d.) offers an excellent refutation of this image. See also Atkinson (1983).

2. See Atkinson (1979: chapter 2) for a more detailed account of Wana history.

3. Since the time of my fieldwork, the New Tribes Mission, a fundamentalist Christian organization, has established a base in the Wana interior. Mission airplanes and evangelical zeal may be enough to overcome the geographical and cultural isolation of the Wana.

4. Readers familiar with Kruyt's (1930) report on the Wana will note a difference between his rendering of *kajori* and my own, *kiyori*. The different transcriptions of the glide represent Dutch and new Indonesian spelling conventions, respectively. Transcriptions of the vowel reflect dialectical differences in the Wana area. I am following usage current during my fieldwork among a Barangas population living east of the Bongka River. The frontal vowel appears after initial consonants when followed by a glide in words of more than two syllables. Coastal Taa speakers and some of the more westerly groups of the interior favor a back vowel /a/ in such contexts.

5. Mention should be made of an aesthetic performance called *makiyori* that involves both men and women who stand in a circle with their arms linked and sing *kiyori* in a beautiful and haunting way. Such performances were rare in the areas where I worked, and I observed one only once early in my field stay. How this aesthetic rendering of *kiyori* intersects with the political use analyzed here is not yet clear to me.

6. Michelle Rosaldo (1975: 201 – 202) has made a similar claim regarding creativity in Ilongot magic spells.

7. It should be noted that my examples of *kiyori* come from interior Wana areas. In foothill settlements with closer ties to the government, *kiyori* may reveal different emphases. See, for example, *kiyori* no. 5, which was composed by a Muslim Wana from a settlement near the coast.

8. This observation was made during the events that provoked *kiyori* no. 17, when many suspected that N. was acting in collusion with government representatives in a plot to trick Wana into cooperating with official resettlement plans.

9. In keeping with other Indonesian cultures, Wana attribute great magical powers (*baraka*) to the former *raja*.

10. This point raises an issue too broad to be considered here, namely the intersection of Wana politics with those of the hierarchical state. Upon meeting outsiders who are thought to be powerful representatives of foreign authorities, influential Wana elders are expected to deliver *kiyori*. As a foreigner whose mission in the area was ever a source of consternation and speculation (see *kiyori* no. 13), I was often the recipient of *kiyori* from senior men of the communities I visited. The presentation of *kiyori* to an important visitor establishes the authority of the speaker in the eyes of his fellow Wana, as well as conveying to the visitor that the speaker is a representative of his community. Indonesian

officials commonly designate such men *kepala adat*, "leaders of customary law."

11. Sometimes a *kiyori* is phrased as advice to the child of an influential man. Such a poem identifies that man and the composer as jointly concerned about the welfare of the young person. The authority of both men is recognized, and their common interest is asserted. The strategy also avoids the appearance of patronizing an equal by presuming to tell him what to do.

12. This chapter has treated the manner in which *kiyori* pose dangers coming from coastal authorities. By definition, this is what millenarian movements in the Wana area are about. Shamans and, to a lesser degree, rice specialists deal with hidden powers that both help and harm human beings. The legal code carries dreaded disease sanctions for those who abuse it.

13. Alternatively, in some relatively egalitarian social systems, differences of gender and age are not denied but instead are heavily ritualized. Aboriginal Australia, New Guinea, and the Amazon provide obvious examples of this.

14. McKinley (1979) is my inspiration for this point.

15. This point is well illustrated by shamanic invocations of spirit familiars that are laced with references to attributes of both wilderness and royalty. How traditional definitions of exogenous powers and new political powers are related in these cultural syntheses varies widely. Anna Tsing points out that the Mbuti oppose the forest as the ultimate authority to everything Bantu; the former is treasured, the latter derided (cf. Turnbull 1961). This opposition could have to do with the highly collective nature of Mbuti society in contrast to the entrepreneurial quality of Wana authority. For the Mbuti, the forest represents traditional band life. Young Mbuti men who go off to find adventure among the villages are deserting the Mbuti collective. By contrast, Wana society promotes the individual pursuit of powerful knowledge through quests for spells in the forest as well as through travels to the coast. The personal knowledge they bring back is highly prized. Myers (1979), in Australian work, shows yet another accommodation of exogenous secular powers by Pintupi Aborigines.

2. Straight Talk and Sweet Talk: Political Discourse in an Occasionally Egalitarian Community

Donald Brenneis
Pitzer College

This chapter presents an analysis of two varieties of public performance in Bhatgaon, a Fiji Indian community. The first — *parbacan*, "religious speeches" — occurs at the weekly meetings of local religious groups.[1] All "religious speeches" deal ostensibly with sacred topics, but speakers often convey a second, political message as well. These political meanings are quite opaque, and not all members of the audience will understand them. The second type of performance is the *pancayat*, an ad hoc "arbitration session" organized to deal with a specific conflict in the community. Issues, events, and individuals that would be buried deep within a "religious speech" are discussed openly in the "arbitration session;" sweet talk becomes straight talk.

Anthropologists concerned with political discourse have become increasingly interested in the distribution, characteristics, and effects of indirection as a speech strategy. When does a speaker say exactly what he means, and when must he resort to metaphor, irony, double entendre, or other subtle devices to signal that he means more than he has said? In what types of societies is oblique reference the predominant mode of political speaking, and where is candor possible? Indirection is clearly a strategy for critical junctures, that is, for situations in which overt comment or criticism would be improvident or improper but that demand some action on the speaker's part (see, e.g., Fisher 1976; Gossen 1974: 112 – 115). In any community such critical junctures often occur in private encounters. In some societies, however, public occasions recurrently pose the same dilemma; one must both act politically and avoid the appearance of such action. This dilemma is most marked in societies characterized by anthropologists as egalitarian and acephalous, in which clear-cut leadership does not exist and decision making is consensual.[2] The perils of direct leadership and confrontation in such societies often foster indirect, metaphoric, and highly allusive speech. Understanding political discourse requires both the interpretation of texts in themselves and the unravelling of well-veiled intentions (see, e.g., M. Rosaldo 1973; A. Strathern 1975b).

Bhatgaon presents in most respects a clear case of the association of oblique oratory with an amorphous, flexible, and egalitarian social order. Bhatgaon village men share a public belief in their social equality; there are no formal offices or leaders within the community. In times of conflict, direct confrontation is avoided, and speeches that can be understood as political seem to have little to do with the conflicts that engender them. In certain situations, however, direct speech is not only allowed but required. My purpose in this chapter is to investigate the relationship between direct and indirect speech in Bhatgaon with particular concern for the public occasions of their use.

"Religious speech" provides a clear example of indirect political discourse; "arbitration sessions" are characterized by straightforward and obvious reference. These two types of events by no means encompass the full range of public politics. Focusing on interpersonal contention, neither is used in dealing with questions of community policy. In Bhatgaon, however, the effective management or containment of personal conflicts is necessary for the success of any larger venture. These events are clearly important to the immediately involved parties, but they have important implications for the larger community as well.

"Arbitration sessions" and "religious speeches" are parts of the larger speech economy of Bhatgaon and must be considered in relationship both to each other and to the range of other available ways of speaking.[3] Both are tightly intertwined with less public communicative events, and particularly with *talanoa*, "idle talk," a principal adhesive in the web of social life in Bhatgaon. While one's general status as an equal derives from sex, age, and residence in the community, specific standing vis-à-vis others is not based on such fixed criteria but comes, in part, from individual accomplishment and, in larger part, from "talk." Here I use "talk" to refer both to the fact of talking with someone and to the contents of conversation. Through conversation one provides accounts and evaluations of people and incidents; by the act of talking one maintains relationships.[4]

Disputes between villagers usually break important strands in the social web; such disruptions in accustomed interaction signal to others that something is amiss. In addition, during a dispute partisan versions of conflict-related incidents proliferate in "idle talk" sessions. These are private and individual accounts and are unlikely to be accepted by everyone concerned. "Religious speeches" provide important opportunities for the public expression, however oblique, of these positions. The "arbitration session," on the other hand, forces the public construction of an official account against which the later behavior and talk of disputants can be measured.

After a brief ethnographic description of Bhatgaon, I will discuss "religious speeches" and "arbitration sessions" in some detail. In these discussions I will be concerned not only with the texts, textures, and contexts characteristic of these events but also with the question of how they are politically effective. I hope to demonstrate that successful performance is compelling for sociological reasons specific to Bhatgaon as a community and because of features inherent in the organization of the events themselves. Finally, this analysis should show the necessity of considering the interdependence of varieties of political performance within a community. At one level, the characterization of political speech among equals as indirect is a powerful and suggestive insight. A full understanding of this association, however, requires the consideration of oblique discourse within the context of available genres.

Bhatgaon: A Fiji Indian Community

Bhatgaon is a rural village of 671 Hindi-speaking Fiji Indians located on the northern side of Vanua Levu, the second-largest island in the

Dominion of Fiji.[5] The villagers are the descendants of north Indians who came to Fiji between 1879 and 1919 as indentured plantation workers. Bhatgaon was established in the early 1900s and now includes ninety households; there has been little migration to or from the village for the past twenty years. Most families lease riceland from the government of Fiji, and, although they may work as seasonal canecutters or in other outside jobs, most men consider themselves rice farmers. Rice and dry season vegetables are raised primarily for family use, although surplus produce may be sold to middlemen. Leaseholds are generally small, and rice farming does not offer Bhatgaon villagers the same opportunities for wealth available in sugarcane raising areas.

The political activities of men and women are often directed to the same ends but usually take place in different forums. "Religious speeches" are male performances; women may participate in the "arbitration sessions," but the sessions are organized and run by men. This study is concerned with male politics. Women's political participation generally occurs in less public settings,[6] as does much male politicking through such genres as "idle talk."

Among males an overt and frequently articulated egalitarian ideology prevails. Although ancestral caste appears to influence marriage choice (Brenneis 1974: 25), it has few daily consequences in Bhatgaon. As one villager said, "*Gaon me sab barabar hei,*" "In the village all are equal"; men frequently point to this ideal as a major difference between India and Fiji. This public ideology is manifest in such practices as sitting together on the floor during religious events and equal opportunity to speak in meetings. The roots of this egalitarian outlook lie in the conditions of immigration and indenture;[7] the belief is reinforced by the relative similarity in wealth throughout Bhatgaon.

Such egalitarianism, however, is problematic in several important respects. First, not every villager is a potential equal. Sex is a crucial dimension; women are not considered to be comparable to men in this respect. Age is also consequential. Adolescent boys are accorded less respect than older, married men. As there are no formal criteria or ceremonies to mark the transition to social adulthood, disagreements about how one should be treated are common and often lead to serious conflict.[8]

A second problematic aspect of Bhatgaon egalitarianism is the delicate balance between people who should be equals. Individual reputation (*nam,* "name") is central to one's actual social position. A man's "name" is subject to constant renegotiation through his own words and deeds, and through those of others. Villagers are quite sensitive to perceived attempts by others to lower their reputations. They are also attuned to the successes of others; too much success is seen by many as both a personal affront and a violation of egalitarian sentiment.[9] *Jhaln*, "envy," is often cited by villagers as a source of constant conflict within the community, especially between men of roughly equivalent standing (cf. Foster 1972). In disputes reputation management is a constant concern, for conflict often arises from apparent insult, and the remedy lies in the public rebalancing of a man's reputation with his opponent's.

A number of men are recognized as *bada admi*, "big men," because of their past participation in village affairs, religious leadership, education, or other personal success. They also gain respect through the successful management of the disputes of others. Their position is always under stress, however, as obtrusive attempts to assert authority or to intervene in others' problems may be seen as socially presumptuous. Successful "big men" do not exercise their informal power ostentatiously. Continued effectiveness as a respected advisor depends upon an overt reluctance to assume leadership. Even when requested to intervene in a dispute, "big men" are often unwilling; they fear both being identified with one party's interests and being considered overeager to display power. The willing exercise of authority leads to its decline.

There is a police station three miles away, but there are no formal social control agencies in Bhatgaon itself. The village has a representative to the district advisory council, but he is not empowered to regulate affairs within the village. With the decline of caste as an organizational feature of Fiji Indian life, such bodies as caste councils are no longer available for conflict management. Conflict in Bhatgaon remains largely dyadic, the concern of the contending parties alone, yet as long as disputes are dyadic, the chances of settlement are slim. The face-to-face negotiation of a serious dispute is usually impossible, as open accusation or criticism of another is taken as a grievous insult. The offended party may well express his displeasure through vandalism, by cutting down his neighbor's banana trees, for example. While such mischief would not be positively evaluated, other villagers would see it as the natural result of direct confrontation and would not intervene. Only a *kara admi*, "hard man," would risk such revenge through direct discussion; most villagers resort to more indirect strategies.[10] It is difficult to enlist third parties in the management of a conflict, but such triadic participation is crucial. The recruitment of others, not as partisans, but as intermediaries and arbitrators is a central political goal of disputants. Compelling the interest and involvement of disinterested parties is therefore a major end in dispute discourse.[11]

The most salient organizations in Bhatgaon are religious associations. Two Hindu sects are represented, the orthodox Sanatan Dharam and the reformist Arya Samaj. Their local-level organizations are called *mandali,* a term referring both to the groups and to the weekly prayer and fellowship "meetings" that they hold. The "meetings" are run by committees of officers elected yearly. There is one "meeting" for the twenty-nine reform households, and there are three for the fifty orthodox families. The number of orthodox "meetings" reflects several schisms within that community, resulting from unmanageable conflicts between members. The seven Muslim households belong to a mosque association, but they gather only for special events such as festivals and weddings.

Conflicts in Bhatgaon may involve the members of several religious groups, or they may be restricted to coreligionists. Interreligious disputes frequently lead to long-term avoidance, although they may occasionally result in public events such as insult song sessions (see Brenneis and Padarath 1975). Here, I will deal with disputes between men who are members, not only of the same religion, but also of the same "meeting." Such shared membership implies a particular range of constraints on, and opportunities for, public politicking.

Matters of Common Knowledge

Before proceeding to specific discussions of "religious speeches" and "arbitration sessions" a brief digression on knowledge in Bhatgaon is necessary. In those north Indian communities from which Bhatgaon villagers' ancestors emigrated, various types of knowledge were differentially distributed along lines determined by the caste system, just as were more tangible resources. Brahmins, for example, had a virtual monopoly on many types of sacred and ritual knowledge, while black-smiths controlled a range of technical information forbidden to brahmins. A great deal of knowledge, both sacred and secular, was status-specific. Who one was determined what one knew; what one knew demonstrated who one was.

The radical leveling of Indian immigrant society in Fiji had obvious implications for the allocation of knowledge. While in north India the differential distribution of knowledge had both reflected and helped maintain a system of ranked but interdependent groups, in Fiji the groups were at best ill-defined, and the division of labor in part responsible for the division of knowledge no longer existed. Secular knowledge became, in effect, open to all.

In Bhatgaon, at least, there was a corresponding democratization of sacred knowledge as well. The reformist sect has as a central tenet the notion of *sikca*, "instruction." Members are expected to educate both themselves and others in religious practice and understanding. Although reform Hindus are a minority in Bhatgaon, they have a considerable influence on orthodox villagers as well as on reformist villagers.

The generally egalitarian nature of social life in Bhatgaon has a counterpart in the relatively equal opportunity of all villagers to pursue knowledge, both sacred and secular. The sacred has become common knowledge; it is no longer, in most cases, the property of a particular group. It is important to note, however, that, where egalitarian ideals are stressed, continuing symbolic expressions of one's membership in a community of peers are necessary. One must not only feel membership but be able to maintain it publicly. Apparent exclusion is taken very seriously, and knowledge continues to define social identity.

A crucial way of demonstrating one's membership is through sharing in what is "common knowledge" in the community—what "everyone" knows. Although sacred and technical knowledge can be included in this, they are relatively unchanging. The real action lies in the dynamics of everyday life; familiarity with local individuals and recent events is necessary. No one, however, knows everything, and some villagers are considerably better acquainted with particular incidents than are others. This differential participation in common knowledge is, as I shall argue below, an important political fact and a resource for disputants.

"Religious Speeches": Strategies of Indirection

"Religious speeches" are oratorical performances with ostensibly religious content given at the weekly "meetings." Although members of other religions are welcome, the participants in a "meeting" are almost all members of the same Hindu sect. "Religious speeches" are part of a program that follows a ritual butter sacrifice or a reading from the *Ramayana* epic; programs also include religious songs. The program is set by the chairman of the "meeting." Anyone in the congregation may be called upon for a speech, but those who want to speak may ask beforehand to be included. Not all "religious speeches" have a political intent; many are spontaneous speeches on purely religious subjects. "Religious speeches" do, however, offer an important medium for political performance, and I will focus on those speeches which are designed to exploit such opportunities.

The apparent content of "religious speeches" deals with sacred themes. Sometimes speakers celebrate a particular epic hero or cult leader; more frequently a speech focuses on a moral quality considered essential to a good Hindu. There is a great disparity between overt content and intention in politically motivated "religious speeches," however. Although I understood Hindi well and was on the lookout for conflict, during my first few months of fieldwork I saw no reason not to interpret "meeting" speeches as purely religious discourse. A friend's comment on the successful political attack a speaker had made in an apparent homily on the virtues of "meeting" attendance suggested that I was missing the point. The contents of "religious speeches" are not ambiguous in themselves. It is easy for the Hindi-speaking outsider familiar with Hinduism to follow an analysis of, for example, the fidelity of Sita, the wife of the epic hero Ram. The relationship between text and intended function, however, remains quite opaque;[12] the audience knows that some speakers have no hidden agenda and that others are using "religious speeches" for political ends.

In considering the contexts for "religious speeches," a distinction between primary and secondary audience is helpful. The primary audience is composed of the individuals or group at whom the performance is chiefly aimed, that is, those whom the performer hopes to influence directly. The secondary audience includes others who are present. It is not merely a residual category, however, as the secondary audience provides both evaluation and an element of control. The spectators limit and shape the performance.

The primary audience for "religious speeches," when they are being used politically, is those members of the "meeting" not directly involved in the conflict. Spectators sit quietly on the floor while the orator speaks from a standing position. The speaker's goal is to provoke their interest and to gain their support for the future. "Religious speeches" are an important means of recruiting third parties to intervene in, and bring an end to, one's dispute. The secondary audience is one's opponent or his supporters; if the enemy is not present, one can be sure that word of what is said will reach him rapidly. This secondary audience constrains by intimidation. The fear of revenge for overt accusation makes speakers wary. "Religious speeches" are quite indirect in conveying their political messages. This indirection derives from two strategic responses to the "meeting" audience. First, speakers use a strategy of avoidance vis-à-vis their opponents; oblique oratory forestalls revenge. Second, as I will discuss in greater detail below, indirect reference serves a strategy of recruiting third parties. Their interest can be pricked and, at times, their concern compelled.

Bhatgaon villagers recognize two general varieties of Hindi. One, śudh Hindi, "sweet Hindi," is characterized by such features as gender, carefully inflected verbs, and a heavily Sanskritic lexicon. The other code in the village is the local dialect, referred to as jangli bat, "jungle talk"; "jungle" vocabulary includes many English and Fijian items, and its inflectional system is much less complex. "Jungle talk" is the mother tongue for villagers; "sweet Hindi" is learned at school, by reading, and by listening to the radio and to formal speeches.[13] "Religious speeches" are given in "sweet Hindi," or at least in as elegant a code as the speaker can manage. Villagers' competence in "sweet Hindi" is quite variable, but limited knowledge of the code does not limit the effectiveness. Audiences consider the attempt to speak properly to be more important than the results.

Given that "religious speeches" used for political purposes are intended to convey multiple meanings, a crucial question is how speakers cue their audiences to the secondary, covert meanings. When does the audience understand that it is not to take a speech at face value, and

what features guide it to this understanding? "Religious speeches" are
not metaphoric. They contain few figures of speech that by their stylistic features or conventional associations suggest hidden meanings.
Speakers rely instead upon the mention of particular topics such as
anger, jealousy, and contention, and upon several types of syntactic
devices. Chief among these is what I have labeled the "coy reference."
Coy references employ the indefinite pronouns *koi*, "some(one)," and
kya "some(thing)," and occasionally relative pronouns such as *jo*,
"who." They are used to provide vague antecedents for the later use of
the third person pronouns, as in "There are some people who do not
go to "meetings"... they are not good reform Hindus." One can be as
derogatory as desired about an unidentified malefactor.[14]

Even when the entire audience understands that a quite secular
motive underlies a sacred text, some members will recognize only the
fact that something is up, whereas others will be aware of the specific
facts of the dispute. It is here that the differential participation in
matters of common knowledge discussed above becomes important.
People in the audience are concerned about their acceptance as members of the "meeting" because the "meeting" is an important and
relatively stable reference group in the fluid social structure of Bhatgaon. The audience feels that it should be able to uncover speakers'
motives, to unravel their allusions, and to interpret the social as well
as the literal meanings of their "religious speeches." Audiences have
an investment in the interpretation of events within the "meeting"; the
failure to understand suggests less than full participation. They therefore work, often quite subtly, to investigate and comprehend the hidden
meanings.

Speakers have mixed motives in those "religious speeches." In part,
they hope to recruit supporters or at least to promote some sympathy
for these positions. The successful association, however oblique, of
their opponents with the absence or distortion of important virtues
can be effective in giving the enemy a bad name and lowering their
reputation. A more important goal is bringing a private conflict, previously discussed only in sessions of "idle talk" around the *yaqona* bowl,
to public notice through acceptably indirect means. Speakers hope
both to alert fellow "meeting" members to an ongoing dispute and to
convince them that it is serious enough to demand their assistance as

third parties. A successful speech not only arouses interest but also catalyzes community involvement, often through the convening of an "arbitration session."

"Arbitration Sessions": Constructing Public Knowledge[15]

Ad hoc "arbitration sessions" are usually convened by the elected officers of a "meeting" after considerable, albeit indirect, prodding from disputing members of the association. "Arbitration sessions," in marked contrast to "religious speeches," involve quite direct talk about specific events and personalities. Allegations that in most contexts would lead to revenge are discussed at length and without repercussions. Given the egalitarian character of life in Bhatgaon and villagers' consequent avoidance of overt confrontation, the "arbitration session" poses interesting questions: What makes such direct performances possible, and what are their implications for the future relationships of the involved parties? These questions can be answered by outlining the process by which "arbitration sessions" are arranged, their participants and audiences, the formal organization of the session as a communicative event, the content of testimony, and the effects of the sessions.

The sessions are planned and convened by the elected officers of the disputants' "meeting." These officers meet at the *antarang samiti*, "confidential committee," and very deliberately discuss the case, choose appropriate witnesses to summon, and otherwise prepare for the session. Often committee members will interview witnesses clandestinely before the session is held. While they are concerned that factual evidence will be presented, they also want to manage the evidence in such a way that neither party will be totally vanquished. Reinstating the good reputations of both disputants is a central goal. Committee members are also concerned with the public evaluation of their own behavior. They must not appear to be too eager or to dominate the proceedings. The successful management of others' conflicts requires at least the appearance of reluctance; the committee remains as far backstage as possible.

The "arbitration session" itself is held on neutral ground. Both parties attend along with their supporters, the witnesses, and the committee members. The session is often the first occasion since the beginning of the dispute that is attended by both disputants; such joint participation is important in itself.

The audience for such sessions presents a complex picture. Discourse in "arbitration sessions" chiefly takes the form of testimony under oath, and various deities constitute an important secondary audience insuring the truthfulness of witnesses' accounts. The committee members also play an important role in asking questions and maintaining fairly close control over the issues that witnesses can pursue. The primary audience for the entire event, however, is not present. This audience includes other "meeting" members and the village as a whole, and it is from this audience that the "arbitration session" derives a great deal of its effectiveness. Before the session is held, an individual villager's knowledge of the case comes through private and frequently partisan lines. Such knowledge is unauthorized; it can be discussed with close and trusted friends but cannot be drawn upon in public talk. Villagers fear being drawn into the conflict and being treated as a partisan. Through "arbitration session" testimony, an official and definitive account of events crucial to the development of a dispute is publicly constructed. It becomes the basis for later discussion and a new baseline against which the subsequent behavior of the disputants can be measured. It also lets everyone know what happened between the parties and answers those critical questions raised obliquely in "meeting" speeches.

The interrogative form of these proceedings is another important factor in the success of such sessions. Members of the committee interview a series of witnesses, each of whom has sworn to give truthful testimony; such oaths are taken quite seriously. In marked contrast to the American courtroom, there is no adversarial questioning. Only members of the committee may ask questions, and they ask only those questions to which they already know the answers. Women, who rarely figure in other public events, are called as frequently as men. The question-answer format has two features of critical importance for the sessions' success. First, questions compel answers (cf. E. Goody 1978).[16] An unanswered question is an interactional vacuum; response is necessary, especially in public contexts. It is likely, furthermore, that the style and degree of directness of an answer are patterned on those features of the question (see Conley, O'Barr, and Lind, 1978 for some suggestive findings in this area). The direct questions put by committee members draw forth terse but equally direct answers.

A second important feature of the question-answer format is suggested by the work of Keenan, Schieffelin, and Platt (1978). In interpreting the extensive use of questions by mothers in speaking with very young children, they suggest that the question-answer pair be considered a single propositional unit. By answering the question — whether verbally or nonverbally — the infant completes the idea begun by its mother. If this notion is applied to the "arbitration session," one effect of the interrogative format can be seen as the reduction of third-party responsibility for the emerging account. Such evasion of personal accountability and the concomitant shared resolution of contention fit well in the acephalous and egalitarian context of Bhatgaon. The public narrative is constructed through the propositions collaboratively stated by questioner and witness together. The committee is not presenting an account of its own but is contributing to its composition.[17]

The orchestration of "arbitration sessions" as events is a delicate job. The appropriate witnesses must be located and their accounts compared and checked. The planning involved, however, cannot be overly evident to the disputants or the neutrality of the committee might be challenged. The witnesses also must be closely controlled. In contrast to arbitration sessions in many small-scale communities, the "arbitration session" by no means involves a full airing of the issues involved in a dispute (cf. Gibbs 1967; Nader 1969; Cohn 1967). Instead, testimony is confined to a particular incident from which the dispute is considered to stem. The committee has a clear prospective interest in the future relationships between the disputants, but a limited and retrospective focus is the most effective way of insuring a successful outcome.

A final crucial feature of these sessions is the manner in which they end. After the last witness is heard, there is no summing up, no discussion, and no decision by the committee. The disputants are not embarrassed by any directly suggested solution,[18] and the committee members do not overstep their roles. Testimony establishes a single and noncontradictory account of crucial events; these publicly accomplished facts stand on their own. The disputants usually shake hands without much conversation; this serves both as a ritual and public statement of the resumption of amicable relations between them and as a signal that the session is over. The participants may linger, but they talk about other subjects. It is important to understand that no consensus is reached or even attempted; no decision is made. A cooperative and binding account of a contested incident is accomplished, and interested villagers are left to draw their own conclusions and interpretations.

Conclusion

In this chapter I have argued for the interdependence of a range of political performances in an egalitarian Fiji Indian community. The dominant mode of conflict communication is indirection. Public political messages are deeply buried in religious speeches, and individual speakers cannot be held responsible for such secondary meanings, which accords well with the notion that oblique reference is characteristic of political talk among equals (see M. Rosaldo 1973; Irvine 1979). In contrast, the "arbitration session" provides a forum in which contentious issues can be overtly raised. Such sessions are carefully managed to guide and control the information presented and to protect the interests of all the parties involved. Although the talk is open, its subject matter is restricted. No one bears sole responsibility for the public discussion; instead, a cooperative account is created through interrogation. Reference is direct, but the event itself is oblique, providing a legitimate and public version of a case, yet one for which no individual can be held accountable.

"Religious speeches" and "arbitration sessions" are clearly important communicative events in the political life of Bhatgaon. They afford people the opportunity to resolve specific grievances and to repair troubled relationships. Beyond these immediate effects, however, these performances, particularly the "arbitration sessions," speak to broader tensions and contradictions inherent in any egalitarian and leaderless community. Bhatgaon men want to be equals but recognize that much of the time they are not. They also want to live in an orderly social world and understand that the maintenance of order may threaten their equality with their fellows; direct leadership is dangerous to all involved.

In convening an "arbitration session," the committee creates a context for public equality, an occasion within which right relationships among peers not only are enacted but emerge, fostered by carefully edited testimony. Order and amity, however fleeting, are established through cooperative effort. The disputants themselves are given the chance to meet again as equals and to resume their disrupted relationship. More important, however, all the participants experience the compatibility of order and equality within this special context. If, in everyday life, differences between individuals and the effects of unresolved conflicts are all too evident, in the "arbitration session" social reality, cleverly constructed as it is, matches the ideal.

Notes

This chapter was originally presented as a paper in the symposium, "Language and Politics in Oceania: The Social Ecology of Speech Events," at the 1980 Annual Meetings, Association for Social Anthropology in Oceania.

Research in Bhatgaon and subsequent analyses were supported by The National Institutes of Mental Health, the Comparative International Program (Harvard), the Center for the Study of Law and Society, Pitzer College, the Haynes Foundation, and the National Endowment for the Humanities.

Wynne Furth, Fred Myers, Ronald Macaulay, Richard Bauman, Edward Schieffelin, Roger Abrahams, and Judith Huntsman provided valuable criticisms and suggestions for which I am grateful.

1. A detailed discussion of *parbacan* can be found in Brenneis (1978).
2. This dilemma may actually be common to any relationships among equals, whether in an egalitarian society or within a particular stratum in a hierarchical society (cf. Albert's [1972] discussion of Burundi oratory).
3. For a discussion of the notion of speech economy see Abrahams and Bauman (1971).
4. For a fuller discussion of this point see Arno (1976).
5. These data reflect the situation in early 1972.
6. Wynne Furth, who also conducted research in Bhatgaon, has noted that women carry out considerable public politicking through discussions with other women at

weddings and similar events; men are not privy to such performances, as they sit separately.

7. A fuller discussion of the development of egalitarianism in Bhatgaon may be found in Brenneis (1979).

8. This problem and its implications for conflict in the village are considered in Brenneis (1980).

9. Jayawardena (1963) found a very similar phenomenon in his study of overseas Indians; a chief cause of conflict was the "eye-pass," a perceived affront against one's standing as an equal.

10. In speaking of the verbal characteristics associated with direct and indirect conflict strategies, villagers often use the terms *sidha bat*, "straight talk," and *śudh bat*, "sweet talk," respectively. "Sweet talk" is polysemic; it also refers to a prestige variety of Hindi discussed on page 77.

11. The problem of third-party recruitment is discussed in detail in Brenneis (1979).

12. The indirectness of the relationship between text and situated meaning is by no means restricted to Fiji Indian politics but is a constant feature of human communication. The recently burgeoning field of linguistic pragmatics is concerned with mapping out patterned associations between intent and the form of utterances in a range of societies.

13. The situation of "sweet Hindi" and "jungle talk" is quite close to diglossia, albeit, in its specifics, of quite recent origin (see Ferguson 1959).

14. A more detailed explication and examination of the coy reference is in Brenneis (1978:165).

15. It is important to remember that a "religious speech" is a particular genre located in the larger context of the "meeting" as speech event; the "arbitration session" is an event in itself.

16. Bloch (1975) has proposed that "formality" is the crucial coercive feature of political language. The effectiveness of public interrogation in Bhatgaon suggests that different forms of political discourse compel in quite different ways.

17. For a somewhat comparable case of the public construction of an account see Lévi-Strauss (1967:166–69).

18. The avoidance of another's embarrassment is particularly important here. For a general discussion of this concern linguistic strategies employed in meeting it see Brown and Levinson (1978).

3. Who Speaks Here? Formality and the Politics of Gender in Mendi, Highland Papua New Guinea

Rena Lederman
Princeton University

Consideration of male/female relations in Mendi poses problems for a general understanding of the politics of gender in the New Guinea Highlands. Highlands societies are famous in the anthropological literature for sex antagonism and male dominance, and yet, in Mendi, women cannot simply be considered socially subordinate to men. While throughout the Highlands political values emphasize equality, consensus, and individual autonomy among men, in Mendi, relations between men and women appear to be balanced too. For example, in Mendi, unlike in the Mount Hagen area (M. Strathern 1972) or in Mae Enga country (Meggitt 1974), women have their own exchange partners and may be involved in exchange autonomously from their husbands and brothers (Lederman 1979). But, despite the fact that they are involved in the daily give and take of pearl shells, pigs, and Papua New Guinea currency on a footing apparently equal to men's, Mendi women are on the sidelines at large-scale ceremonial prestations. Just like women elsewhere in the Highlands, Mendi women are not orators, and they do not publicly distribute wealth on these occasions. How are we to understand female reticence at formal exchange events? Are the exchanges in which women participate merely means to the end of public male distributions, or do they have their own rationale? Have ceremonial, male-dominated events been overvalued by anthropologists, misled by the bustle and fanfare that attend them?

Questions were raised in my mind about the significance of such formal events in Mendi by a very large community meeting, held in late June 1978, in the main ceremonial ground of the Suolol, the Mendi tribe with whom I lived.[1] The meeting was held ostensibly to discuss the organizing and timing of the Suolols' *sai pombe*, an important parade festival that would signal, to other tribes up and down the Mendi Valley, the tribe's intention to hold a major pig kill in the next year. At the meeting, which I will describe below, the preeminent big-man of the locality spoke eloquently, advocating a course of action differing from that of other leaders attending the meeting. His words were very well received, and his last contribution closed the meeting. It seemed that he had carried the day. Two days later, however, I was surprised to find people doing the opposite of what they had, apparently, been firmly set on doing at the end of the meeting.

On the face of things, this pattern is a familiar one in anthropological discussions of decision-making, political meetings or "councils," and oratory, especially in "egalitarian" societies (see, e.g., Bloch 1975; Kuper and Richards 1971; and several chapters in this volume). In consensus-oriented polities like Mendi, effective decisions (i.e., ones that make a difference to the people involved) appear to be made in informal contexts, not at formal public meetings, which frequently frustrate anthropologists either with their inconclusiveness or with their seemingly predetermined outcomes.

In this chapter, however, I will argue that the meeting mattered and that the Suolol leader's speeches there were quite effective. Despite their relative egalitarianism — even for the Highlands — an ideology of gender hierarchy constitutes the tacitly accepted background of belief for both men and women in Mendi. In what follows, I will show how this ideology is used to structure certain formal meetings so as to give special cultural weight to male, corporate group action. Effective speechmaking in this context defines and constrains individual action in particular ways that informal discussions do not. This conclusion echoes certain points made by Maurice Bloch in his Malinowski Memorial Lecture (Bloch 1977) about the relationship between formal or ritualized events, "social structure," and the amount of instituted hierarchy, but brings to bear on his thesis material from an unlikely source.

Veiled Speech and the Politics of Consensus

In his early discussion of leadership and consensus in the Eastern Highlands of New Guinea, Kenneth Read (1959) noted two "antithetical orientations," perhaps generally present in Highlands societies: "strength" and "equivalence." They describe the tension Read observed in Highlands political life between assertions of personal autonomy and of the need for concerted group action. In the Highlands, this tension is not resolved by the existence of a centralized political authority that can be turned to in disputes and decision making. The social control of violence, as well as the social possibility of collective action, becomes in effect everyone's responsibility.

Andrew Strathern (1975b) argues that the use of indirect, allusive language is a tool that makes social control in this social context possible, and his discussion applies equally to the Mendi case. Strathern describes how indirect, "veiled" speech is used in a range of situations, from children's games and courting songs to ceremonial oratory. This kind of speech can be used effectively to focus attention on the speaker and perhaps thereby enhance his prestige. But it has a further important role to play: "veiled" speech in the context of disputes is used "to express ... suspicions and aggressive intentions while at the same time not revealing these so openly as to provoke violence or to preclude a settlement," (199). Strathern argues that whereas direct questions, challenges, or insults may provoke violence, indirect speech preserves social relationships while still conveying information about the contentious issues. This sort of language, he wrote, "is part of the total set of controls over, and cues about, the aggressive intentions of the parties at the meeting" (193). Elaborate, indirect speech puts a damper on aggression in the context of disputes and makes possible amicable settlements in the absence of a mediating authority.

The political significance of "veiled" speech in decentralized, egalitarian policies, standing in for central political authority in more hi-
erarchically organized political systems, has been widely noted (see,
e.g., Brenneis 1978; Keenan 1974; M. Rosaldo 1973). New, "direct" forms
of political discourse, associated with the imposition of modern national governments and centrally controlled court systems, contrast
with traditional forms of speech that aim, through slowly drawn out
discussion, to arrive at a settlement of complex disputes. This contrast
highlights the apparent close fit between indirection and egalitarianism. As Rosaldo observed of the Ilongot (Philippines), the differences
between direct, "straight" speech introduced by central government
representatives and circuitous traditional speech heard in egalitarian
meetings accompany different attitudes toward human motives and
truth. While direct speech in the modern context refers to a higher
authority (to the courts, to God) as the source of truth and legitimacy,
the use of indirect language in traditional dispute settlement refers to
the community and reflects the idea that people are "equal, individual
and difficult to understand."(M. Rosaldo 1973:221) For the New Guinea
Highlands, in particular, "veiled" speech resolves the tension Read
described between "equivalence" and "strength." The ambiguity inherent in this form of speech makes possible a certain *flexibility* of
response on the part of people addressed by it.

But allusive speech is not used in relatively egalitarian societies only.
It is also used in hierarchic systems of traditional authority such as
that of the Merina of Madagascar. According to Maurice Bloch, formal
oratory of Merina leaders is highly indirect. But these allusive speeches
constrain the response of those who allow themselves to be addressed
in this way. Like Strathern, Bloch considers indirect speech as a
mechanism of social control, but he describes a very different relationship between speech and social relationships from that implied by
Strathern:

It is because the formalization of language is a way whereby one speaker can
coerce the response of another, that it can be seen as a form of social control.
It is really a type of communication where rebellion is impossible and only
revolution is feasible. (Bloch 1975:20)

Indirect speech, then, appears in a range of political types, and is
not associated exclusively with egalitarian societies. Wherever it appears, it merely reflects and helps to support the existing political

relations. Thus, its ambiguity serves coercive ends in Merina society and noncoercive ones in Mendi. It might be added that the effect of direct speech also varies with existing political relations. While all direct speech is characterized by some degree of pressure by the speaker for a response, it facilitates modern authoritarian relationships in some cases (Rosaldo 1973) and relationships between equals in others (Brenneis, this volume; Bloch 1971). Neither indirect nor direct speech is a political fact in itself.

However, the *formality* of discourse—those special conventions and ritualized restrictions on participants, place, and behavior that make discourse proper and unquestionable or sanctified because it is "traditional" (see, e.g., Bloch 1975, 1977) — may be quite important politically. Like allusive speech forms, formality occurs in both authoritarian and egalitarian societies. While Bloch (1975) is right in stating that formality in the Highlands is not as elaborated as in Merina, still, some Mendi situations are relatively more formal than others. But unlike the speech forms discussed above, the effects of formality do *not* vary with political type: it will be seen that formality in Mendi is constraining in ways similar to formality among the Merina, even though it is conveyed differently in each case. Indirect speech itself makes a situation "formal" in Merina society. But, in egalitarian societies like those in the Highlands where "veiled" speech styles comparable to Merina oratory operate in both formal and informal settings, formality is mostly conveyed by nonlinguistic aspects of events, as I will show in the next section.

In Mendi, consideration of formality will reveal that individual autonomy and flexibility and competitive balance among equals are only part of the political picture that also includes sex antagonism and an ideology of male superiority (see, e.g., Brown and Buchbinder 1976; Meggitt 1964; M. Strathern 1972). Looking at how access to formal contexts of discourse is restricted — asking who can and who cannot speak here — we see that formal Mendi meetings are male and that women as a group are excluded. To discover what difference this exclusion makes—what it is that women can and cannot do and how these things are valued—is to identify the "political" meaning of gender in formal settings.

For the purposes of this chapter, "political" relations refer not only to the way access to a given set of culturally valued resources is restricted for certain people (or "statuses") and not others, or the way in which a particular given social order is maintained and enforced; they also refer to the way in which this social order and these valuations are themselves created and reproduced or are denied and transformed. Formal occasions may help to reproduce these valuations and differential restrictions in the face of other values and relationships implicit in informal contexts (cf. Bloch 1977). The significant political distinction between egalitarian societies like those in the Highlands of Papua New Guinea, and traditional nonegalitarian societies like that of the Merina, may have to do with differences in the relationship between formal and informal contexts within each society.[2] These assumptions imply that while attention will be focused on an account of a formal meeting in the present discussion, the significance of that event for an understanding of Mendi political relations cannot be appreciated without also considering the informal social context in which women are active and verbal participants, and to which the apparently "unconstrained" response of men to the big-man's speeches related. What this informal context is will be elaborated in the next two sections. The existence of such contradictions does not show the meeting up for a fraud. However, it does enable us to go beyond Read's (1959) early hints about the complexity and tension upon which Highlands egalitarian polities are built.

A Mendi Meeting

Sai pombe refers to a parade of two or three days' duration held to announce the inception of the last (approximately year-long) phase of preparations for the pig festival (sai le) in Mendi. Pig festival preparations comprise a series of events extending over about twelve years for any particular tribe. Neighboring and distant allies are invited to participate in full dress at the sai pombe and are rewarded for doing so with pearl shells and money. This payment is partly a reciprocation for payments made to the current hosts when they were invited as guests to the sai pombe of their allies, years earlier. Preparations for the parade involve readying sugarcane and sweet potatoes for guests, renting feather headdresses, buying tree oil and accumulating pearl shells to be used as body decorations and as gifts for invited paraders, organizing invitations, and preparing the parade grounds. It is, in other words, a large mobilization of wealth and energy. Converted into modern Papua New Guinea currency, their final *sai pombe* was estimated to have "cost" the Senkere community and their allies about K20,000 (or approximately U.S. $29,000 at 1978 exchange rates).

In Senkere, past parades have been marked by a degree of competition between allies, expressed in two ways. First of all, the current hosts may try to surpass the past hosting performance of their current guests in the overall scale of their parade by inviting more contingents of paraders from a wider array of clans. People in Senkere were planning to invite, among others, members of a branch of Suolol who live outside the Mendi Valley in Ialibu, quite some distance away.

Competition may also be expressed in attempts by the guests to set the parade date for their hosts, forcing the hosts into holding the event before they are really ready with their own self-decorations and with wealth to give to guest paraders, and so embarrassing them. Thus, twelve years before the meeting in question, some men from two Suolol clans had paraded in the ceremonial ground of an allied tribe, Surup, members of which were planning their *sai pombe* prior to their own *sai le* pig kill of 1967. This Suolol parade had overtones of a sneak attack, since no Surup ("not even a dog" in some Suolol accounts) were present, having gone off to participate as guests in another a parade elsewhere in the Mendi Valley at the time. During Suolol's victorious parade in Surup's empty ceremonial ground, a trade store was alleged to have burned down, and ever since, according to Suolol informants, the Surup had hung a tin of fish from the store in the rafters of one of their men's club houses as a reminder of the insult — much as they might have hung up the bones of a prominent clansman killed in battle to remind them of a death to be avenged.

The meeting in question followed several months of heightening discord between members of Surup and two Senkere subclans over a series of recent deaths and sorcery accusations (see Lederman 1981). Surup leaders (partly at the urging of at least one member of a third Senkere Suolol subclan who had sided with them in these disputes) had been threatening for some time to set the date for the *sai pombe*, and had announced that they would parade at Senkere at the end of that week, while even the most eager people in Senkere were arguing for a date two weeks after that. The meeting was called on a Monday to discuss community policy with respect to Surup's intended parade. It contrasted with *ad hoc* meetings that had preceded it in that members of interested neighboring groups were invited to attend and in that it was announced widely within the Senkere community (indeed, more than 100 people came, an unusually large gathering). It took place in Senkere *koma*, the main ceremonial ground in the area. Some of the shells intended as payment to parade guests were publicly displayed and counted at this meeting, and members of two subclans, whose wild pandanus trees happened to be bearing then, made a harvesting expedition to bring back nuts to bake at the meeting especially to draw people to it.

The main question to be settled at the meeting was to what extent members of Suolol were going to sanction the almost inevitable Surup parade at Senkere.[3] The most important big-man in the community, Olonda, had been arguing for some time that only Surup should parade this time and that Suolol and its other allies should parade later on. A possible explanation for his position was his history of poor relations with Surup stretching back fifteen years. The leverage he brought to bear on his side was that (1) he was organizing the collection of shell wealth that would be given to Surup *if* they came to the *sai pombe* sponsored by Suolol and (2) he had taken another initiative, making the long trip to Ialibu to inform the people there when they should plan to come (i.e., on a date he wanted, not on Surup's date). He recognized, as did everyone, that he had no control over when or whether Surup came (short of violence, that is). But, he believed firmly that no one else should join Surup if they came that week, and if they came then he was determined that no shells would be distributed to them.

On the other side, members of Surup had also met and conveyed to observers from Suolol that they wished their parade to be the final one before Suolol's pig kill. Using their geographic position as leverage, they threatened to close the road to the Ialibu contingent if the latter came to a Suolol parade held after the Surup affair. The few Surup who came to the Senkere meeting arrived late and spoke little. They expressed both their group's readiness to parade and their perplexity at Suolol's state of disunity and unpreparedness that week.

A third position, advocated by Pua (an influential man and subclan brother of Olonda, but no orator), was that some people ought to dress up and participate when Surup came to parade in Senkere but that a second, Suolol-sponsored parade should also take place later. Some such participation would be a way of admitting good-spirited capitulation by conferring some legitimacy on Surup's parade and would help to right the balance of intergroup relations.

The discussion preceding Olonda's speeches concerned the preparations remaining for the Suolol *sai pombe*, and a full range of attitudes to Surup's plans. Many outsiders from neighboring clans expressed confusion about why more Surups were not in attendance (there were only two present, clan brothers of the wife of one local man). They asserted that Surup and Suolol were important allies and, as "brothers," must decide together about when the parade should take place. Several of them commented that dissension like that between Surup and Suolol boded ill for the parade, since the parade's purpose was to strengthen alliances between groups.

When Olonda rose to speak, he reviewed the history of Surup/Suolol rivalry, simply noting that Suolol had paraded twice during the Surup *sai pombe* twelve years ago. "What will happen now?" he asked the few Surup men present; they did not answer. In this way, he deemphasized Suolol's first, aggressive parade at Surup's place by emphasizing that Suolol had also paraded with Surup at the parade Surup themselves had sponsored afterward. He implied that Surup ought to do the same, this time. He then addressed members of the other tribes in attendance directly, summarizing the discussion, but adding his own twist: only Surup would parade that week because Suolol was not ready. This was because the branch of Suolol living in Kuma, a large community in the northeastern part of Suolol territory, had not yet repaid twelve shells that they owed to Senkere Suolol. These were shells that the residents of the Senkere neighborhood had presented to Kuma residents on the occasion of Kuma's own *sai pombe*, which had been held six months earlier. Just before that parade, a respected member of the Senkere community had died, a death in which Surup and one Suolol subclan were purportedly implicated and that prevented men from Senkere Suolol from parading at Kuma as they would have liked had they not been in mourning. The Kuma Suolol, as every-

one present knew, had to make their repayment if they were to participate without shame. Furthermore, a parade without the Suolol resident at Kuma was not possible. Coordination with the Kuma Suolol in
the completion of the pig kill cycle had been a central concern all year.
Without such coordination, the pig kill would not compare favorably
with other recent ones. This was a principle with which everyone in
the community agreed. The point Olonda was making was that, regardless of the readiness of individual Senkere men with their own
personal parade decorations, Suolol as a proper, unified *sem onda*
(tribe) was not ready to hold its parade that week. There was a general
fear in the Senkere community that if the coordination with the Kuma
community was dropped in this parade context, it might fail over the
pig kill as well, which would be devastating for Suolol's reputation,
already damaged by the political disputes previously mentioned.

This speech had the effect of galvanizing the outsiders, who confirmed that they would parade at the second Senkere *sai pombe*, not
at the one Surup was sponsoring that week. They emphasized that
Suolol and Surup were brothers, that they wanted to contribute to a
large and good festival, and that they would help bring other groups
of paraders there. They clearly supported Olonda's position that the
parade that week was Surup's affair alone.

Some people present thought the meeting should have ended right
there, and they raised their shovels to the pandanus nut oven, but they
were stopped by others who had more to say. Much divisive talk
referring to intra-Suolol conflicts followed, during which Olonda tried
with great flourish but no success to reassert control over the discussion. He repeated his point that the matter was out of the hands of
Senkere men. Participants from other tribes strongly supported this
argument in their speeches as well, and, after a while — and one final
performance by Olonda — harmony was restored. One of the men who
had sponsored the pandanus collection applauded, others joined him
(perhaps following Western custom), and the meeting ended with the
opening of the oven and the distribution of the nuts.

Although there was no definitive summary statement and no vote
taken, it seemed clear (and the discussion subsequent to the meeting
confirmed for me) that the parade that week was considered to be
Surup's affair and that no one from the Senkere area would actively

participate in the event. If the outcome of the meeting was not completely predetermined, it did seem to illustrate the centrality of the preeminent big-man and of speechmaking in shaping collective decisions.

Two days later, on Wednesday, however, I became aware that many men in the Senkere area were busily preparing their wigs and feather headdresses for the Surup parade. On Monday evening and all day on Tuesday, Pua and others privately argued that people in Senkere should parade with Surup; as it turned out, they did exactly that. It seemed to me then that Olonda's well-received speeches had had no practical effect and that the meeting had had no particular importance, despite all the fanfare. People had acted as individuals and had taken matters into their own hands as events of the moment moved them—a practice perfectly in keeping with the ethos of autonomy I had come to appreciate in Mendi. Not only did more than a quarter of the young and adult men of Senkere Suolol parade with the Surup (even going to some Surup localities and accompanying the Surup paraders to Senkere on Friday), but Pua found a way to make a shell payment to some of the Surup on Sunday, after the parading was over. At that distribution (a compensation for a ceremonial ax broken during the parade), the Surup —who included two big-men, important exchange partners of Pua's— expressed pleasure that Suolol men had participated with them in the *sai pombe* and satisfaction in repaying Suolol for the latter's previous parade aggression. Most significantly, they agreed, at Pua's insistence, not to close the road to the Ialibu contingent whom Olonda had invited to come to the Suolol *sai pombe* (which took place at the beginning of September and far outstripped Surup's event in size).

Responding to my expressions of confusion during the following week, Pua explained the outcome to me by saying that Olonda had not done enough "quiet," private lobbying. The implication was that it was in private contexts that practical decisions about action are made, not in public meetings. He recounted other times when leaders got up to speak without first turning over the ground privately. His comments and those of other participants in the Surup parade suggested to me the practical importance of informal talk in individual decision making.

However, these comments did not answer my questions about what the meeting had accomplished. This was because private and public

discussions concern two different categories of social relationship —
that of the personal "network" (*twem*) and of the corporate "group"
(*sem onda*, what I have been calling "tribe" or "clan") — each of which
constrains individual action, sometimes in mutually contradictory
ways (see Lederman 1982).

Private, informal discussions concern obligations people have to
their personal networks of exchange partners, though group affairs
may also be spoken about in this context. Both men and women, and
adults as well as unmarried people, take part in these discussions all
the time. Obligations to exchange partners (who may include affines,
cognatic kin, and unrelated people) center around debts and credits
in pigs, pearl shells, Papua New Guinea currency, or other items required in marriage and death payments and other minor transactions,
but also involve general hospitality and mutual aid, including support
during parades. If it was true that Olonda had not done enough private
lobbying, then perhaps he did not appreciate the current extent of
such personal obligations between particular Senkere Suolol men and
members of Surup. On the one hand, had he lobbied intensively, he
might have been able to convince or pressure more Suolol men into
not parading that week. On the other hand, given the extent of Suolol's
internal conflicts and coordination problems, it is doubtful that his
public rhetoric could have been much softened in any case. He was
consistently concerned about Suolol's strength and consistently identified his own standing with that of the tribe. It is possible that, if he
had not argued so strongly for a separate Suolol *sai pombe*, it might
never have happened.

Thus, the private lobbying to which Pua referred concerned decisions about personal obligations of Suolol men to their Surup exchange
partners, and not any new consensus about the timing of Suolol's *sai
pombe*. Those who participated in the Surup affair were people like
Pua who had important obligations to their Surup exchange partners.
These people had indeed acted "as individuals": the point is that
Olonda had done his best at the meeting to insure that they *could not,
in fact, do otherwise*. Even Pua's pearl shell distribution to the Surup
did not make the participation of Suolol men anything more than

personal, although it did create enough ambiguity to save the face of his Surup big-man exchange partners and thereby enable them to back down from their threats to close the road.

Public discussion concerns *sem onda* (group) action almost exclusively: large pig kills, war death compensation payments, large "fertility" cults. During formal, public discussions, attention is focused on the group significance of events, even though the personal obligations of clan members to exchange partners in other groups may also be fulfilled at these events. The meeting was not, then, merely a ratification or summation of many individual decisions; nor was it undone by the individual actions that followed. The successful staging and harmonious outcome of the meeting were significant, not so much because they could determine what actions would take place, but because they shaped a particular and widespread public understanding about the group meaning of subsequent actions.

These understandings were, of course, considerations in the private decisions for action that individuals made and had many practical effects on the lives of both those who paraded that week with the Surup and those who did not. At the least, the new timing and the general importance of Suolol's own *sai pombe* at Senkere two months later (in which most Suolol men participated, including most of those who paraded the first time with Surup) created problems of resource allocation for many people. Men with Surup exchange partners and affines had to manage their debts and credits very carefully in order to be able to participate in two separate parades. Personal exchange relationships were strained, and a few appeared to break down as a result.

How Formality Conveys Group Goals

Compared with formal meetings in more hierarchic societies (see, e.g., Bloch, ed. 1975; Kuper and Richards 1971), the Senkere meeting was anarchic and unstructured. There was no "chair" to control access to the floor; no vote was taken; and people were not bound by any of the recommendations men made. In contrast to some formal meetings elsewhere, too, matters of substance, over which participants had some control, were discussed, and opposing points of view were aired directly (cf. Bloch 1971). But, like formal, institutionalized "council" meetings in other societies, the structure of the meeting was different from the more common sort of discussions in which people in Mendi engage. The participants, also, insisted that the meeting was different from smaller, informal discussions about the parade that preceded and followed it. But, to my knowledge, they did not distinguish formal from informal meetings by citing characteristic *speech forms* associated with each. Rather, they explicated the distinction by pointing to the *social contexts* in which discussion occured. People referred descriptively to "quiet talk" (*ngail sub*) in a person's house being different from talk in the ceremonial ground, before everyone's eyes — something for which big-men are known.

I will now consider how the content of the meeting was reinforced by its formality and, in particular, by the exclusion of women as participants. This will help to explain the particular value inhering in group discussion and the particular compulsion behind obligations men have to clansmen.

Irvine (1979) points out that the analysis of formality is often marred by a conflation of its several meanings. Sometimes it refers to increased structuring of the linguistic or nonlinguistic "code," sometimes to aspects of the social setting, to the level of the analysis of behavior, or to some mixture of these features. Irvine suggests that we analytically separate four aspects of formality that do not always occur together: (1) increased structuring of the codes that organize behavior in a situation; (2) centralization of attention at a gathering; (3) increased consistency of the codes used, which gives activity a sense of propriety; and (4) a tendency to invoke public or social rather than "personal" identities of the participants. I will consider the Mendi meeting from these vantage points, in order to explicate what "formality" is about in this case.

Discourse was "structured" or restricted more than usual in that the assembly spoke about a narrowly defined problem, expressed in terms of *"sem onda"*: Suolol, Surup. The topic of this discussion related to collective action on the level of *sem onda* (the *sai pombe*), rather than to action appropriate to individuals, sets of exchange partners, or households (like marriage). In informal contexts, discussion may range over many topics and may refer to anything from personal names and families to *sem onda*.

This explicit thematic emphasis on corporate groups was reinforced indirectly by means of references to eating together (an action that signifies good relations). For example, one minor big-man announced that he could have eaten the pandanus nuts he had harvested in his wife's house (the site of quiet, private discussion). He did not, he explained, because the pandanus is for all the people at the meeting. Other men referred to the pandanus to make a similar point: it was meant not merely for the Surup affines of one Suolol man to share but for all Surup and Suolol men together.

Apart from these themes and the narrow focus of the discussion, speech at the meeting also differed from everyday talk in that there was more attention to turn-taking and more than the usual emphasis on hearing what certain respected men like Olonda had to say. In general, there was more reference to procedure than in ordinary contexts: to who had or had not been heard from, to what should come next, and so on. Olonda was the only speaker whose performance was stylized, however. For example, whereas speakers either remained seated or stood in place, Olonda used the spatial organization of the crowd, coming to the center as he spoke, and sauntering to the far periphery as he finished. While the speech of a number of men was "veiled," this was not a striking feature of the meeting. Remarks were frequently direct and angry, though, admittedly, the situation might have been different had more members of Surup been present.

The most strikingly structured aspect of the meeting was not linguistic but spatial. The meeting took place in the main ceremonial ground, which is this dispersed community's social center and the site of large-scale group events like pig kills and pearl shell displays. This fact was explicitly mentioned to set the meeting off from other discussions, even though people find themselves in the area during the course of any normal day, and small-scale events may take place there as well, from time to time. Adult men sat together in the central area between the pandanus nut oven and the line of pearl shells. Women and young people sat on the periphery. Speakers addressed and came entirely from the central male group that included members of Suolol and of the other tribes. While in informal discussions men and women may often sit separately, there is generally not quite so sharp a distinction between male and female groups as such. Rather, people may sit in groups of friends, and there are usually several separate clusters of men and women.

This organization created a central focus of attention at the meeting. The single line of pearl shells was not only a physical boundary, focusing attention on the men, *but* also a concrete demonstration of the common purpose of the men of Suolol. The shells were counted together, and individual contributions were not identified. In fact, many members of the assembly could not accurately report how many shells were contributed by particular people but knew only the aggregate figure announced by the man who had made the count. During the Suolol parade two months later, these shells were given en bloc by a Suolol big-man to a big-man in a group of parade guests, who would later redistribute them to his clansmen. The pandanus oven also focused attention on the men at the same time as it was referred to in speeches to underscore a similar point. Discussion began in earnest when the oven was closed up. When all appeared satisfied that the discussion had ended, the nuts were distributed. This activity focused attention temporarily, and references to the nuts further reinforced messages concerning group coordination and harmony.

Women, for the most part, concurred with this focusing by not forming a separate focus of their own at the meeting, but rather, sitting on the outskirts and listening to the talk. But attendance by women was much lower than that of men. When I asked a few women why they had not been there, they answered with comments like "Why should I? That is men's business." and "I had garden work to do."

"Code consistency" has to do with what conveys a formal event's "seriousness." Few Mendi discussions emphasize "consistency," for most are punctuated with purposely inappropriate contributions such as sexual joking. In contrast, this meeting was quite proper and serious. Restrictions on who might speak and about what they might speak were matched by the location and the focusing features to give this effect. At the handful of such meetings I witnessed during my stay in

Mendi, women did not make speeches. A "female" voice is inconsistent, inappropriate. Women do not form part of the primary audience: they are not even addressed.

But what aspect of "femaleness" is being ruled offstage? The social identity of women in Mendi is not narrowly defined in ordinary circumstances. Normally, they are quite vocal, although it is significant that there are no specifically female "councils" or issues that require collective *female* decisions and action, unlike the situation described, for example, by Bloch (1971). Mendi women are, compared with women in the Highlands generally, unusually autonomous participants in exchanges. As I have noted, they have their own exchange partners and not uncommonly conduct transactions in shells, pigs, and other items independently of their husbands. In particular, some of the shells on display at the meeting had been contributed by women, and some of the talk concerned the allocation of those shells. Furthermore, the talk concerned allied groups, that is, the natal groups of many of the resident wives. From these facts, it would seem that women ought to have been involved directly in the proceedings.

Yet they were not. That women's "public" identities are antithetical to *sem onda*-oriented formal occasions is illustrated by the behavior of one of the most remarkable women in the community. In her late forties in 1978, Tenpuri had a roster of exchange partners and active debts and credits quantitatively equivalent to the two most important big-men in Senkere and was, from the point of view of informal exchange, more active than her husband. However, if a pearl shell distribution in the ceremonial ground was in order, or if pigs had to be slaughtered and speeches made, her husband officiated (sometimes accompanied by her insistent sotto voce instructions and comments). In these formal contexts, her personal identity as a prominent member of the community was not relevant. Moreover, her public identity was characterized by restriction — by what she could not do, *despite* her desires and abilities. That *any* woman should give shells or make a speech at a tribal gathering — unless explicitly as a "place holder" for a dead or absent male — is not proper in Mendi. Action by a woman, and female imagery in men's speeches, both may be interpreted, or intended deliberately, as an affront. For example, in boasting or challenging speeches during intergroup competitive displays (*tanol tukim pila*), men call their opponents "women" or "our wives" when they claim victory.

In contrast, the participation of men in formal, *sem onda* affairs is normal, appropriate, and valued highly. Men, like women, participate in household production activities and have obligations to their networks of exchange partners. But men, as members of *sem onda*, also have obligations to their "brothers" to contribute to the large group displays. Men may sometimes see transactions with their exchange partners as means to the end of formal group display, and sometimes value the latter over the former. For women, in contrast, network transactions and obligations are ends in themselves because, regardless of how they value group activity relative to network activity, their active participation is confined to their networks.

In Mendi, the male/female distinction can come at times to stand for this group/network distinction and, furthermore, may give group action a positive cultural value. It follows from this, then, that in formal contexts, *not only* women are ruled offstage, but so *also* are the "personal" identities of men. Men who bring up inappropriately personal issues at a meeting concerning tribal affairs are overruled or ignored. At the meeting in question, this was alluded to, for example, in the criticisms made by participants from outside groups concerning why only the Surup affines of one Suolol man had come. The significance of Olonda's speeches has to be seen in this light as well. Olonda's contribution was appreciated and consented to because he had skillfully framed his arguments in appropriate group terms.

Political Ideology and the Significance of Exclusion

As Irvine and others have noted, formal political meetings do not reveal much about decision-making processes in either egalitarian or hierarchic systems. As she wrote (1979: 782), formality "has to do with what can be focused on publicly, and so can connote the publicly recognized and legitimate social order." In her view, the "organization of these formal meetings reflects political ideology," not processes by which decisions are made.

Individuals make decisions about action outside formal contexts in Mendi, too. These decisions reflect compromises between the obligations and needs individuals have with respect to their exchange partners on the one hand and their clansmen on the other. But while individuals are free to make personal decisions about how to balance these obligations, formality *is* constraining in two ways in Mendi, and perhaps generally in the Highlands. First, as Andrew Strathern puts it (1979a: 103), assertions about individual autonomy that Highlanders make must be understood in their sociocultural context of morality, judgment, and ambition where they "inevitably involve a group context and an evaluation of individual achievement in that context."

Moreover, he notes (1979a: 104) that actions during public ceremonial exchanges — a central context for speechmaking in Mount Hagen — "mean something simultaneously and inextricably at both the group and the individual levels." Wherever this duality exists, while a person is free to make personal decisions about action on his own, he will not be in control of this second, group-level sense in which his actions will also be understood unless he takes part in the process of shaping those understandings in formal meetings. There is some compulsion to participate. Not participating reduces the sphere of control a man exercises to his personal relations and makes him more like a woman, who also exercises control only over personal network relations. But not participating constitutes a choice for a man, because all men have access to the forum where group policy is discussed. Here, all men are on an equal footing and are different from women.

This leads to the second way in which formality in Mendi is constraining. While there was no individual authority, *all* the men at the meeting were acting quite explicitly to control who could and who could not speak. That no woman tried to speak at this particular meeting reflects their passive acquiescence to the values expressed in the form of the event. This form both demonstrated and validated the (uneasy) dominance of the group meanings of action over those of the network in Mendi, a relationship most potently reinforced by gender symbolism. *In this context of formality*, symbolism devalues both "femaleness" and the individual network transactions of both women and men at the same time as it gives special weight to the male, corporate group significance that that action can also bear. There is a compelling redundancy at formal events: talk concerning *sem onda* is reinforced by formality, by those features which focus attention on men, who actively constitute the groups that their "maleness" represents. The particular matters at hand are, in this way, suffused with a familiar and approving glow. Reminiscent of the manner in which authority cannot be challenged in Merina society, this effect cannot be challenged because it is never explicitly articulated. It is, in sum, "veiled" and implicit. What is left unsaid at the meeting is closely related to who could not speak.

It is ironic, then, that the most explicit and frequently reported (but least convincing) expressions of "male superiority" in the Highlands come in those personal contexts where it does not, in fact, hold (where it is not reinforced formally) in Mendi: for example, in talk between husband and wives. Reactions of Mendi women to these expressions vary greatly, from laughter and scorn to anger and even to divorce. But their reactions do not seriously challenge the cultural source from which expressions of male superiority issue, since they occur in the very same personal contexts in which those expressions are meaningless and inappropriate to begin with. Women in Mendi have no "legitimate" collective forum from which to challenge the existing male social structural ideology and, for the most part, do not express a need for one. Their frustrations over the way in which group events affect their lives are also acted upon in personal settings.[4]

The literature on Highlands exchange and politics has been dominated by descriptions of formal groups. This emphasis may accurately reflect explicit political ideology there but may not sum up the entire system of political meanings. If politics refers not only to the maintenance of a particular social order but also to the continuous process by which that order gets defined by both the people who control explicit ideology and the people not in control of it (Thompson 1975), then the extent to which the dominant ideology is only passively acquiesced to by women, and not actively shared and supported by them, is significant. In Mendi, women can perhaps more easily leave oratory and group ceremonies to men because their own sphere of activity is positively valued, informally. As I have noted, Mendi women are actively involved in exchanges and discussions that take place in informal, private settings; where networks are positively valued and where the symbols, men and women, especially as brothers and sisters, have many interests in common. In Mendi — although perhaps not so clearly elsewhere in the Highlands — these interests find formal, ritualized expression in the marriage ceremony, in which Mendi brides distribute their own marriage payment. The more balanced cultural emphasis on networks and groups in Mendi may partially explain the greater autonomy of Mendi women as compared with Hagen women, and may account for both the greater emphasis on network exchanges relating to marriage and death and the lower frequency of group-level exchanges in Mendi, also as compared with Hagen women.

This particular Mendi situation may also be responsible for a less antagonistic relationship between the sexes there than elsewhere in the Highlands. However, even those acts of personal rebellion, in which women actively oppose men's definitions of the social order, such as M. Strathern describes (1972), raise questions about the extent to which male ideology can be understood fully without appreciating how this ideology is an argument *against* women's ideas, rather than simply a positive, independent statement.

However, the importance of formal, explicit political ideology cannot simply be discounted just because informal powers and alternative meanings exist. Consideration of the power of our own explicit ideology of gender hierarchy in muffling certain voices and devaluing certain acts should convince us of this. The point is that we cannot merely note that women are restricted in this context and not in that one, as Irvine argues (1979: 784) when she writes, "any restrictions on participation in formal meetings do not necessarily apply to other contexts, which may be the ones where political decision making actually occurs and where political freedom is, therefore, more at issue." These contexts are all part of a single social experience and have to be examined *in relation* to one another. More attention needs to be paid to the tension between formal and informal situations — both to the ways in which certain talk becomes inaudible politically and to the processes whereby the formal ideology is eroded and questioned by the existence of alternative perspectives alongside it.

And, if we agree that formal meetings, in particular, have to do with what is recognized and considered legitimate, connoting a social order, as Irvine also argued, then the restrictions on participation also inherent in formal contexts may create an asymmetry that is culturally loaded and constitutive of political hierarchy. Such formal contexts and facts about who is included in, or excluded from them, are central to both the understanding and the transformation of political systems.

Notes

Reprinted with some changes, from the *Journal of the Polynesian Society* (1980) 89: 479 – 98. By kind permission of the publisher.

The research was carried out in Upper Mendi, Southern Highlands Province, Papua New Guinea, from November 1977 through March 1979, and was supported by National Institute of Mental Health Predoctoral Research Fellowship 1-F31-MH06068 and National Science Foundation Predoctoral Research Grant BNS77-10555. I thank both institutions for their support.

I thank Michael Merrill for participating in the research with me, and for commenting on drafts of this paper. Thanks are also due to the other participants in the symposium, "Language and Politics" (Association for Social Anthropology in Oceania Meetings, February 1980), and to L. Brock, G. Coleman, A. Rosman, and P. Rubel for their comments. Any slipperiness remaining in the argument presented here is my responsibility. Mendi names have been changed in this account.

1. Some background on the Mendi area may be necessary. Mendi fits the central Highlands pattern of closely managed pig herds and intensively cultivated sweet potato gardens. Mendi clans (in which membership is often with that of one's father and of which idioms of unity are "agnatic") are the basic exogamous and territorial units, and within each fighting is rare. Mendi tribes (or "clan clusters" in the terminology of the previous ethnographer, Ryan 1959) are political alliances of geographically contiguous clans. They may have up to 1,500 members and act together to fight against major enemies, to make major war compensation payments to allies, and to hold pig festivals. While the marriage rules disperse ties, one usually marries one's allies in Mendi.

Women generally move, on marriage, to the place of their husband. Residence in Mendi is dispersed within named localities but is conceptually centered around a ceremonial ground belonging to the resident clan. The Senkere "community" referred to in this paper—which is a government census unit—had a population of approximately 350 and was composed of several subclans of two Suolol clans living in three neighboring named localities, each with a ceremonial ground. The ground at the locality called

Senkere was the largest, since it had been augmented, ten years before, when it was decided that it would be the site for the next pig kill. Several other subclans of the Suolol tribe lived in another cluster of named localities at Kuma, another census unit five hours' walk over a forested ridge in the northeastern part of Suolol territory. Members of still other subclans affiliated with the Suolol tribal alliance lived outside the tribal territory, in Lower Mendi and in other districts of the Southern Highlands like Talibu.

2. However, I do not think that what I have called "informal" experience can be equated with Bloch's "infrastructure" or "practical" activity, at least as those terms are commonly understood. Both "formal" and "informal" relations are culturally constructed, and both have practical effects in the world.

3. Unfortunately, I did not tape the meeting. My account is based on my own and my husband's written notes, taken during the meeting, and on commentaries afterward by a number of Suolol and non-Suolol participants, including Pua and Olonda.

4. This may be changing already in some parts of the Highlands, perhaps especially in the context of missionization and economic "development" (see A. Strathern 1979b).

4. Putting Down Roots: Information in the Language of Managalase Exchange

William H. McKellin
University of British Columbia

Political activity among the Managalase[1] is focused on the exchanges between affines and between their communities. A young man's primary exchange partners are determined when he or his sisters marry. Either their marriages reinforce existing alliances, as part of a cycle of marriage exchange, or they force members of the two groups to redefine their political affiliations. Consequently, marriage negotiations are very sensitive activities, even more delicate than plans for pig exchanges and feasts. If any of the parties is publicly embarrassed during the proceedings, disruptions of political relations by quarrels, sickness, or open conflict are likely to result. To reduce this possibility, the Managalase politicians use metaphorical rhetoric, particularly *ha'a*, "oratorical allegory," to avoid direct confrontations during negotiations. Indirect discourse such as allegory also enables them to hide the substance of their discussions from others who are not directly involved. Furthermore, metaphorical rhetoric is a means of testing the opinions of exchange associates and partners before taking a public position on a political issue.

After his marriage a young man actively participates in community affairs and must learn to take part in the rounds of negotiation, planning, and exchange that characterize Managalase political life. Initially he depends upon his father or on his *kajuha*, "sponsor," to reach him the strategies and etiquette of affinal exchange. He must learn how and when to present game or the first fruits of his garden to his wife's kinsmen. Also, he needs to learn the protocol involved in hosting his various affines at large intercommunity feasts. At the same time, he will acquire the ability to compose and intepret allegory. Each gift presented by a young man to his affines provides an opportunity to hone his skills and contributes to his political maturity; he is *zinum saman*, "putting down roots."   This chapter is primarily concerned with one aspect of oratorical rhetoric, the structure of information in Managalase allegory. By organizing the story in a form described as "overlay" by Grimes (1972, 1975), the orator is able to "highlight" portions of the story, placing some information in the foreground for his listeners while allowing the remainder to fade into the background. An orator can present a number of allegories with different messages by using one plot structure but varying the highlighted portions of the story. Consequently, members of the audience must be familiar with this structure of information to accurately interpret the speech. If a young man intends to maintain an active role in politics or to achieve prominence as a big-man, he must learn this subtle aspect of allegorical oratory.

Rhetoric

Ha'a, or allegory, is the most widely used genre of metaphorical rhetoric performed by the Managalase.[2] It is similar to forms of metaphorical discourse found elsewhere in Papua New Guinea: among the Melpa of Mount Hagen (A. Strathern 1975b), Central Province's Taude (Hallpike 1977), the Benabena (R. Young 1968), the Enga (Brennan 1970), and various groups in the Eastern Highlands Province (Aufenanger 1962). Allegorical speech is also found in Tok Pisin, where it is referred to as *tok bokis* (Brash 1971).

Allegory is only one form of Managalase communication that employs *súara kúaraman*, "indirect speech." In addition to oratorical allegory, *gú*, "tokens," and two different kinds of play or pantomime, *siribe saim* and *matauraman*, are presented as metaphorical forms of rhetoric. Dreams, in which people see or hear messages from spirits of kinsmen and some lyrics to songs, are also considered indirect communication.

Presentation of a token such as a betel nut by one man to another may be the opening presentation to a more important transaction. By offering a betel nut with designs scratched into the outer skin a man may signify that he has a pig he wishes to exchange with the recipient or that his daughter is ripe for marriage. But a man who gives betel nut fruit with the skin removed warns the recipient of impending danger from others. The various tokens employ the elemental forms of metaphors used to construct more complex plays and allegories.

Siribe saim and *matauraman* are two different types of theater. *Siribe saim* is a comical version of a hunting expedition in which the actor, spear in hand, searches for his prey in the middle of the village. Scouring the ground for signs of his quarry, the hunter tracks the game to the house of the person intended as the target of the performance. When asked where he is going by the man in the house, the actor responds by telling an allegory. A performance of *siribe saim* expresses a general message of dissatisfaction with the conduct of an exchange, but it relies on the *ha'a* at the end of the hunt to make specific accusations. *Matauraman* is a pantomime with a plot similar to that of allegory. It, too, appears to be comical and amusing to the general audience, but it masks a powerful underlying political statement that the performers direct to a specific portion of their audience.

Ha'a, however, is the most widely used form of indirect rhetoric. As we shall see, its range of plots and themes, combined with its system of overlay, makes allegory the most flexible genre of indirect discourse. Managalase men and women, who engage in exchange, trade *ha'a* with those who share equivalent standing in the exchange system. The temporary inequalities between partners that result from the phases of the exchange cycle are insignificant as long as the participants do not default in their portion of the cycle. If this happens, any parity between the parties is destroyed and the delicate balance safeguarded by allegory is broken; direct insults rather than indirect speeches become the appropriate form of communication between the two.

Ha'a are used in negotiations not only to avoid directly embarrassing a potential ally; they also enable individuals to criticize others and still avoid the charges and consequences of slander. In negotiations, *ha'a* might be considered a form of politeness. In other circumstances, *ha'a* can produce the same devastating effects as biting satire.

Telling *ha'a* is also a competitive activity. Men vie with each other to tell stories that their listeners will find difficult to interpret. This game has a serious side to it, however. First, as we shall see in more detail, the meaning of a *ha'a* eludes an audience unless its members are familiar with its structure as a form of discourse. Second, they must know a wide variety of plots and metaphors used in constructing allegory. The interpretation of these metaphors is not necessarily fixed but may vary from village to village and from story to story, depending on the myths, songs, and oratorical conventions of the particular community. Third, the listeners must be privy to the activities of the speaker and his social group's concerns; that is, to the gossip that might have provoked the speech. Therefore, to interpret the *ha'a* the audience must attempt to reconstruct the speaker's presuppositions based on the structure of the story, the type of allegory and metaphors used, as well as other information derived from the social context. Any failure to interpret the allegory demonstrates a shortcoming of the audience, not of the speaker.

Metaphors and motifs for *ha'a* are drawn either from myths that are widely known or from those owned by the storyteller, his rights to them based on his claims to land established through his kinship ties. Some songs, associated with specific places owned by groups of individuals, are a second source for metaphors. In either of these two cases, the knowledge of metaphors is largely dependent on the speaker's kinship relations and his ownership of land. The land that yields a man food for exchange also furnishes him with the lore upon which to base his *ha'a*.

A man is not restricted to the use of his own songs and myths, but through participation in various exchanges, with affines and others, he develops a familiarity with their allegories and learns to weave them into his composition of a *ha'a*. Some appealing and useful metaphors that were invented by a *ha'a* speaker at one time have become part of oratorical convention and endure in use. They are usually identified with the village in which they were invented. A man, skillful at telling *ha'a*, does more than exhibit his oratorical ability; his choice of metaphors implies his rights to land and illustrates his extensive exchange alliances. Allegory represents the sources of a man's political power.

The Tarop Ha'a

The Managalase classify *ha'a* (and other forms of indirect rhetoric) by general motifs or themes. They identify these motifs by their characteristic participants, settings, or events. Often a storyteller will not explicitly name the actors in the story; he forces the listeners to identify participants through other clues. For example, stories describing the activities of birds are generally known as *magite* stories after the trees in which particular birds roost. Rather than naming the bird and identifying th. theme associated with it, the storyteller may mention only the kind of tree used by that bird as a roost. The listener must determine which bird is referred to from the kind of roost mentioned to be able to identify the corresponding allegorical theme.

Plot structure can also be used to identify a motif. The series of events, without the typical participants, may indicate the relationship between a story and a particular theme. The allegory considered in this paper is a *tarop*, "tree kangaroo," *ha'a*, based on the events of a tree kangaroo hunt. When a man spots a tree kangaroo, he chases it until it climbs up a tree. While it is up there, the hunter goes for assistance and returns with men who help him build a fence around the base of the tree. Together they catch and kill the animal after it is frightened out of the tree and into the enclosure. This basic sequence of events provides the basis for a *tarop ha'a*. The motif is the interruption and resumption of some activity. We will see this theme in the *tarop ha'a* presented here, accompanied by additional metaphors that are emphasized by the structure of the story.

The following allegory was told by Ninivera, a man in his late fifties and noted for his oratorical ability. He has become a prominent member of his clan, Ugese, and his village, Dea, where he is very influential. Originally the story was told to the people in the village just before daybreak after something wakened Ninivera from his sleep. From his

doorway he saw a series of events that form the subject of this *ha'a*.
The text presented here was recorded that evening.

Tarop Ha'a Ninivera

1. Nú gahie *va'erenemere'o*./

2. *Va'e* give gahie/ajinemi'e give
   jahe./
3. Va'e vúan'e arare va'e
   va'erenemere
4. ke ve inidore *ajinemire*./
5. *Ajinemi'e* / ijie hije'e givahe/

6. ariro vere kiravore./
7. Ee ize ume vere kirame
   va'erenmere'o./
8. Nami'ero ajive'ero /
9. ibite udu usenemi'ore
10. "Ijie hanuhe gehebe duseme
    arininave
11. gimerere ijie kani'eje" kúa'ero./
we said./
12. E'ero/ ibiteja udu usenemi'ero

13. vere kiramere'e iji nami'ijo'e/
14. ajive gahahe hirinemi'e dusevo'e

15. give'ero / kuniremere'e /
16. rome vene sirire'e/ rone'e
17. ibite'e udu usejie *ke kani*ore./

18. E *ke kani*arenemere'e /
19. kege dovesahere'e nahuzeme

20. Ega'e vúeho / meva'ejome/
21. nú bagave'erone/
22. ni núne gehe hanuge'e hijeja/

23. bane givare
24. e nu meva'ejome / medusevare./

1. We went up there and did something./
2. We went up/saw something
   climbing up there.
3. We went up the path chasing
   after it
4. until it was above us, climbing./
5. While it was climbing/ we stayed,
   watched
6. and came down to build a fence./
7. We should cut tree branches to
   build a fence.
8. Stay, climb up the tree/
9. cut branches and lay them down
10. "Those animals up there will
    jump down,
11. we will see them and kill them,"

12. And so we should/ cut branches,
    put them down/
13. build a fence, and watch/
14. While someone will climb up the
    tree to chase the animals so they
    jump down;
15. we will see them/ catch them,/
16. hold them by the tail,/
17. pick up the sticks we have cut
    and kill them.
18. Take them and kill them./
19. Take them, tie them and wrap
    them up.
20. But suppose / they just ran away/
21. We were not watching,/
22. our eyes were not turned up
    toward the animals
23. We would not have seen them
24. While we just wait along/ the
    animals simply jumped down.

25. Enere are sise ijime nume va'erenemere	25. Then the animals could run away through dangerous places:
26. rare kahe ijime va'e / vú isohe ijime	26. go down a cliff / or through a valley
27. nú meva'ejome	27. While we were walking

This *ha'a* is about a marriage or, more accurately, about an elopement that Ninivera witnessed. Two related but different interpretations were offered of this allegory. The first is by a woman, Avota, a kinswoman of the girl involved in the elopement. Avota was a politically astute woman who participated in exchanges in her own right in addition to assisting her husband, who is one of Dea Village's influential men. Her experience in exchanges gave her some familiarity with *ha'a*.

What did he talk about? A woman whose husband's family live up at the top of the village and whose own family live in the lower part of the village. We didn't see what happened and so we didn't understand the story when Ninivera told it this morning.

The girl just got up and went into the boy's house and said "I want you to be my husband." She climbed down out of her own house, went up to her husband's house and went in. None of us saw this because we were asleep. But Ninivera saw what happened, then he went back to sleep. Early in the morning, before the sun was up, Ninivera came down out of his house and told this *ha'a*. Everyone up in the new husband's house heard him, as did the girl's relatives down below. They didn't know what happened, so they just sat in their houses and didn't say anything.

This is what Ninivera said. This is the *ha'a* he told.

Avota's interpretation of the *ha'a* is based on her familiarity with the events to which it refers and on a general understanding of some metaphors used in *ha'a*. Her lack of complete expertise is evident from the superficial rendering of the story. Her brother, Aresa, discovered a much more subtle message in Ninivera's story. He explains why the parents of the young man and woman did not openly respond to the *ha'a*.

Jas (the girl) went up to Sakura's house and just went in and married him. Ninivera saw what happened and told this *ha'a*. Sakura's sister married a man from Eneje, but Jas married Sakura. Ninivera thought that the marriage should be allowed. That is why he told the *ha'a*. He wanted the parents to agree to the marriage to protect them. Otherwise, both parents would quarrel. For this reason, Ninivera wanted them to agree to the marriage.

How can we account for the different interpretations? The text is the same for both interpreters, and the social context has not changed. The difference arises from the first interpreter's failure to appreciate the information that is communicated by the structure of the *ha'a*. How do the metaphorical figures, the social context in which the *ha'a* is told, and the strategy of the speaker expressed through the structure of the text produce a coherent communicative message?

The structure of the text, with its system of cohesion, offers the first clues for an interpretation of the message of the *ha'a*. From it, the listeners are able to determine the metaphors that are central to the interpretation of the story and, correspondingly, what social information is most relevant for an understanding of the orator's speech.

Cohesion in Managalase Oratory

The systems of cohesion found in *ha'a* are distinguishable from those used in other genre of Managalase speech. These patterns enable the listeners to identify a speech as *ha'a*, and they help the audience to intepret the allegory by emphasizing key portions of the oration. The first system, linkage, is common to *ha'a* and other narrative forms. Linkage can be readily identified by its use of repetition. A clause or portion of a clause from one sentence is repeated at the beginning of the succeeding paragraph or sentence (Thurman 1975). In Managalase the sentence-final form of the verb in the first clause appears in a sentence-medial form in the repeated portion of the clause (e.g., *va'e* in lines 1 and 2). In the initial position of a sentence or paragraph the repeated clause becomes the theme of the sentence or paragraph, telling "what it is about." Linkage presents a clause as the marked theme and "represents a foregrounding of the speaker's point of departure" (Halliday 1967:214).

Linkage

Linkage occurs between the following lines in the illustrated *ha'a* thematizing the following events:

1. va'erenemere'o	[we] went
2. va'e	
3. ajineemire	something climbing
4. Ajinemi'e	
7. kua'ero	we said [we should do this]
8. E'ero	we should do this
11. ke kaniore	kill [them]
12. E ke kaniarenemere	
19. mebevarorovome giverejahe	they surprise us and we will
20. Bevarorovome giverejahe	see them
20. kuniremerene	catch them
21. E kuniremerene	
31. ijie kegero'ore iji'e ijahe	take them and kill them
32. Ijahe kegero'ore ijie	

Two systems of cohesion in addition to linkage contribute to the structure of the allegory: the delineation of information units and their focuses and the pattern of overlay. The characteristic that most readily identifies a narrative as ha'a is the speaker's use of many short, studied phrases. These phrases, or "information units" (Halliday 1967:200), are indicated by a falling pitch at the end of a word followed by a pause and the beginning of another utterance — a new information unit. An information unit does not necessarily correspond to the grammatical clause or sentence of a discourse. In its unmarked form found commonly in standard narratives in Managalase, the information unit is coextensive with the clause or sentence. The focus of the unit is the information presented as "new" (Halliday 1967:204). But, in the marked form, used extensively in ha'a, the information unit does not correspond to the grammatical clause. Consequently, one clause or sentence may be composed of several short information units, each with its own primary focus. Short units enable the speaker to emphasize the importance of the material in focus by treating it as if it were new information. A similar pattern is also found in English oratory and news broadcasts (Grimes 1975:275). In Managalase, short information units draw the attention of the audience to the speech itself and to particular information in the speech. This characteristic gives ha'a a formal, poetic style.

The third system of cohesion found in *ha'a* is overlay. Overlay, like the blocking of information into units, draws the listener's attention to particular pieces of information in the story. But overlay, unlike the focus of information units, is concerned with larger portions of discourse.[3] Overlays are superimposed over information units to highlight particular elements of paragraphs or discourses. Overlay provides an additional option — "highlighted information" — to those of "given" and "new" information that operates at the clause and units levels (Grimes 1972, 1975).

Highlighting by overlay is achieved by repeating portions of the text, similar to the way thematization is achieved by linkage. Overlay, however, repeats larger sections of the discourse to produce a different result. In overlay the events are told, not in a single sequence, but in clusters or planes. Each individual plane presents events in their chronological sequence, but the events of two successive planes will not form a sequence. Instead, some events of the two planes will overlap, each plane repeating some information found in one of the preceeding planes. Planes, linked together in an overlay by the events they share, produce a three dimensional layering of information.

The information which is repeated by the overlay is "highlighted" by the speaker. The events which are told in one plane and reappear in succeeding planes are placed in the foreground for the audience while those which are deleted fade into the background. The highlighted information makes the speaker's message more explicit by drawing his listener's attention to specific metaphors which complement the motif of the allegory. An inaccurate comprehension of the overlay structure of a *ha'a* often results in a plausible but incomplete or inaccurate interpretation of the orator's message. In some instances, however, members of the audience play upon this characteristic of overlay to redirect the original speaker's intentions towards a politically more acceptable target as part of the process of negotiation.

Ninivera's *ha'a* is composed of several sets of overlay. His story can initially be divided into two parts. The first (lines 1 – 19), provides an account of what the participants in the hunt said they should do or what they did. These lines provide the basic information of the *ha'a*. The remainder of the story presents collateral information by way of alternative solutions to the hunter's situation and the possible consequences. Essentially, the second half reinforces the earlier message and makes its point more explicit.

The events of the first portion of the *ha'a* (lines 1 – 19), as organized in chronological order, are found in Table 4.1. These events are organized into planes or layers of information (Table 4.2) that Ninivera uses to highlight particular events in his *ha'a*. Each plane is composed of only a subset of the total number of events that occur in the story. In each plane, some events of the total series are deleted, as in the case of event 7, climbing the tree (to cut a branch). This event is not repeated in a retelling of the sequence in line 12. The overlay structure, showing repeated and deleted events, is presented in Table 4.3. The lettered rows represent the planes of the story beginning with plane A, which corresponds to the first line of the text. The columns indicate the events of the story in chronological sequence. Reading across the rows of the matrix, we can see the events that occur in each plane of overlay. Thus, in plane F, events 5, 7, 8, and 9 are mentioned. An examination of the columns reveals the events that are repeated on various planes of overlay. These are the highlighted events that tie the planes of the overlay together and present the information the speaker wishes to emphasize. For example, event 10 (build a fence) appears first on plane D and is repeated in planes E and H.

The three instances of repetition produced by linkage must be considered before the structure of overlay is examined more closely. Linkage accounts for the repetition of event 2 in planes A and B; of event 3 in C and D; and event 18 in planes G and H. If these repetitions are considered primarily as the consequence of thematization rather than of overlay, we find that there are two overlays to this portion of Ninivera's *ha'a:* planes A through C and D through J. The first three planes are a separate overlay because none of the events except the linkage occurs in the other planes. Plane J does not form a separate overlay, because event 15 also occurs in that plane. Thus, linkage joins two separate overlays, the end of one overlay providing the theme or point of departure for the next.

Now we are prepared to examine the structure of each overlay. In the first, two events and their participants are highlighted: "we went up there" and "something climbing." One, the initial activities of the

Table 4.1
Events in Chronological Sequence

Participants	Events
we [hunters]	1. went up there
	2. saw
animals	3. something climbing [continuous action]
we	4. chased after it
we	5. stayed and watched
	6. came down [to get help]
	7. climb up the tree
	8. cut branches
	9. lay the branches down [for a fence]
	10. build a fence
	11. climb up the tree
	12. chase the animals
animals	13. they jump down
we	14. see them
	15. catch them
	16. hold them by the tail
	17. pick up sticks
	18. hit and kill them
	19. tie them and wrap them up

Table 4.2
Planes of Overlay

Plane	Text Line
A	1
B	2
C	3,4
D	5,6
E	7
F	8,9
G	10,11
H	12 – 17
I	18
J	19

Table 4.3

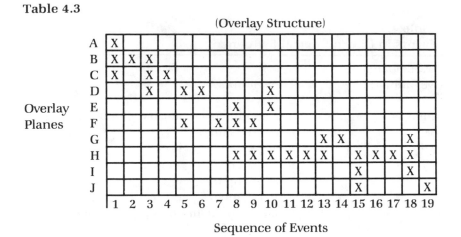

(Overlay Structure)

Overlay Planes	1	2	3	4	5	6	7	8	9	10	11	12	13	14	15	16	17	18	19
A	X																		
B	X	X	X																
C	X		X	X															
D		X		X	X			X											
E							X	X											
F				X		X	X	X											
G											X	X			X				
H						X	X	X	X	X	X		X	X	X	X			
I													X		X				
J													X						X

Sequence of Events

hunters, is also presented as the theme in line 1 and, through linkage, as the marked theme in line 2. The overlay is therefore concerned primarily with the hunters and secondarily with the animals. Two events (2 and 4) are not repeated in the overlay, left in the background by the speaker. Understanding the significance of the two highlighted events will be crucial to the exegesis of the allegory. The background information, however, may only supplement the highlighted portions or may be totally inconsequential for the allegory's interpretation.

The second overlay begins with a change of theme, or point of departure, from the hunters to the animals. This shift is produced by the linkage that joins the two overlays. Having stated what the animal is doing by linkage, Ninivera sets out to describe the hunter's response to the situation. He describes the process of finding help and building a fence characteristic of his *ha'a* with the *tarop* motif. The overlay that he uses to describe the events of the hunt focuses the audience's attention on several activities. The activities listed in Table 4.4 are presented more than once in the overlay.

These events are the highlighted information in this overlay. Those events which receive the greatest prominence are "cutting branches," "building a fence," and "catching the animals." If we consider events

Table 4.4

	Events	Number of occurrences
5	stopped and watched	2
8	cut branches	3
9	lay branches down	2
10	build fence	3
13	they jump down	2
15	catch them	3
18	hit and kill them	2

8, 9, and 10 as one activity, building a fence with the sticks, then the branches and the fence are pointedly drawn to the audience's attention as the most important information in the overlay. Once again, the events that are not repeated serve as the background for the important information; they are inconsequential for the interpretation of this portion of the *ha'a*.

The last two lines deserve some additional attention (lines 18 and 19). Here we find another event thematized by linkage: the killing of the animals. The conclusion of the sequence in this portion of the story is emphasized by overlay in addition to its status as one of the marked themes produced by linkage.

The alternatives that Ninivera presents in the remaining lines of the *ha'a* further stress the importance of the branches used to both trap the animals and kill them. The events repeated in the planes of the third overlay (lines 20–36) highlight the difficulties hunters would have in finding a branch if they were surprised by the animals because they had not been attentive. The hunters would not have help finding a stick with which they could kill the animals.

The fourth overlay (lines 36 – 50) details the consequences if the hunters cannot find a stick once they finally catch the escaping animals. The highlighted events in this overlay are "blinding the animals," "returning to the tree" mentioned in the first overlay, "cutting branch," and "killing the animals" with the stick they cut. Finally, lines 51 and 52 serve as a coda, drawing the story to an end with the hunters killing and eating the animals they have caught.

In three of the four overlays of the story, in both the initial set of events and the alternatives, one piece of information is consistently highlighted, "cutting a branch," either to build a fence or to kill the animals. This information, highlighted by Ninivera, and the events thematized by linkage are the keys to interpreting this *ha'a*.

Interpretation

Initially, three questions must be dealt with to interpret Ninivera's *ha'a* accurately. First, what is signified by the thematically marked portions of the text – the hunter's trip, the animals climbing in the tree, and the killing of the animals? Second, what is the importance of the tree and its branches, which are used to build the fence and to hit the animals? Finally, why did Ninivera decide upon the *tarop* motif for his story about marriage rather than another, such as the betel nut motif? These questions can be answered only by stepping beyond this story and into Managalase village life.

The hunter in the story is clearly Ninivera and other men, since it is told as a first person narrative. The identity of the other men is clarified by their relationships to one of the thematized portions – the animals. The hunters are the men who should be watching the animals. The animals are the two young people identified at first as the thing(s) climbing in the tree. Ninivera based this on his initial observation of the girl going up into the house where her future husband was sleeping. Killing the animals, the third theme marked by linkage, directly reflects the Managalase attitude toward marriage.

Marriage to a young man brings an end to his carefree bachelorhood and thrusts him into the responsibilities of affinal exchange and parenthood: he must put down his roots. In the past, when tattooing and seclusion were practiced, only single boys and young men were allowed to participate in these rites, which were intended to strengthen them. They were isolated from women and their weakening polluting influence. Also, during their bachelorhood, young men sharpened their skills as hunters and learned the different forms of magic that increased a hunter's success. Marriage reduced young men's time for hunting and made avoidance of women, necessary for hunting to be effective,

more difficult. Finally, Managalase men draw a direct connection between siring children and the aging process; the strength of one generation is passed on to the next.

Young women also approached marriage with ambivalence, although they are often more anxious to marry than men, as we have
seen here in this instance of elopement. Marriage frees a girl from her
mother's domination and allows her to establish her own household.
But, at the same time, she must show deference to the wishes of her
husband's coresident kinswomen. Marriage also may reduce the contact that a girl has with her siblings and other childhood friends,
especially if her marriage takes her to a distant village. Finally, marriage
makes her more aware of the dangers of childbirth. Thus, for both men
and women "killing the animals" as a metaphor for marriage is deeply
rooted in the Managalase conceptualization of marriage.

These elements of the story — "the hunters," "the animals," and
"killing the animal," thematized by linkage — are the figures that Avota
considered to arrive at her interpretation of the *ha'a*. To her, it was an
allegory about the activities of the two young people, told to inform the
girl's parents of the elopement. Her exegesis is not wrong, for the story
is concerned with these events, but Ninivera has said much more about
this marital arrangement. His opinion about the marriage is presented
in a subtle way, in overlay. Here we must turn to the information
highlighted by Ninivera's construction of this *ha'a*.

The interpretations of the second and succeeding overlays hinge on
the significance of the tree and its branches used to build the fence
and to kill the animals. Ninivera has used *ize*, "tree" or "wood," and
ibite, "branch," interchangeably in his story. These alternatives were
not selected randomly. He might have chosen a more common phrase,
ize dom, for "branch" (*dom* meaning branch of a tree or river). *Ibite*
(or *bite*), however, has a specific usage; it is the name given a tree or
large branch cut down in preparation for a feast. The branch is brought
into the village and erected in front of the host's house. Coconuts, betel
nuts, bananas, and other gifts for the guests are hung from its small
branches. At the base of this festal tree, yams are stacked around a pile
of cooked game and pig. Thus, the branch in the *ha'a* signifies exchange
or, given the circumstances, marital exchange. Actually, we have two
possible interpretations. Either Ninivera is concerned with the ex-

change of food that accompanies Managalase marriage ceremonies, or he may refer to the initial prestation in a cycle of exchange marriages between two social groups. Aresa, in his explanation of the *ha'a*, has chosen the latter interpretation. A close look at *ibite* and exchange explains his choice.

Managalase feasts are part of a cycle of exchanges. Usually, new exchanges between two groups grow out of the group's mutual exchange ties with intermediaries. If this is the case, the new cycle of exchange is considered as the outgrowth of previously existing obligations between allies. But new exchanges do occur without prior exchanges or obligations between two parties. To begin a new exchange partnership an opening prestation is made without any prior commitment from either party and with an avowed disregard for the repayment of the gift. The term used for this initial gift is *mebite venan*, formed from *ibite*, "festal tree," the prefix *me-* and *venan*, "to do." The prefix *me-* may be translated as "simply," "just," or "without concern." Aresa's interpretation of the *ha'a* reflects his understanding of the elopement as the opening prestation to a new set of marriage exchange.

A Managalase marriage is understood as an exchange between two *agan*, "kin groups," composed of people who share lineal affiliations, have some common territory, and assist each other in exchanges (McKellin 1980). The model marriage involves the exchange by men of their *makine*, "opposite-sex siblings," which for this purpose may be parallel- and cross-cousins in one's kin group as well as actual siblings. These marriages usually occur within several years of each other and involve people of the same generation. Since only two groups are involved, these marriages are not politically complicated.

Indirect marriage exchanges are a more complex variation of sister exchanges. They involve three or four kin groups divided between two different villages. Marriages of this type provide a basis for intervillage political alliances, particularly if they are negotiated by big-men attempting to reinforce their exchange networks.

In contrast to arranged marriages, elopements, including the one that gave rise to Ninivera's *ha'a*, threaten the alliances produced by exchange marriages. Young people elope for three basic reasons: to avoid an unappealing arranged marriage, to overcome parents' objections to a specific union, or to evade parents' delays to a marriage that would be acceptable at the proper time. The respective kin groups of the couple may respond to the elopement in one of the several ways. Their first option is to prohibit the marriage and attempt to keep the couple apart. This is rarely successful, particularly if the two kin groups do not agree. The second strategy is to interpret the elopement as part of an existing marriage cycle. Because this approach does not disrupt any existing alliances, it is the preferred solution.

The last option is the one proposed by Ninivera in his *ha'a*; to consider the elopement as the beginning of an altogether new cycle of exchanges. This is necessary only if the marriage cannot be worked into an existing pattern of alliance. A new cycle may disrupt the political affilition of the couple's kin by forcing them to realign themselves into two new sets of affines or two sets of exchange partners, which might divide the kin group(s) of the couple. Yet, in the case we are examining here, Ninivera contends that this potentially divisive solution is the best way to deal with the elopement.

The tree and the branches (*ibite*) represent the beginning of a new cycle of exchange (*mebite*).

The alternatives Ninivera sees to a new exchange are described by the third and fourth overlays. In the third, Ninivera suggests that if the current situation is overlooked and the couple do not marry now, the parents themselves may have the difficult task of looking around later to find other spouses for the two young people. This could lead to disputes and the loss of face ("blinding") for all parties concerned. In the end, after both sides have quarreled, the only solution may be to return to the marriage originally desired by the two young people. Thus, the events highlighted by the story identify the information that Ninivera wishes to stress as essential for an accurate interpretation of the allegory.

The final question remains: Why has Ninivera chosen the *tarop* motif in this situation? The *tarop* motif tells of a chase that is interrupted while the hunters go for assistance before they attempt to catch their prey. By focusing on the branch and the fence in his overlay, Ninivera is also drawing attention to the cooperative aspect of the *tarop* hunt. He is asking that the other men, kinsmen of the two young people, accept his suggestion and join with the kin in recognizing the marriage.

Conclusion

In this chapter we have examined an allegory told in the process of negotiating a marriage. Ninivera, the storyteller, used this indirect form of rhetoric to test his opinions of marriage and to elicit support for his position without taking a public stance and without directly confronting the parents of either young persons. Ninivera may have restricted the number of people who understood the story by his use of allegory to the point that even the two young people he was talking about did not know what he meant. In the end, Ninivera's proposal that the elopement be formalized by marriage was accepted, and after a month's preparation a feast with bridewealth was given for the young woman's kinsmen.

In his allegory, Ninivera has demonstrated some of the subtleties of *ha'a* that young men entering the web of politics must learn. Though he chose a common motif, the *tarop ha'a*, his use of cohesion — short information units, linkage, and overlay — enabled him to draw competent listeners' attention to the most important figures in his allegory. Rather than searching through the possible associations and significations of the many potential metaphors in the story, the listeners were presented with the story's essential metaphors. These were placed in the foreground for their interpretation by the orator's construction of the speech. The speaker's intent is expressed not just by the metaphors he chooses but also by the ways he uses them.

Political oratory, as Bloch has noted (1975), is often repetitious, formal, and overly stylistic. Here, in this study of Managalase allegory, we have seen that the complex discourse structures that produce the impressions Bloch has described are essential if a speech is to be properly understood.

Notes

This chapter was originally prepared as a paper for the symposium "Language and Politics," at the 1980 Annual Meetings of the Association for Social Anthropology in Oceania, February 1980.

The fieldwork on which this paper is based was conducted between February 1976 and December 1977 under grants from the Canada Council and the Social Sciences and Humanities Research Council.

I would like to thank William Samarin, Ivan Kalmar, Tom McFeat, David Turner, John LeRoy, Brenda Beck, Don Brenneis, and Roy Wagner for their comments on an earlier draft of this paper. They cannot be responsible for the remaining deficiencies.

1. There are approximately 6,000 speakers of Managalase, a language of the Koriarian family, who live in the Northern Province, in the Plateau region to the southeast of Popondetta and to the northwest of the Owen Stanley Range.
2. The orthography is based on J. Parlier 1964, except that /Z/ is used for the voiced prenasalized alveolar affricate and voiced stops /b/ /d/ /k/ /g/ replace /p/ /t/ /?/ /k/.
3. Overlay is very similar to "symbolic obviation" discussed by Wagner (1978).

II. Autonomy: Language, Objects, and the Limits of Control

5. Words That Are Moving: The Social Meanings of Ilongot Verbal Art

Michelle Z. Rosaldo
Stanford University

I learn with my ears and through language. Happily, the Philippine people I studied in 1967 – 69, and again in 1974, were enamored of verbal performance.[1] It was my misfortune, however, that as my linguistic skills increased to the point where I could understand the elaborate verbal displays associated with magic, song, and, in particular, oratory, these genres lost their appeal to a people who once had enjoyed them. Once beautiful, they were seen as conducive to discord. And Ilongot informants who carried my tape recorders and batteries to the sites of political meetings never ceased to confirm my impression that the "true oratory" I hoped to discover had died with the fathers of men who themselves did not think to teach their traditional skills to their children. I might look for the past in the present, but the quest was at best problematic. Simultaneously idealized and distrusted, classical oratory had come to be coupled with a violent style of life.

Whether men once spoke more beautifully than the orators I heard at peace meetings and bridewealth confrontations during close to three years of fieldwork from 1967 to 1969 and again in 1974 is, of course, impossible for me to determine. Certainly, my recordings include examples of speech that Ilongots recognized and evaluated in terms of the canons of oratorical skill. But what is clear is that from at least the mid-1960s the art of traditional oratory was increasingly called into question. Ilongots argued about whether to conduct debate in the elaborate oratorical style or, instead, in the manner of lowland author-ities. They criticized metaphorical turns of phrase in the name of a Christian God who desires "straight speaking." And, in response to my disappointment at the lack of artful speech in a bridewealth meeting recorded, men told me that talk in the "old style" would have bred conflict. Concerned to display their "new knowledge," they all had, as Christians, submitted to the dictates of a pistol-waving young "Cap-tain," who directed participants to eschew "curvy speech," "name" their objects, and follow the way of "the law":

As you speak to one another, what I am against is such words as might count as a challenge, words that ask your fellow to match them in force; yes, I'd criticize you if, well, you returned in that way to old customs, especially since you now have knowledge of the word of God; yes, I will recognize old ways, curving speeches, and if I hear them, well, I'll be opposed to that kind of talk.

Few agreed with my sense that his gun was in fact more conducive to violence than the balanced and delicate phrases associated with ora-tory in the past.

My goal in this chapter is to begin to interpret these changes. I seek to come to terms, first, with traditional oratorical style — by linking aesthetic to ethic and showing the sense in which "modern" critics are right in their view that "curvy speech" may breed violence. I then suggest — much more briefly — that present evaluations of oratorical convention are themselves rooted in changes in Ilongot culture and social relationships, with consequences for Ilongot views of their so-ciety, their speech, and themselves.

Certainly, Ilongots in 1974 saw themselves at the brink of a definitive break with past "custom." Barely recovering from the loss of close to one third of their population during World War II, Ilongots had, since the late 1950s, accommodated increasing incursions of settlers who farmed their abandoned swiddens and began cultivation of forests where Ilongot men used to hunt. Through the years of the 1960s, the majority of the Ilongot population converted to Evangelical Christian-ity. And, with the declaration of martial law in the Philippines in 1972, schools were established in interior Ilongot settlements; young men began to engage in wage labor; and elders found confidence in asserting that "we now are a part of the lowlands" and, more particularly, that sons would not follow their fathers in severing human heads. In such a context, it was hardly surprising to witness the decline in traditional art forms we have learned to associate with processes of "moderniza-tion" and the ravages of "social change."

Far more elusive, however, was the Ilongot sense that the past was not dead but disruptive; for them, verbal arts were called into question, not because they had ceased to be lovely, but because they embodied old ways. Old songs were abjured because they bred thoughts of be-headings; oratorical graces were criticized for engendering anger and chaos — as inappropriate to play and to politics as they were unac-ceptable in church. Traditional art forms made sense, I was told, in a particular kind of society — and Ilongots, in challenging traditions, were questioning as well those patterns of social relation that gave sense to the art of the past. In order to understand the changes in Ilongot aesthetics, it proved necessary, in short, to look backward, to follow the Ilongot critics who were rejecting old skills because of tra-ditional meanings — and read art as a social text.

The Story of Tubeng

Having written on oratory at some length after our first period of fieldwork, I was anxious, when I returned to the field in 1974, to explore my conclusions in detail, by reviewing older recordings and collecting new samples of public, political speech. A first opportunity arose with news of a bridewealth meeting in Ringen, a settlement some two days distant from our established Ilongot home. We set off with guides and recorders. All thought I would hear fine speeches, because the parties to the encounter all came from localities known for their verbal skills. The subject of the meeting was a claim, by young Tubeng, to recom-pense. While courting the beautiful Dila, he had spent several hundred pesos for gifts that she and her kinsmen received. The matter was delicate and heated; Dila had recently abandoned poor Tubeng, and he sought a return on his futile investment from Kayul, the successful groom.

As it turned out, this was the meeting initiated by the pistol-waving young captain. But, while initially distressed by his message, I took heart in the moments that followed as speakers from both sides, acknowledging the former's directives, yet adopted conventional rhetoric and spoke not of real claims and conflicts but instead of their style of talk. So, Dura, the speaker for Kayul, first asked why he was called to the meeting:

If you are finished Captain, there. The course of his words are good, we all know that. Now, what I want, what I want is that I myself be the one who starts things by asking my uncle, Inanu, what it is, what it is that people are to speak about this evening. Listen all of you people collected here, you who are inside this house. You, Uncle Inanu, what did you call me for, to this place. And I want to hear that, since I wouldn't just wildly say what I may say if I don't know the course of your thoughts, you my brother. I'm finished there.

And Inanu, father to Tubeng, gave an appropriately indirect response:

Okay, don't go on, brother Dura. Just as our Captain has said, to those who are reached by his words. Well, don't think you alone were the one pointed to. Even I, well, the words were, in part, also pointed at me. That is why he spoke like that. And so, before I let you know why I called you here, to be together, both of us, since both of us know what is proper, let's recall that we both know of straight speech. So, don't think there is anything bad I called you for. What I wanted, the reason I called you here, is so that the two of us might truly know one another's thoughts. And surely, we need not return to our talk of an earlier time, our talk when we happened to meet at the [church-sponsored] conference...We need not return to the beginning of things, where our talk will be painful and hard....

Inanu proclaimed that he would not "use the oratory of the past, when we channeled our words on winding paths," and boasted of Christian conviction. But, at the same time, he displayed a most conventional reluctance to give public voice to his purpose, "go back to the name" of his grievance, and say what was on his mind. Friends who listened with me to the tape, and discussed, as they helped me transcribe it, commented that Inanu showed himself a "knowledgeable" man in so setting forth his case "slowly." By avoiding the "names" of political goals, he could hope to avoid confrontation and permit the "discovery" of what in fact were quite troublesome wishes and claims, not as threats, but instead as the deep revelations of an "open" and well-meaning "heart."

As it turned out, however, Inanu's delicacy cleared space for Dura, who — like the recalcitrant "owner" of "rice seed" some other man seeks as his bride — then declared himself unable to construe the meaning of Inanu's "slow" and still cautious petition. He too was a Christian, a man who opposed "crooked" words, "angry" hearts, and deception — but he did not know what Inanu was asking. He did not understand why he was called:

You're finished there. Well, don't go on. What you have said there [about straight speech], I know. But the reason I won't, as you have asked, give you an answer there, well, is because I do not know what you are talking about. No, you must explain to me what it is that you are asking, what you are referring to...

Although their language lacked the flourishes of metaphor and verbal skill that make high art of politics and mark a memorable performance, the speakers then proceeded for some time in a manner that conformed to my "traditional" expectations, with kinsmen of the hapless suitor, groom and bride, proclaiming their good faith while at the same time feigning ignorance and denying indirection, and then again refusing to reveal their "hidden thoughts." Small details, points of fact — the memory of the speakers' prior meeting at a Conference of New Christians; the claim by Dura that he could not be responsible for an unruly "son's" romance — would be acknowledged and then brushed aside while speakers boasted of their "cool, clean hearts" and showed a taste for verbal fancy. One man declared that "like a pup, I will jump into this fray" and was then silenced by a fellow; another "decorated" his plea for straight, clear speech with what he labeled a conventional turn of phrase, "now then, rattan it is ; much as our elders said, we must cut to the core of things like slashers of rattan."

As in all oratory, business was cloaked, in part, in verbal wit and play. But, as the hours passed, all present came eventually to agree on common terms for serious discussion. No man could deny the "shame" experienced by an unsuccessful suitor, nor would any challenge Tubeng's right to recompense for goods "thrown out" on flaunted love. It was at this point that the youth — who by his move quite changed the conduct of the meeting — spoke for himself and, when encouraged by his elders in the room, produced and read aloud a list enumerating the damages of his now futile suit. As if recounting all the names of inlets on a river's course, he managed to announce in turn the watches, shirts, new radio, restaurant meals, and gold-plated teeth that he had given Dila's kin. He read. And as his audience became aware that he was naming well over U.S. $100 worth of goods, the room was stirred by nervous murmurs that gave way to an alarmed and almost fearful silence. Tubeng demanded, not a return of now used gifts whose values had accordingly declined, but the precise equivalent of his expenditures in money. And the very fact that Tubeng's written list could conjure such an amount of cash was itself a sort of testimony to the righteousness of his claim.

In traditional oratory, men speak of "hidden thoughts," but all participants know well such memories as may be brought to bear, and so their politics hang less on points of fact than on their strategies of revelation and denial. Conventionally, Ilongots used plays of wit to try to temper an intransigent stance, protesting "anger" at another's show of strong intent, denying that accusing words were meant as challenge. But, when confronted with young Tubeng's list (a set of facts that all believed but none had guessed), no member of the audience could envision a response. In desperation, Dura took a querulous stance, protesting certain items in the boy's long count — but his quibbles, in this regard, seemed almost comic. Friends told me later that the family of the groom should quite simply have bowed to their fate, and then, perhaps, requested "pity" in the hope that Tubeng would relax his claims, in knowledge that his "poor" opponent had no cash to pay, and so, confronted with the stunning list, would offer up the only thing he had to give — his life.

But as it was, Dura's pettiness seemed only to strengthen Tubeng's cause. He spoke; Inanu snapped back a response; and then an uncommitted man, positioned (as he put it) "in between" the two, declared that Dura's words were lacking tact and "thought," that he had spoken "to no purpose." Another took the opportunity to "criticize" and so "instruct" poor Dura in more appropriate turns of phrase. And then Inanu, in an artful move, argued that his son's demands for cash repayment were, in fact, far from extreme, and hardly cause for what he thought to be their most "confused" reception. Thoughtful and kind, the child was—his father claimed—a model of Christian restraint, a paragon of good reason. In order to support his claim, Inanu asked his fellows to reflect upon a story meant to contrast Tubeng's straight and Christian ways with the happily abandoned customs of the past.

Inanu told how he had, years before, acquired a wife (much as the happy Kayul had) by "skipping ahead" of his own uncle, Gading, and making off with the woman whom his uncle had intended as a bride. A kerchief given to the bested groom was not, Inanu told, enough to soothe the latter's "angry" thoughts and wounded feelings. Instead, as a repayment for the insult suffered and his loss of love, Gading had insisted that he dip the cloth in human blood and so required that his nephew lead him on a headhunting raid where he could satisfy his "anger" by taking a human life.

To this unsettling anecdote of the past, Inanu then contrasted Tubeng's sane and Christian wishes. His son, he said, did not require a "return" to satisfy his sense of being wronged; he did not, as had been customary once, demand a payment for his "anger." What he desired was, instead, the wealth invested in a futile quest; he sought the money wasted on a woman who betrayed him. And as a proof, then, of his modern ways, young Tubeng measured out his fellows' debts in terms, not of the "heavy" feelings slights in courtship cause for all, but in the far less laden and much more objective terms of an explicitly calculated expense. The question, Inanu told the group, was not if Tubeng was correct, but when it was that Kayul, Dura, and their presently assembled kin could promise to accumulate the money; in order to avoid "old ways," he hoped his interlocutors would soon agree to give his son the poor boy's proper due in cash.

So the case rested. The hours that remained were devoted, in large part, to a discussion of just how and when Kayul and the others could begin to earn the sums that Tubeng mentioned. At one point, Tubeng tried to get his opposites to sign their names to an agreement he wrote down, but Dura's fellows said that they were "blind men" who did not know how to read, and managed in their turn to criticize young Tubeng for his rash attempts to emulate the lowland forms of law. But while several of those with whom I spoke after the meeting felt that Tubeng had, perhaps, won more than he should, none quarreled with the conduct of the meeting. Instead, my friends inclined to reaffirm the moral of the story that Inanu told, and so insist (when I would try to disagree) that quarrels over courtship almost always led to violence in the past. Thanks to the captain's leadership, the speakers had — informants said — been careful to avoid the violent pitfalls of an old and "crooked" style of speech, which would most certainly have led to fighting. Abjuring metaphor, they had managed to maintain a civil peace.

In their manner of deciding Tubeng's fate, these Ilongots were, in short, concerned with more than the just recompense for unrequited love and generous giving; they were deciding too about the *forms* of their political life; of their verbal art; and of such mundane facts as disappointment, gift, exchange, in what they saw to be a "new society." I have recounted Tubeng's case at length because I think that in the contrast that Inanu's story raised — between a payment for lost goods and a "return" for rightful "anger" — lies a clue to current changes in Ilongot life and to the reasons that traditional oratorical forms are seen as dangerous and violent.

The written list of hitherto unknown expense; the captain's plea for direct speech; and even more, the notion that our human bonds and disappointments can and should be measured out in numbered sums — all these are antagonistic to a genre whose artistic qualities, I will claim, are rooted in a very different view of human beings and their relationships in society. In Tubeng's story lies a text on art and changing social contexts. But in order to understand the reason that Inanu's vivid and yet hardly representative tale (the events that he recounted occurred in 1942, when Ilongots, like Filipinos elsewhere, had begun to find their lives disrupted by the ravages of a global war), could be accepted by Ilongots as an adequate account of marital politics in the past, it will be necessary to consider in detail the nature of "true" oratory, and its affinities with Ilongot understandings of their traditional social life.

Oratory as Exchange

Purung, the Ilongot word for oratory, describes at once a public meeting and an elaborate, public style of speech; in *purung*, art and politics are combined. As such, *purung* is comparable to other kinds of speech involving "elaboration" (*bēira*), "witty flourish" (*'amba'an*), "crooked" speaking (*'asasap*) and display — to invocations, boasts and magical spells, and in particular, to songs. "Gossip" (*bērita*), "tale" and "myth" (*tadēk, tudtud*) contrast as genres where what counts is more a matter of knowing *what* occurred than of the way in which one tells it; narratives are communicated in what is recognized as "straight," unmarked and often quite dispassionate and unelaborated verbal form. A story told in songs could make men pound their chests with thoughts of violence, love, and age, but the same events recounted as prose narrative on our tapes did not compel attention or response. This stylistic contrast was reflected in the otherwise surprising fact that Ilongots who loved to hear our taped recordings of songs and oratorical debates would tend to find the myths and stories on our tapes quite boring. Ilongots told stories to inform, convince, illuminate, and entertain; but though they would, in daily talk, find cause to dramatize and enliven their accounts of past events, the fact was that they did not think to find the signs of verbal skill and beauty in a story. Their narratives, considered by themselves, were more concerned with the report of temporally ordered points of fact than with the speaker's feelings and desires to move or shape his fellows' hearts. And it was this interactional and affectual concern that seemed for Ilongots to lend both social relevance and aesthetic force to genres readily associated with verbal performance.

Beauty—be it in ornaments or youthful grace, in oratorical speeches, public dance, or casual singing — is something that arouses feeling and inspires heartfelt response. Hardly the detached and tranquil object of much Western aesthetic thought, Ilongot art is seen as something that addresses and makes claims upon real persons in an immediate social world. A lovely ornament stirs one's fellows with an envious hope to kill; a song of longing wakens "pity" for an "empty-handed" youth in thoughtful "fathers." Oratorical flourishes give rise to witty and elaborate forms of speech. *Purung* is, as we shall see, a matter of "exchanging" words; good singers "answer" one another in their songs. And much as orators will hope to bind an interlocutor's heart through words, so men and women in their songs and spells attempt to taunt, cajole, and otherwise stir their listeners' hearts to sympathy, fear, desire, or violence. By contrast, narrators pretend to make no special claims—a fact revealed when orators will themselves deny the weightier implications of their words with the insistence that "I am not orating to you now; I am just gossiping, telling a story."

Disinclined to think of myths or tales in terms of canons of aesthetic grace, informants would recount their memories of bloody killings on our tapes in what appeared to be a sort of catalogue of the places visited, deeds accomplished, rituals performed — without, it seemed, a view to how one might engage an abstract audience in story. Narrative, unlike oratory, was not evaluated as a verbal art because its *form* did not—like that of truly stirring speech—give rise to feelings bound up with recognized consequents in society. Thus, when I asked informants to tell stories for our tapes in something of the more vivid manner I had heard in their spontaneous exchange among friends, they would require an interlocutor to respond, not as an audience to a tale, but as a coparticipant who, by "exchanging words," could help to reenact events recalled. Turning tales into performance meant, in short, converting narrative events arranged in time and space into the dialogic form of oratory. Well-told stories were, in fact, quite likely to make rich use of dialogue in their accounts; and my friends, when asked to turn a narrative into an art, were quick to draw on oratorical conventions and, in particular, on the model of declamation and exchange associated with recognized canons of verbal performance.

The point is that, for Ilongots, true verbal art has social force. Aesthetic value and artistic form are bound up with a view of how and why to move men's hearts, a view uniting studied pose with hopes for dialogue and reciprocity. Artistic skill, in oratory and in song, requires a combination of display—the presentation of one's heart in words— and sociality, or exchange; and furthermore, as I will try to show, the oratorical "exchange of words" can be beautiful only because it gives expression to and helps to organize and shape feelings of "anger" that — much as Inanu's story told — are central to Ilongot understanding of their traditional society.

Given the multiplex, overlapping, and unstable nature of cooperative groupings in everyday Ilongot social life, Ilongots are well aware of the discontinuity between their ordinary alliances and social bonds, and the dyadic, confrontational form of oratory. Days and even months of careful talk may be required to negotiate (at times only apparently) the united stance of people who need not themselves have common motives for their joint affiliation to a single cause. Disputes about the diverse claims of individuals who together will constitute one of the two opposed *tupak*, "sides," may in and of themselves retard the opening of a meeting — as in fact happened one night when the gift-laden supporters of a hopeful groom were left to wait in rafts on the river while the kinsmen of the bride took hours to decide among themselves just who of them deserved a bridewealth gift. The difficulty, in the case at hand, was that an uncle, Mundu, claimed that he was entitled to a "hooking pollarder's rope" — an expensive round of ornamental wire — not as a bridewealth gift *per se* but instead as a return for insult suffered when a "brother" of the groom happened to cast aspersions on the sexual behavior of his "daughter." And, while his fellows hoped to silence these demands, they recognized that such claims as his must be reckoned with (and Mundu, in fact, won his point), all local differences quieted or dismissed, if kinsmen are to be effective in what is always an event involving contest and displays of unity and strength alone with the exchanges through which disputes are — hopefully — resolved.

Good speakers claim that "when I left the doorway of my house, there was no rustling in the roof," or yet again "there is no twitching in my heart" — that no one of their kin opposes present efforts. And Ilongots tell of parties who failed to achieve their goals because of bickering among themselves that gave unwanted "forks" to what became most unconvincing "tongues." Thus, while the members of a "side" occasionally "jump in" to speak at will, displaying hopes and making claims that fellows fault and find distressing, each *tupak* will tend to be united behind some one or two key speakers (and these are always adult men of middle age), who can declare themselves the "tongue" or "voice" of a much larger "body" and use the singular form of the pronoun to suggest the unified and collected strength of both their own and their opponents' "sides."

These speakers claim that they are "giving," "handing," "setting down," and even "feeding" one another words. They use reciprocal forms of the verb — *meki'upu kita*, "we speak reciprocally, I to you" — instead of forms denoting undifferentiated, plural or collective deeds

—*pemen'upu kisi*, "we speak together, all of us"—which would suggest more of cooperation than of exchange or contest. They say that they will "go and speak" (*rawengku dimu ki'upuwi*); they cast their words as actions. And they will frame pronouncements with such phrases as, "I will go after that," "well, I am finished now," "let me add feathers here," and in so doing cast each utterance as a movement that responds to words that came before. One speaker asks:

What did you come here for, into my house. Tell me, truly, why it is that you have come. That is what I would hear.

And then his opposite responds:

I came to see what is happening to your neighborhood, to find out why it is that so many mortars can be heard together pounding rice, to seek out some of those working hands. ...

Or then again:

Okay, I will not hide from you. I came to see if I could share some rice, to join with you in planting. I came because my dogs when hunting heard the bees which told that you have sweet flowers in your forests, and I hoped to make your honey mine. ...

To which the answer is, as one might guess, that dogs and ears are readily deceived and that the host has no "sweet flowers," no "spare rice," "no extra hands to pound" — or, stated in more "direct" terms, no daughters who are ready to be married.

This patterning of response upon response is equally clear in the following fragment of an actual *purung* called because word had it that the brother of a new bride required bridewealth prestations from the groom, who was, in turn, the former's "father." Adopting something of the surly stand that Dura chose in Tubeng's case, the brother "started things" by demanding that he learn the reason he was called to talk:

what is it that you ordered me for, well, I came to hear ... and I can't speak wisely, so I just said to myself, "go only to hear, in case, perhaps, there is some reason, something he called me for, well, I'll just go to hear its name; and that is what I came for, and really, if I had not heard that you wanted to speak with me, well, you know I have lots of work at home. ..."

To this, the uncle could respond:

okay, if you are finished there, then let our brothers and our parents hear it all. Don't think I am hiding anything. The true reason that I called for you is that there is this that reached me, some gossip that the wind brought to my ears. There it is. Look now my child, don't think I am hiding from you; don't think I have any mix of disguises. The true reason that I called for you is that ...when it reached me, that gossip...I did not know if I was to take it to heart....

And then the nephew answered back:

well, since I am the one you are looking for, and you want to hear what I have to say, I will say yes, I will be the one to talk to you, and since we are father and son, I will not hide my thoughts .... Well, it is true, there is some little bit I said, something I said before. But even if I said it, I will not continue since I know that we are father and son ....

The uncle found in this good cause to "offer thanks," and yet, upon acknowledging his nephew's worthy thoughts, he voiced again his yet unsatisfied (and, as the subsequent hours showed, quite justified) concern:

I give thanks, yes, I will say thanks, because you have said yes, you are my child. ... But still I wonder if there is not a seed, a bit of substance, in your words that came before.

These speakers echo one another's words, repeating that they will not "hide" their hopes, that in their hearts are no ill thoughts, that in their breath they know that they are kinsmen. They offer to "distribute knowledge" and to "share" their thoughts, to counter "words like arrows" with a speech that is "as soft and sweet as ripened fruit," and in adopting a magnanimous pose, they may "give thanks that you have given me the things you know." But if there is a sense in which they are engaged in an exchange of words, the fact is that exchange itself depends on caution, poise, and contest. Men are reluctant to "move quickly," to appear unduly "anxious" or concerned and so expose themselves to ridicule or abuse. The goal of oratorical events is an exchange of words that should, ideally, lead to an exchange of goods and then to a common meal in which both sides are joined as kinsmen; but the achievement of these desired ends works through deception, pretense, wit, and the display of unity and strength by "sides" that are, initially, opposed. What is negotiated is, as we shall see, not justice but equality in *liget* — a word combining elements of ideas like "anger," "passion," "energy," and "force."

No mediating party can decide the form or outcome of an oratorical event, nor do participants themselves appear concerned to judge their fellows right or wrong. Instead, their speech emerges as a sort of artful duel of revelation, hinted meanings, verbal parry and response, wherein a diverse collectivity is divided in two "sides" so that, through the reciprocal gift of words, real differences can be named and reconciled. The give and take of verbal statement and return is paralleled by the fact that the reciprocal gift of words gives way to an "exchange" (*ta'rat*) of goods for wrongs, and furthermore, by the fact that most oratorical events themselves are moments in an ideally balanced or "reciprocal exchange" (*tubrat*) wherein both parties demonstrate that they are ultimately "the same" and over time display their balance. Thus, at the one peace meeting I was able to attend, the dynamics of exchange dictated that, after the victims had been given recompense for their beheaded kin, the killer-hosts accused their guests of speaking behind pointed guns and so demanded payment for *this* threat upon their lives. And, not surprisingly, our records show that most wife-takers one day give a sister as a wife, and equally, that most killers find an opportunity to demand an "exchange" *purung* from the men whose "lives" they stole, because these latter — as is overwhelmingly the case — are likely to themselves have harmed their murderers in the past. In fact, one-sided killings rarely lead to resolution in an oratorical event, because the oratorical form depends upon, as it asserts, a sense of reciprocity.

The point is that, through oratorical display, the representatives of opposed sides can first give voice to their divisive claims and then demand "exchanges" or "returns" (*ta'rat*) by gifts from their onetime opponents. Claims are asserted, recognized, and recognition is itself "returned," and it is through such movement, from display to giving and ultimately, to reciprocal exchange, that grievances are both legitimized and resolved.

Oratorical Style

But if exchange emerges as the form of an oratorical event, it remains for us to probe its meaning. Why does, or did, exchange make sense?

Why can a gift help onetime enemies to "forget" longstanding conflicts? And finally, why is it that exchange requires strength and "angry" shows of force (the possibility that an "exchange" of blows will supersede a calm "exchange" of goods), and how is this, in turn, related to the style and organization of Ilongot verbal art?

Ilongot *purung* contrasts with ordinary speech in that — informants say — good orators do not move directly to their points but speak in lengthy phrases. Where narrators list event upon event (a style described as "constant," *sinaredted*), the orator is apt to "punctuate" (*bētek*, "to write, to decorate, to mark") his speech with repetitions; phonological flourishes; and obscure phrases, metaphors, and puns. Ilongots see in truly artful speech an analogue to a race, a duel, a contest, or — some men suggested — lovely song. And just as songs with tremolo can stir the heart, and quivering music of the violin give rise to feelings that bespeak a sweet and "twisting" inner longing, so good oratory inspires at once feelings of awe and admiration and the desire to achieve a yet more beautiful response. Oratory may, in fact, resemble song in that both use the style known as *'amba'an*, "witty speaking"—a style combining lexical and phonological elaboration (or *bēira*) with allusive, metaphoric turns of phrase that "circle round" unspoken "names" of hopes that lie within one's own or one's opponents' hearts.

Thus, a headhunter who boasts of his success in song employs the artifice of *'amba'an*, adding syllabic flourish (e.g., *-al-*, *-ar-*, to *'anin*, "oh dear"; *bētaling* to *kurut* "course, flow") to his words; selecting unfamiliar terms (*tanung*, "to talk, question"; *sumal*, "come together"; *rekwat*, "to emerge, come from"); employing indirection ("we went to carry you on our backs" denotes the fact of beheading), and word mergers or puns (*bētanabē lingkayatmu* combines *'abēka*, the name of a river, with *kayat*, "to kick"):

'al'alaranin tarda ngu'dek 'anin yaman'ikalagintanungki pa ngun

oh dear victim alas oh dear, talk together [i.e., answer victim in preceding song], now

ta kaginsumalmunmu pan ya 'ed mu pentalaginamaya'i

of how you met [came together] with someone [of whom] you did not know [*bēya*, "to know" is here embedded as *maya*]

ta naraligwatantun sika ngu rinawmi kadi pen'ignakut bētalingkurut where he came from. You, yes, we went to carry you on our backs; it was along the course

kadi nu bētalnabēlingkayatmu pa ngu ta bēlagune nana'bēdēnmu mana tagda

sir, of your kicking Abe:ka river, that the novice got to carry you, you victim ....

And, though much less elaborate by far, it is in terms of similar canons of artistic skill that a man declares intentions toward "that whose name is woman" when he comes to seek a bride:

'inmatmadkun ma talagan 'ipengramakku ma ngadentun bēkur

I performed the preparations [usually, "recited the headhunting spells"] for my truly wanting that whose name is woman ....

The suitor thus makes known his hopes, and then, uncertain of acceptance, such a man is likely to go on:

'angēn kaw 'ikayabumuwak mad 'utlek nima bisa'ulsa'ul 'idē'idēmuamēntaka

even if, perhaps, you have me climb to the peak of the deceptive rattan, I will keep following after you....

Here the speaker merges *bitakur*, the name of a rattan, with a repeated word *sa'ulsa'ul*, a term used deferentially in oratory whose meaning is, appropriately, "to deceive."

Again, it was with fond and almost tearful eyes that Wadeng told me of the artful words of Dēkdēk — the best speaker he had ever heard — when that orator, now dead, had come to speak and so to "rediscover" kinship with once estranged men of Wadeng's local group:

sa kunuy 'inan'u'undikayangku mad 'anikur nima kalēnepampatuy

so it is, they say, that I am searching out in the curves of the Kanuwap River of thought

ma pen'adiralawku ma sinambuanakan ma betrangku

that I look for/go after the monthly replenished fullness of my body

'imendengerengku nem ma pendēnunen kemamau'muwi ma ma'eng

that I hear, perhaps, is forever causing showers of thorns [going headhunting]

duten 'ipen'iwangirku

but I cast that aside.

Without a moment's hesitation or an awkward pause, Dēkdēk wove together metaphor (the falling thorns) with puns (*kalēnepampa* speaks both of the Kanuwap river and *nepampa*, "reflective thought"; *'adiralaw* combines *'adiwar*, "to seek" with *raw*, "to go"; and both include the extra syllable, *-al-*, as simple flourish); the use of "deep" and unfamiliar words (*'undikay*, " to seek," is used only in oratory); and such deferential particles as *nem*, "perhaps," and *kunu*, "it is said." The overall effect of Dēkdēk's speech was both, of course, to indicate the speaker's genuine goodwill and to make known his fearless stance and verbal prowess. "Pierced" by his words, admiring opposites then found themselves as if "struck down" and so inspired to engage in interchange by offering an equally "well-aimed" response.

None of the speeches that I heard and taped was considered by my Ilongot friends to equal Dēkdēk's in skill (and even Dēkdēk's speech falls short of the *'amba'an* heard in song). But many made good use of what informants saw as the most important characteristic of *'amba'an* style — an ability to advance argument while yet "avoiding names" and so, through artful indirection, to define the situation in a manner corresponding to one's goals. What is accomplished by such artful speech is a display combining deference and daring; good speakers "give" in graceful words a statement that makes known at once their "soft" and humble thoughts and their capacity for potent shows of *liget*, "energy, passion, anger." And underneath sweet words are almost always subtle threats of "angry" strength and sometimes violent force.

Good oratory is deferential and the phrases indirect because the speaker fears an outburst of such "anger." A cautious speaker will preface his words with such disclaimers as, "don't think I am accusing you," "I do not claim to answer back," "I do not criticize, my heart is cool" — while yet accusing, challenging, and making claims. Because all are concerned to tame the "angry" *liget* in their fellows' hearts, Ilongot *purung* winds a delicate and "curving" course; it is, in one familiar phrase, a measured, "slow" proceeding — the word "slow"

(*lipalipa*) referring, not to the pace of speech, which is ideally mellif-
luous and unbroken, but to a lack of "sudden" outbursts of "intense"
concern and feeling, a quality of respect that avoids calling things by
name. The true or "big" names (*'usikena ngaden*) of things can be
experienced as an affront and excite passions. Thus, in oratory, one
moves "slowly" out of a desire to "find" the words that can at once
contain the *liget* of the youths for whom one speaks and yet be in-
offensive, "hitting" aptly on the grounds for "softened" feeling in an
opponent's heart. Orators through indirection show their "respect"
and wisdom. They speak of "tasted objects" rather than of weapons,
of "rice" instead of women, of "young pups" when they have in mind
a hopeful husband—much as all adults are careful to avoid the names
of affines, call death an "absence," burial a "handling of dirt," and say
that "something kind of happened" (*kimu'kuyen*) instead of "he got a
little better" (*pimi'piya*) when reporting progress in a fellow who was
ill.

But practically, there is, I think, an even deeper way in which "slow"
speech is necessary to oratorical encounters, something I mislabeled
in earlier work on oratory (cf. M. Rosaldo 1973) as an ability to persuade.[2]
What happens in an oratorical confrontation is not in any familiar
sense a "trial" in which one musters facts to help decide a case and
so, perhaps, negotiate its outcome. Orators confront one another's
intransigent and separate hearts and must attempt, with "curving"
words, to "hit" and so to bind them. When an opposite will not be
moved, a speaker may have the wit to "answer" each denial with new
insistence, swearing to climb rocks, drink streams, or manufacture
untold gifts for would-be brides and so confront, with passionate "anger" of his own, a "hard" opponent. But equally, the seasoned orator
may, in delicacy, claim to set forth "soft" words, words "sweet as fruits"
and "without arrows." Through lovely speeches, one hopes opponents
will "get used to" one another—and since, Ilongots say, it is impossible
to "know" what "flows" inside the hearts of "equal humans," a cautious
pace is required if people are to find real pleasure in, and come to
trust, each other's words.

At times, then, artful speakers deprecate themselves; they talk of
kinship and the "pity" that one's kin should show in answer to sincere
petitions. Thus, Rumyad men, at the peace meeting I attended, de-

scribed themselves as crippled "fathers" of the younger orators from Butag, hoping that, in sympathy for old men shivering in the night air, the Butag speakers would — without first "seeing" a return for stolen objects — enter and enjoy the comfort of their onetime killers' homes.

But then again — and in particular when confronted with intransigent opponents — the "knowing" voice may seek to strike a chord relating less to sympathy than the "anger" that the speaker — or his opposite — yet keeps hidden in his heart. This was, in fact, what happened at one of the most disturbing *purung* I attended, where Lundi, a recent widow, living with her brother-in-law and sister near our settlement and quite far from the majority of her close kin, was sought as a bride by Bē'rak, an aging bachelor who many reckoned *depyang*, an "incompetent," "worthless man," or "clod." Present when we first arrived, Lundi stayed only briefly in the house where men were speaking, long enough to learn that the male orators desired her to speak her mind—but if, as a woman, she felt herself unable to broadcast the things she felt, she could trust them, as her "brothers," to look out for her concerns. Lundi listened silently, and then, reluctant to remarry, she protested that the noise disturbed her tired children and left the house.

What eventually happened was that Lundi was persuaded, as a hostess, to reenter the house, at which point Bē'rak, misunderstanding a suggestion that he give Lundi a drink, tried to embrace her. In fury, Lundi left again, again returned, and this time let herself admit the "name" of what it was that had just recently made her "angry." But, since she had thus "let out" a cause of *liget*, Bē'rak could insist, "in shame," that he be allowed to pay her in return for his offense. This accepted, Bē'rak's speakers took the opportunity to offer to enhance their gift. The *purung* ended with the agreement that Bē'rak would be allowed to visit the house where Lundi was staying and help her brother-in-law in garden labor — apparently, a step toward marriage, although on last report we learned that Lundi had fled to distant kin.

Several women I knew berated the men who were involved for disattending Lundi's stated wishes, but most agreed with those who argued that much courtship takes something like this form. A woman resists and a man hopes, through labor and repeated gifts, gradually "to accustom" his lover's heart to interaction. And Ilongots say that if a man has *liget,* or "passion," necessary to persevere, he is unlikely to fail to win his suit. The artful and committed suitor manages to "find" the things that keep a woman's feelings at a distance, and if she or her brothers "name" their reasons for dissension, the young man's party can insist on giving gifts and so initiate further talk. Much of the art of *purung* consists, in short, in such attempts to "hit upon," make public and so accessible to resolution what were divisive, hidden thoughts — to find a source of "anger" and repay it. Slow and careful speech seeks to facilitate what may be critical revelations. By "laying out" his words and proclaiming against deception, the orator works to ease and open out his fellows' hearts.

The careful speech of *purung* is, thus, predicated upon a particular view of people's hearts and thoughts, a view that claims that troubled feelings can be quieted if their source, once "hidden," is made known. One tries to find the words that will occasion revelation, just as in medicinal spells one tries to "hit upon" the words that "find" the things that made a person ill. In both cases, the "knowledge" that leads to a success is something one assumes to be already there, requiring only revelation; and so, practitioners seek to make the "names" of troubles public because in giving voice to "hidden" founts of "anger," one makes them manipulable, subjecting them to social action and control.

But if the knowing speaker seeks, in slow and cautious terms, to let his opposite "make known" a hidden feeling, if speakers value openness and claim that they "lay out" their hearts and lack disguise, good orators are also men who can "hold on" to tortured thoughts and anger. While protesting revelation, they will attempt to "hide" in metaphors and "crooked" speech their deeper meanings. Avoiding names of things in order to befuddle and exhaust their interlocutors, they hope to dazzle and in general display a quality of *liget* that indicates the mettle of their side. The rounds of boasts and dueling that in the past preceded peace negotiations — and made it something of a show of courage for men to ask for peace — are themselves testimony to the fact that orators require "passion" as a necessary complement to knowing subtlety in their speech.

Thus, successful orators hear their fellows' words and then turn them to their purpose — as did Lundi's "brother" when he first asked Bə'rak's speakers what sort of "rice" they hoped to find in local gardens, knowing that if they said *mabu'u*, "plain rice," he could name other families who had a surplus, and if they spoke of *deyeket*, "glutinous rice," he could insist that in his household full of children, hungry youngsters had long ago consumed his small supply. Some brothers will "pretend to anger" (*rayag*, "to make a show of anger, make an unconsummated threatening gesture") at a sister's marriage, in order —others claim—to provide a cause for payments. Some see the subtlety in their *purung* as a device for "testing" (*pabēyabēya*, "making known") their opponents; through ruses meant to cause confusion and frustration, they hope to intimidate those speakers who, for lack of *liget*, can be summarily dismissed.

In 1973, when men from Dekran came to announce their hopes to marry Binsing, Katan's daughter, they were intimidated by the "angry" speeches of her kin. A history of enmity as well as rumors to the effect that men from Dekran never helped their wives, gave Binsing's father and brothers sufficient cause to feel, at best, ambivalent about the union. And, so according to reports, the "angry" pretense in her uncles' speech — as they declared that before a Dekran man could move into their homes, the latter would have climbed on ladders runged with knives and sipped till dry the local rivers — caused the suitors such confusion that they could not decide among themselves a telling answer, and thus humiliated, withdrew. The Dekran version placed a different value on the same proceeding. They saw themselves behaving in the manner of the Christian ethic they had recently accepted, demonstrating "knowledge" without "passion," and when, faced with *liget*, showing themselves willing to "give in."

In short, then, without *liget*, without firm words and stunning speech, one's *purung* is unlikely to manage "to reach" its mark; young men thus lose their hope for brides; the brothers of new brides receive no payments; and enemies continue killing rather than redress a history of wrong.

And yet, ideally, "anger" is, with time, revealed and "answered." As the *purung* proceeds, speakers are constrained to "give" more of their "hidden" thoughts, articulating demands and hopes, yet trying to avoid a compromising revelation. An awkward turn of phrase may permit an opposite to say, "you speak as though my sister were wild game, waiting to be hunted" — and so shame the careless speaker. More serious, if clumsy speeches are seen themselves to call forth "anger," if words or gestures meant to be convincing can be construed as boasts or threats, the offender will confront demands for payment "in return" for the distress he caused.

Thus, for example, at a bridewealth transaction in Pugu we heard complaints to the effect that not only was the groom's party very large but that some of them had brought "even Americans" to "beautify" their presence and had, furthermore, flown with us from Kakidugen to a mission airstrip near the bride's family's home. So accused of showing off, the speakers for the groom then managed to answer the attack by setting forth a set of tokens of our voyage: brass wire, with which, they said, they "telephoned" the airplane; red cloth with which they flagged it down. And finally, in playful flourish, they claimed the bride's family, now overwhelmed with goods, to be the real "Americans" while they themselves were poor and groveling "Japanese"—who should be given gifts "in return" for their excessive loss!

More difficult, because of deep distrust, the Rumyads in the peace meeting that we saw were also criticized for their numbers. Before the *purung*, Butag fear of Rumyad strength led to the loan of a bachelor hostage whom the Butag men had thought to hold at knifepoint, "by the tail," as they walked on the trail toward Ringen — and if they had so used the boy, they would have had to pay for threatening his life. Instead, the Butags chose to show their firm goodwill and fearless daring, to treat the youth as a companion, and then, "in anger" find the Rumyads at fault for what appeared to be excessive "bodies" on their side. But once Rumyad had paid recompense for "tasted" goods and killings, and the Butags, fully satisfied, had entered and set down their weapons in the ready Ringen homes, it was time for a return prestation. The Butag men were "criticized" (*pekiw*), and forced to pay for holding loaded weapons, an unnecessary show of "anger" in the presence of unarmed and friendly hosts. Something of the reverse occurred when, at the celebration of a youth's beheading, the hosting Kadēng happened, in a boastful dance, to call to mind a death that visiting Da'sa caused his distant kinsman. The boast was seen by all as dangerous — an irresponsible and thoughtless challenge. Da'sa grace- fully gave an arrow in recompense for the killing. But then all thought it just that Kadēng was required to reciprocate for so defaming Da'sa with a still larger gift.

Violations of this sort — occasioning *ta'rat*, a "return," "repayment," or "exchange" — tend to appear casual and accidental. But they in fact emerged in every *purung* that I heard. Unable to negotiate acknowledged differences in the "knowing" terms appropriate to kinsmen, orators are bound in a dilemma. Demonstrating potent *liget* and conviction in their speech, they inevitably occasion *liget* in the men whose gifts or sympathy they seek — and such "anger" requires a "return." While speakers hedge — "don't think I am accusing you," "don't think I put sharp prongs onto my tongue" — affronting words are rarely masked by protest. Proclaiming honorable means and goals, men nonetheless give voice to challenge and accusation. Yet such affronts — which may themselves call forth "returns" of physical assault — are what in oratory provide the basis for exchanges through which differences are often best resolved.

Through a balancing of "angry" claims, individual offenses and returns become aspects of a *tubrat*, "reciprocal exchange" (a word that characterizes the exchange not just of goods but of beheadings and of women in marriage) in which members of both sides assume what often is a genuinely dangerous and violent stance, in hopes that, having proved themselves "the same," they can both pay and be paid for past wrongs. *Purung* thus requires that adults align themselves on opposed sides, disguise their "different" hearts, and in their artful words display their *liget*, in order that complaints can be "revealed," acknowledged, and redressed.

In the course of an encounter, both parties will display their strength and both may receive payment. Oratorical elaboration is the condition for an exchange through which a group of "angry" men, acknowledging the "anger" in their fellows, allow that all are "equal humans" who have no further cause for strife. A form of discourse dominated by the dual form of the verb — *maki'upu kita*, "we speak, one to the other, I to you" — *purung* moves ideally from antagonism to a more fluid style of interaction. The ultimate suspension of opposing claims is symbolized by youths who hand-feed one another rice (*tubu*); collective participation in a concluding feast; and, if portions are sufficient, by gifts of food (*'ising*) that individuals offer one another to indicate their mutual concern. As fellows and recipients of "equal shares" of meat and rice, they will conclude with speech in the collective form — *pemen'upu kisi*, "we speak together" — suggestive of the diffuse reciprocity that should obtain in civil dealings among relatives and friends.

The skillful indirection of oratorical discourse—of speech that strives at once for delicacy and respect and for the strength implied by dazzle and deception, a style of talk that seeks to call forth secrets and yet makes strategic use of hidden motives of its own — itself provides a challenge to, as it facilitates, such outcomes. Achieving what is at best a delicate balance (and forever vulnerable to the man or woman who feels "twisted" by a thought still unaddressed), orators enact a sort of mediation between the separate hearts of "angry" and potentially un-equal men and the far less passionate claims of those who share a "body," and, as equals can cooperate in day-to-day affairs. Their speech — like daily living — affirms the fact that Ilongots can live in civil peace only if they see themselves as "sharing needs" as kin and equals. Yet oratory makes clear, as daily life does not, that equality itself is an achievement, always tenuous and dependent on a sense that would-be "equal men" are capable of potentially destructive "anger" — which, displayed and celebrated as it is, is hopefully resolved in formal speech.

Oratorical Art and Ilongot Society

My point in the preceding section was to suggest that oratorical elab-oration, and in particular, the indirection characteristic of the 'amba'an style of speech, serves to permit a mediated display combining both humility and "anger"; and furthermore, that such display makes sense because it is through verbal shows of "angry" *liget* that exchange is motivated and difference is — at least potentially — resolved. The form of *purung* thus depends itself upon 'amba'an style, and both of these become appropriate in turn, because the resolution of disputes re-quires negotiations that give rise, not just to order, but to equality. What remains to be discovered is the relationship between the balance sought in oratorical events and the bonds that govern traditional Il-ongot society; only then will we be able to explore the consequences of contemporary developments for traditional verbal art.

The equality (or more accurately, perhaps, the sense of "sameness") forged through oratorical exchange is not, for Ilongots, an abstract and philosophical ideal but is an assumption that pervades their daily living. "Energy" and "anger" are themselves the products, not of inner strivings, but of "envy;" and "envy" is, of course, created when ideals of "sameness" or equality are breached. People are, Ilongots say, in-spired to work, to learn, and even at times, to kill, because they would be "equal" to their fellows; headhunters take the lives of "equal-to-us-human beings"; age-mates speak of one another as their "equal bachelors," "equal maidens," "equal men," and "equal women," and in so doing indicate an orientation to both the hardships and accomplishments of their peers. When game is killed, the meat ideally should be shared in equal portions by all those living in a settlement; and when food is served at mealtimes, men, women, and children may alike expect to be presented with their individual and equal shares.

Although within a local group some men are apt to be more influential than their fellows, no man is recognized as a figure of authority in relation to his age-mates. And even though in daily life adults "command" obedience and labor from their children, and men may be inclined to voice directives toward their wives, Ilongots view compliance as a problematic fact that follows, not from the authority of men and in particular of elders, but instead from the "respect" that grows of love and the familiar bonds of kin. Adults and children can all equally attempt to win their way by pleading, frightening, shaming, or deceiving, but no individual can with certainty pretend to know or rule another's always independent "heart."

This sense of "sameness" and autonomy of one's fellow human beings is, however, qualified by the fact that the autonomy all people desire is in a very concrete way much more available to men than to women, and again, to married men than to still dependent bachelor youths. It is only with a wife and hearth that he can call his own that a man may host his fellows to a meal and so attain political support for his decisions; only married men can draw on private rice stores when they choose to hunt or travel; and only married men can claim a "tongue" in public speech. And if a man requires a hearth and family of his own in order to achieve a voice among his adult fellows, traditional Ilongots believe that men ideally should display capacities for *liget* by taking heads before they move into affinal homes and "sit" or settle with a wife.

The point is not that all Ilongot married men have taken heads — although, in fact, the vast majority had, as late as 1969, achieved the right to wear a headhunter's hornbill earrings — but rather that the equality in terms of which men organize their daily lives involves the shared assumption that all adult men have earned their right to wives and social recognition by a youthful demonstration of their "equal" force. Most adult men have, in fact, "cast off" the heads of fellow human beings; and ultimately, it is because adults are thus assumed to be each other's peers in "anger" that people hesitate to offend or slight their fellows in the cooperative dealings that constitute their daily world.

This stated, it becomes easy to see why oratorical events themselves are typically concerned with either marrying or killing. Furthermore, since both of these entail a recognition of men's claims to *liget*, one can begin to understand why Ilongots associate their killings in the past with competition over women, and finally, why oratory requires that men at once display and then acknowledge their equality in "anger" if the imbalance caused by daring grooms or even more disruptive murders is to be rectified or resolved. Oratorical discourse and the artful indirection of *'amba'an* speech concern an "anger" that alone permits men to establish their equality; the art of oratory is an art with social purpose, and, I have suggested, it is rooted in the particular sense of "being the same" or "equal" that allows for order and cooperation in traditional Ilongot society.

Thus, when Inanu claimed that oratory in the old style led to killings, he was, of course, failing to note the caution and humility that were a vital part of oratorical indirection; he did not note the ways in which the "crooked" words of witty speakers could correct social imbalance and help enemies to come to view themselves as "equal" kin. But, in insisting that conventional oratory was, in fact, concerned with a potentially disruptive *liget*, Inanu spoke with reason, and as my friends who heard his words insisted, he was not far from wrong. Oratory that inspires response can easily give rise to violent "passion" — although it is through verbal art that "anger" born of challenge and opposition is subordinated to exchange and so resolved. It thus remains for us to ask, not why Inanu criticized the past, but what it was that gave him license to reject it. If traditional oratory made sense within a world ruled by particular views of human beings and their social interactions, the rejection of traditional verbal arts is something that, in turn, must be interpreted with reference to the changing tenor of contemporary Ilongot social life.

It is beyond the scope of this study to develop a full analysis of contemporary social changes, but we can point to certain interrelated shifts in modern Ilongot experience that have helped to undermine conventional verbal forms, and lend, to youths like Tubeng, new authority. One might, for instance, note that postwar years have brought to young men education, and their command of lowland languages has enabled them to mediate in dealings with the agents of Philippine government control. Such youths have come, increasingly, to assert their skills and, in so doing, to deny the claims of once esteemed and "angry" elders, while adults are now inclined to bow before the power and prestige of lowland law.

Important, too, is recognition of the fact that Ilongots have for decades been the victims of land-grabbing settlers. But more particularly, the late 1960s were a time when Ilongots who could not hope to hold uncultivated lands against increasing settler populations began to designate particular plots as "private property," which individual owners could, then, choose to give in sale. Their forests daily shrunk by new land-hungry farmers, the individuals who sold their land hoped to attain the carabaos and irrigation ditches necessary to help them shift from a subsistence based on hunts and swidden fields to one anchored in the cultivation of wet rice. But whatever their stated goals, what seemed in fact to be occurring was that individual Ilongots were temporarily enriched with all too rapidly diminishing quantities of cash. At the same time, bridewealth payments — which traditionally consisted largely of the gift of game, along with an occasional pot, a gift of cloth, a knife, or ornamental wire — were inflated to include such things as money, radios, watches, carabaos, and guns. And then, by 1974, emerging opportunities for wage labor at sawmills and on roads were beginning to provide young men with new sources of autonomy and cash.

Clearly, developments of this sort prove consequential for daily social interactions. For Ilongots, they led the way toward a rejection of traditional norms that stressed equality in cooperation in favor of the much more abstract sense of "being equal" that emerges when individuals weigh their worth in cash. Questions arose: If X sells game instead of sharing it with kin, or Y invites a group of lowland settlers to "help him farm" his land, or Z attempts to "sue" his "brother," R, because R's carabao (utterly absent, until recently, on most Ilongot lands) wandered dangerously into Z's growing rice...are these betrayals of the kind of trust expected among kin...and, if so, what is to be done? Here, men like Tubeng and Inanu offered what Ilongots saw as threatening but inevitable sorts of answers. Fearing rightly that the sums that Tubeng named — much like the bridewealth goods they knew themselves to seek — were virtually beyond intelligibility or constraint, they yet rejected a traditional concern for balance among persons who desire to be "the same" in favor of abstract appeals to new and "Christian" ways, and personless and timeless rights and wrongs.

And yet, it was not simply the prestige of modern ways — or the compelling force of economic change — that lent authority to Tubeng's rather horrifying demand for money. The arguments in his defense appeared to have as much to do with a desire to oppose "straight speech" and God to "curvy" words and "angry" ways as with a sense that justice was on Tubeng's side. One needs, in short, to note the cultural form of social change — and in particular, the fact that Ilongots during the time of our research were tending both to abjure headhunting and to affiliate themselves with the New Tribes Evangelical Christian Mission, present in Ilongot country since 1955. Although for some it was the biblical Word, for others martial law, for others settlers and schools that most convincingly bespoke an end to taking heads, the fact is that by the early 1970s Ilongots had begun to find in Christian faith an alternative way of dealing with distressing feelings that, they said, bred violence in the past. Thus, where previously men thought to kill in order to "cast off" the weight of grief, the early 1970s saw death of kin as a most frequent motive for conversion. And yet more generally, Ilongots claimed that their new faith had led them to respond to insult, pain, and disappointment, not with "passion," but with the "quiet" sort of "hopefulness" inspired by a Christian God. Once stirred by "angry" envy to exert themselves in hunts and garden work, Ilongot converts told that with new faith they grew more "lazy," less "intent" and "anxious" in their labor. And then again, once moved to joy, vitality, and health by fancy dress, display, and song, these Christians claimed that one seeks quietude, not excitement, when worldly existence is subordinated to another life.

The very coupling of an end to headhunting with conversion had, in short, occasioned a pervasive stance of skepticism and distrust toward violent possibilities that were part (but only part) of classic emphases on passion, energy, and anger. And Ilongots of the mid-1970s were anxious to reject not only violence *per se* but notions of motivation, forms of art and discourse, and ultimately those forms of social life in which ideas of "anger," "passion," *liget* were discerned. With a logic that defied the liberal wishes of both missionaries and anthropologists, Ilongots thus interpreted their change of faith as the rejection of a past defined by killing. At the time, this turn entailed rejection both of killing and of the arts and pleasures and images of the self associated with an "anger" that, of course, proved incompatible with a "Christian" understanding of the world.

Thus, Christianity, opposed to headhunting, came to be seen as incompatible with a style of verbal art that construed persons in ways alien to the national legal system. Young men, knowledgeable in national speech and ways, could then invoke their newfound faith in the defense of their desires for law or power. And persons who defined their claims in terms of goods (and threatened the supportive intervention of police) could understand and argue for their style and stance with reference to an opposition between things made by men (*betar*) — the customary ways of "anger" — and Catholic Filipino norms of "order," understood, ironically enough, as those dictated by a Protestant God.

In brief, for Ilongots a set of verbal skills that once were used to balance and display the "passion" held by would-be equal men came to be seen as fundamentally disruptive because the sociocultural world that they portrayed and shaped had lost its sense. The convergent power of an end to headhunting, a rise in Christian faith, and almost simultaneous change in the material nature of their concrete daily interactions led Ilongots to come to understand their art and politics primarily as a negation of the art and politics of their past. For Ilongots in 1974, it was because their art made social sense that there was "Christian" reason to deny it.

It was because aesthetics was so intimately bound up with practical and ethical concerns that Ilongot oratory came to be seen at once as socially and emotionally disruptive — unworthy both as politics and as art.

Notes

This chapter was first presented as a paper in Ithaca, New York, at a Social Science Research Council Conference on Southeast Asian Aesthetics.

Although I have been able to respond only minimally to suggestions for revision, I am particularly indebted to Benedict Anderson, Donald Brenneis, Jane Collier, and Renato Rosaldo for their comments.

1. For further detail on the Ilongots and, in particular, their politics, arts, and oratory see M. Rosaldo 1973 and 1980 and R. Rosaldo 1980.

2. The discussion from here to the end of this section draws heavily upon Chapter Six of my monograph, *Knowledge and Passion* (1980); I am grateful to Cambridge University Press for allowing me to use this material here.

6. From Words to Objects to Magic: "Hard Words" and the Boundaries of Social Interaction

Annette B. Weiner
New York University

Introduction

In the third voyage of *Gulliver's Travels* a brief episode occurs in which Gulliver observes the results of a project where professors of the School of Languages at the Academy of Lagado are attempting to abolish the use of all words. Things — utensils and goods — rather than words are to be substituted in social interaction: "since Words are only Names for *Things*, it would be more convenient for all Men to carry about them, such *Things* as were necessary to express the particular Business they are to discourse on." Thus, Gulliver describes the following scene:

I have often beheld two of those Sages almost sinking under the Weight of their Packs, like Pedlars among us, who when they met in the Streets, would lay down their loads, open their Sacks, and hold Conversation for an Hour together; then put up their Implements, help each other to resume their Burthens, and take their Leave. (Swift 1970: 158)

In abolishing words and creating a language of things, Gulliver's professors had decided that objects have certain unique qualities that give them priority over words. Yet, as Gulliver observed, objects have their own innate limitations—the physical burden of their weightiness, making them cumbersome to talk with. This heaviness, however, is precisely the quality that gives objects their formidable power. Objects that are weighty have properties of durability. Before objects decay, they may circulate for a period of time. As they move between individuals, objects take on value, as they represent the histories of their movements through time and the histories of the individuals who fashioned them, owned them, and exchanged them. In this way, objects become rare things, which increases their weightiness.

Were the professors from Lagado correct? Are these attributes of objects unique in relation to words? Or was Gulliver more observant? Are there limitations in the use of objects as language? In this chapter I explore the relation between weightiness and rarity as associated with objects and with words as both or either are exchanged in the processes of social interaction. How do words take on heaviness, and how do they become valued as rare utterances? What are the limitations in the use of words or objects for accumulating these qualities and bringing them to bear on situations that have social and political consequences? How does the circulation of objects or words between individuals define and limit access to the control that one person hopes to gain over another's thoughts and feelings?[1]

Although my analysis focuses on one specific society, the island of Kiriwina in the Trobriand group, Papua New Guinea, the ethnographic examples I discuss point directly to more general theoretical and methodological issues concerned with the epistemological foundations in the constitution of particular forms of social interaction. Edward Sapir (1933) wrote that "Language is at one and the same time helping and retarding us in our exploration of experience." Within the general context of language and experience are specific processes that give to objects and words the abilities to penetrate or maintain a boundary between an individual and others. From a societal perspective, these processes show the limitations that exist within the relation between the autonomous demands of individual will and the ability of anyone to gain domination over others. In this way, the semantic lexicon encoding the acts of linguistic or material exchange not only circumscribes meaning as the result of the exchange event but documents the limitations and the possibilities, Sapir's "help and hindrance," in the processes through which one person's desires become a social fact.

My approach is to demonstrate the Trobriand ways a reordering of reality is achieved through objects or through verbal responses in everyday interactions, political discourse, and in the use of magic spells. The reordering is grounded in the culturally constituted perception of each individual toward others as an individual's will, intent, and desires are brought to bear on the actions of others. Nowhere are the processes of the penetration of individual will onto the thoughts and feelings of others more vulnerable and exposed than at the times when "truth" is publicly expressed. By "truth" (*mokita*) I mean the accepted knowledge of events as they were in the past, as they exist in the present, and as they are expected to obtain in the future. "Truth" is about history, decisions by people that mark past and present events and circumstances. In the public circulation of objects, "truth" is expressed in values such as durability and rarity. These properties define both the nature of the present relationship and past situations in which the object, in its circulation through time, has been involved. Words that are perceived to be the "truth" about past events and historical or mythical circumstances are similarly thought to have values of weightiness. In certain cases, these words are considered rare in that they are secret, guarded knowledge. When such words are spoken in a public setting, they reveal the nature of a present relationship by exposing the "truth" about past events. The disguise of "truth" also must be accounted for in these situations. The "truth" is being created anew in the telling or the giving, as an individual elects to hide or expose her or his private thoughts or feelings as well as the complete circumstances of past events. Through time, each telling gives these words more or less value.

At special times, the force of magic is perceived necessary to effect one's will over others. Under these circumstances, words and objects are thought to take on extraordinary qualities of weightiness and rarity. These qualities differ in degree rather than in kind from the use of words and objects in everyday interactions. Traditional analytical distinctions between everyday discourse, political oratory, and magic spells must to be collapsed insofar as these latter two situations are classified as the sacred, ritual domain in opposition to the profane and mundane (see e.g., Bloch 1975). How Trobriand magic is thought to work can be understood only from a theory of Trobriand language in use, rather than from a theory of magic.

Personal Space

My concern is to express through the ethnographic experience itself the attributes and values that words and objects are perceived to have and the way these attributes and values give meaning to, and act on, the encounters that individuals have with each other. What qualities must be attached to objects or words that will enable either to break through the boundaries between individuals? These boundaries are clearly marked. My informants call them "one's mind," and based on my observations of the way "one's mind" is protected and bounded from the intentions of others, I call these boundaries "personal space" — the locus of an individual's thoughts, desires, and intentions.

In the Trobriands, individuals are faced with the task of protecting their personal space from the influence of others, while simultaneously, they may be attempting to impose their influence on others. Out of the possibilities of wanting and needing, in a never ending scheme of demands, an individual must act as if she or he wants nothing, needs nothing, and will demand nothing. How a person negotiates his or her own desires with the desires of another person is an extemely delicate undertaking. To make someone believe in you is a paramount concern. The accomplishment of such belief, as for example to create a state of love or fear in another person, is far from simple.

The penetration of "personal space" by the use of words or objects constitutes for Trobrianders the basic work of interaction. The ability to influence, control, and gain from another person in situations as diverse as politics or love demands an extremely subtle awareness of psychological processes (cf. Goffman 1967 on American culture). In Western societies, the range of personal space, the private domain in which individuals move, is far broader. It encompasses material possessions and geographical areas, as well as psychological space, all of which are supported to some degree by institutional sanctions, laws, and controls. In Kiriwina, the protection of "one's mind" is a constant concern, for one's personal space is always in danger of being threatened; one's mind is always in danger of being seduced. Physical space and one's material possessions can be taken by others, but one's personal space—one's mind—is bounded culturally by the idea of privacy. Breaking through this boundary "to gain control of someone's mind" is an extremely difficult achievement. Only an approximation of what a person imaginatively desires may be obtained.

The possibility of rejection produces fear associated not only with one's potential rejection by another but also with one's potential failure to reject someone else's advances. Like weighted arrows, words, objects, and magic spells are projected toward another person's personal space. At the same time, words, objects, and magic spells are the very projectiles that others are using to penetrate one's own personal space. Success or defense must be seen in relation to the hardness of the words spoken, the heaviness of the objects that are given, or the rarefied circumstances under which magic spells are performed.

The circumstances under which words and objects are exchanged in interaction are more complex than defining heaviness or preciousness. For the ability to say no is as significant as saying yes. Kenneth Burke (1966: 420) argued that "The essential distinction between the verbal and the nonverbal is in the fact that language adds the peculiar possibility of the Negative" — the ability to say no. In the Trobriand case, we find that the complexity inherent in the possibility of actually saying no leads to ways in which a "no" is verbally disguised. Linguistically, one may tell an alternative story; or say that knowledge of an event is forgotten or unknown; or disguise the truth in words encoded in metaphors, similes, analogies, or riddles. Burke, however, was not considering objects as part of nonverbal communication, for in exchange, objects say no clearly and dramatically. A person either has the object or does not. Although in some cases a linguistic explanation is given to note an absence or shortage, the explanation never removes the negative fact expressed in the visual representation. Both words and objects carry the possibility of the Negative, but the latter carries the possibility without the potential for ambiguity. That the Negative can be disguised gives its use a special power.

Gulliver's sage with the heavy sack could not disguise the quantity of his things, nor, we assume, their quality, in his discourse with another. In our own society, disguise of objects is often achieved through such substitutions as forgery, fakes, and counterfeits. But all these are meant to be the authentic object. In traditional small-scale societies, authenticity can be well identified. Knowledge of the history of a *kula* shell is intimately associated with recognition of the shell itself. As Evans-Pritchard (1940) demonstrated for the Nuer, knowledge of the most explicit physical characteristics of cattle is not only known but is recorded in poetry.

The ability to create disguise, to devise ambiguity, has enormous potential for attempting to rearrange a situation to a person's own advantage while protecting her or his own thoughts and feelings. Such advantage, however, has limitations, in that disguise of the truth may never generate the power of truth itself. The degree of autonomy and domination that an individual may gain over someone else depends upon the weightiness of words or objects or magic spells, but the fact of weightiness is difficult to disguise. Disguise is protection for one's own thoughts. When disguise is thrown off, a person's personal space is exposed.

Herein lies the inherent dilemma. Exposure, although powerful, is deeply dangerous.

The Actions of Verbal Disguise

In Kiriwina, formalized speech codes allow for the ritualization of verbal interaction so that one's thoughts remain disguised and cannot be controlled by someone else. Ritualization of verbal interaction is by no means unusual, as studies in other societies on the use of lying, gossip, rumor, and innuendo demonstrate (see, e.g., Blom and Gumperz 1972; Dundes, Leach, and Özkök 1972; Gilsenan 1976; Gluckman 1962; Irvine 1974; Keenan 1974; Mitchell-Kernan 1972; Szwed 1966; Wilson 1974). In the Trobriand case, special attention is placed on the circumscription of the "mind" (*nanola*) as the area to which no one has access. Among the Melpa of Mount Hagen, a contrast is made between the *noman*, the mind that "is a source of intention and desire," and "what is on the skin" (M. Strathern 1979). An individual cannot ascertain what is on someone's *noman*. Unlike the skin where shame and other attributes may appear (see A. Strathern 1975a), one can only guess at what is in a person's mind. "The interpretation of meaning [the guesses] rests on this dichotomy: do a person's words come from his *noman* and reveal his true intentions, or are they simply 'in the mouth'?" (M. Strathern 1979: 250).

In the Trobriands, speaking what one truly thinks about something is called saying "hard words" (*biga peula*). Even though the truth about something may be known to everyone, saying the truth publicly exposes all the compromises and negotiations in relation to the truth under which individuals operate in their daily lives. For this reason, saying "hard words" is perceived to be extremely dangerous and produces immediate and often violent repercussions. "Hard words" once spoken cannot be recalled; apologies do not carry any power to mute their effects. From this perspective, "hard words" are weighty, carrying the ability to penetrate the personal space of others.

Consider the examples Evans-Pritchard (1962: 221) presented in the Zande uses of *sanza*, "a circumlocutory form of speech or action in which words and gestures have hidden meanings different from their manifest meanings and generally malicious." When an Azande employs *sanza*, the intent is to release one's own "nasty" thoughts about someone, without that person understanding the meaning of what is being said. "The great thing, however, is to keep under cover and to keep open a line of retreat should the sufferer from your malice take offence and try to make trouble" (222). The danger in their use occurs when someone understands what is being said about herself or himself. The reaction may be extreme and dangerous.[2] In Kiriwina, "hard words" are not ambiguous, and their effect is similar to the Azande reaction when the meaning of *sanza* is exposed.

Trobrianders are especially cautious about saying "hard words." My awareness of this situation came about through my own difficulty in using disguise. Although I was taught the importance of disguising my feelings about particular individuals, I could not interact with ease and generosity toward people I thought were taking advantage of me or who were trying to control my activities. My assessments of individuals I disliked often exactly matched what my close friends thought.[3] They warned me, however, that I must never show my anger or openly discuss incidents that I found provoking. I had to hide my "true" feelings, smile, and be generous and friendly to the very people I disliked intensely. Naively, I wanted to confront these individuals; I wanted to speak about things that bothered me in order to find a way to change them; I wanted them to know that I knew what they were doing to me. But the warnings were always the same: "Do not say the words in your mind." I was told to remember that "the words you say to someone are not the words you think."

One day I got very angry, and in the privacy of my village house I accused X of breaking my bicycle when last he borrowed it. As I told him what I thought in a mild tone, I watched in horror as my words instantly changed the reality in front of me. X's face took on hard lines, his eyes flashed with anger, his hands tightened, and he bitterly said:

I leave you now, because if I stay I will be forced to say what is in my mind, and when I say those words we will never speak to each other again.

In the face of what every friend previously had advised me, I still was totally unprepared for the almost violent nature of X's response. He did not apologize, nor did he make any attempts to arrive at an understanding with me. My words demanded an entirely different reaction. By leaving my presence immediately, X gave both of us the option to continue our relationship, but we never discussed the incident again.[4] Later, my informants told me that if I had not been "new," X would have answered me by accusing me of things that I had done to him. The interaction would have escalated into fighting very quickly.

The shock of these possible disjunctures in my interaction with others forced me to realize the complexity in verbal interaction. I began to observe more carefully the face-to-face interaction of villagers with each other, and I found increasing evidence that individuals whom I knew hated and distrusted each other interacted as if nothing were amiss. Consider for a moment that very often one person suspects another of having "poisoned" a close friend or relative.[5] Yet their behavior with each other displays no sign of suspicion. When I commented, for example, that "M is a good man," my informants would say, "Yes, M is very good, but remember he kills [poisons] people. Never forget that M is good, but he is also bad." But I was trapped in my inability to encompass both aspects of behavior in the same person. If someone was a friend, I could not fully comprehend the Trobriand reality that he owned and used dangerous magic. Conversely, if such a person was someone I did not particularly like, I experienced great discomfort when I tried to disguise my feelings.

Recognition of what one is or might be or was pervades villagers' thoughts. In their interaction with each other such thoughts should be concealed, but at the same time one never ignores or disregards them. Once an act of aggression, adultery, theft, poisoning, killing, or breaking a taboo has been committed, even though the act has been compensated for publicly, the affair is never forgotten. Acts once committed survive through generations, so that new acts may be in retaliation for something that occurred several generations before (see Weiner 1976: 66–68). The reality of social interaction proceeds through the constant disguising of many truths, but truths are always recognized and remembered.

"Hard Words" and Speaking the "Truth"

Informants repeatedly said: "The words we speak are not the words in our minds" or "We say words, but our minds do not believe those words." The only answer one receives when questioning why W went here or there or performed an action of some kind is "We do not know what is in her mind." When individuals speak with each other, in all interactional domains — except in the most private recesses of one's house, in the bush, or at the beach, the areas of confiding and secrecy — an awareness always exists that behind each face and each verbal interaction lie the hidden, dangerous, autonomous dimensions of what a person really thinks.

Personal space in relation to social interaction operates as a conceptual entity, surrounded by formal controls connected with contexts in which one's private thoughts either do or do not become publicly expressed. Implicit in the decision is the knowledge that verbal expression subverts and redirects the social realities of the moment. Saying what one thinks, what everyone may already believe to be the truth of a situation, politically, can be a very powerful means of establishing one's hegemony over others. As John Gumperz pointed out to me, in the Kiriwina case, when one speaks the truth, "one goes on record."

Such a verbal act means taking a decisive step, a step that many individuals are unwilling and afraid to take.

The disguise of situations extends into many commonplace areas of verbal interaction, as in the uses of verbal disguise to collapse kinship distinctions between individuals (see Weiner 1976: 52 — 54). For example, although precise levels of semantic contrast operate between terms such as "clansperson" (*veyola*), "blood kin" (*veyola tatola*), and "nonkin" (*kakaveyola*), and even though these contrasts were recognized by all villagers, the most disaffiliative term, "nonkin" (*kakaveyola*), and the most affiliative term, "blood kin" (*veyola tatola*), are seldom used. The most ambiguous term, *veyola*, is used for people who are kin and nonkin (see Weiner 1976: fig. xx). One uses *veyola* (kin) out of "respect" and "friendship." If, however, a person announces that someone he calls "kin" (*veyola*) is not truly related to him and calls him *kakaveyola* (nonkin), he is using "hard words." By calling into public notice the lack of kinship ties, this truth produces enormous shame for the person who has been called "nonkin" (see Beidelman 1963 for examples of changes in terms of address in Indo-European languages).

Trobrianders who have a close relationship may call each other "sister" or "brother" when in fact they are not blood siblings. To call someone "sister" and to announce the lack of a "true" genealogical link by saying, "But your mother and my mother are not the same," is an extremely shameful statement. The use of "hard words" traditionally would have led the recipient of this statement to attempt suicide. The truth of such statements is not a surprise to anyone, because villagers are aware of the genealogical connections. The public statement of the Negative, saying, "No, you are not my true relative," totally destroys the maintenance of disguise and the stability of the relationship. The ability of "hard words" to change an agreed-upon situation, one in which everyone is knowledgeable about the circumstances, into a situation that produces fighting, suicide, or sorcery, demonstrates the power of the weightiness of words.

Using "hard words," however, may put the aggressor in as much jeopardy as the opponent. In an intervillage court case over land tenure that I observed, Z was asked to testify concerning the information he had about his father's land. But Z continually denied knowing anything about his father's land. He said his father had never told him the story of the land (see Weiner 1976 on land tenure), and if he spoke now, the things he would say would be a "lie" (*sasopa*). Most of the men present knew the "truth." Z was afraid that he and his kin would be killed through sorcery if he told the "truth," because the actual story involved a blood feud, several generations ago, in which control of the land in dispute had been given to a man from another lineage (*dala*) as payment for the murder of his relative. To tell the true story now would still shame the man who was trying to reclaim the land. During the court case, some men shouted out at Z:

Why don't you tell the truth? Are you afraid that they will kill you? We are here and no one will kill you. Just speak. Don't be afraid. Don't hide. We are not going to die and that man will not die. If we hide, the people just feel pain.

But Z had few living kin and was much more frightened of sorcery than of fighting. He never spoke the "truth," preferring to "lie" and to "take care" (*kaymayaba*) of his kin.

A range of words, *sasopa*, *kiwola*, and *sinapu*, were glossed by informants as "lying" or "tricking." These terms are used in serious matters concerning land tenure, stealing, adultery, fighting, love magic, poison (sorcery), and questions of kinship relations. The notion of lying or tricking, however, has little to do with our notion of deceit. The actual truth of the situation is not at issue. What is imperative is the public declaration, the act of going on record, to say the way things are or were. To lie or trick allows an individual the option to stay away from confrontation, to remain safe, and to maintain the autonomy of personal space.

In 1976 a high-ranked chief, A, was confronted with a situation of "hard words" by his potential successor, B, who also had the rank of chief. One of A's sister's sons was told by B that he had planted his taro on B's land and he would have to dig it up. A, however, declared the land under his control and sent a message for B to come to his village. The tension in this situation was enormous, as everyone said that if B appeared either A or B would be killed by the other. B never appeared. He sent a message saying that he was going to sleep, and the situation was defused. B was testing to see what kind of support he would have, and then he backed off by telling a lie.

Vagueness and ambiguity are what verbal disguise in the form of lies is about. Lying and tricking enable one to deny knowledge while most individuals know the knowledge. "Hard words" strip away the ambiguity, pushing the heavy dimensions of truth into the public arena. Taking a stand on "hard words" has such danger associated with it that even powerful men are very cautious in their moments of going on record.

In this way, the weightiness of "hard words" generates the power to penetrate deeply into someone's personal space, but "hard words" reveal one's own mind at the same time. To use "hard words" precludes any attempt to disguise what one is thinking. "Hard words" demand action that for either party is dangerous and possibly even fatal. The displacement of "hard words" through disguise such as lies means that other kinds of actions must be available so that intention and desire can be expressed without "hard words" and without ambiguity.

Objects as the Displacement of "Hard Words"

Situations occur when an individual wants to make his or her desires and strategies public. Objects convey unambiguous kinds of information, revealing some degree of intention. Like Gulliver's description of the sage, objects, in their style and manner of presentation, "speak" a language of negotiation, intention, and appraisal. One's private thoughts may be directly transferred into nonverbal statements that publicly convey meaning about the nature of one's past and future expectations of a particular relationship. A range of tactics concerned with what Erving Goffman (1969) has called "strategic interaction" are accomplished through the presentation of objects in specific kinds of exchange situations.

In contrast to my informants' warnings concerning the expression of anger in verbal discourse, I was told that "anger may always be expressed in yams."[6] To anyone familiar with Trobriand ethnography, this statement has vast implications, for yams are the objects that act on the stability and regeneration of all important kin and affinal relations (see esp. Weiner 1978). How, then, can yams express anger when angry words shatter relationships? Yams express the Negative, and this expression is publicly made at harvest when all yam production is displayed for several months.

The harvest period demonstrates the labor that men have committed to other men. Yam houses are filled, not by an owner's gardening efforts, but by the efforts of men who are connected with the owner through a range of kin and affinal links. Each owner, himself, will be working for other men. Not to work too hard in the garden for someone, thereby producing only a meager crop, or not to work any garden at all for a person, are strong public statements of anger.[7] Informants gave similar reasons for not working hard: "He did not take good care of me"; "He did not kill a pig for me when I filled his yam house last year"; "He tried to poison me." Unlike "hard words," the use of the Negative through objects is desirable. One's thoughts are stated without the dangers of exposure.

Given the intensity of these situations, the contrast with "hard words" seems incongruous. In all kinds of exchange situations, from the small things exchanged between lovers to *kula* transactions, each individual in the exchange relationship maintains a high degree of autonomy. Exchange of objects does not penetrate a person's mind directly. Objects influence, but do not control, another's mind. Even in situations where the producer of yams (or the *kula* partner) is of lower rank, age, or status than the receiver, either partner to the exchange, at any time, may publicly show satisfaction or dissatisfaction with the particular relationship. Objects, as they move between individuals, express a range of emotions from fear to anger to love, while the partners to the exchange retain control over their own thoughts and desires.

The power of objects is generated out of the Maussian notion that things are a part of oneself (see Weiner 1983b). The display of yams, for example, addresses the ability of the gardener, his own present and future political intentions and status as a man of renown. To go on record with objects is intimately tied to the presentation of the self. In this way, these actions resemble the values that lie behind the decoration of the self as described for other New Guinea societies (e.g., Gell 1975; A. and M. Strathern 1971).

Among the Melpa, in ways similar to Trobrianders, secrecy of intent, desire, and strategy is the primary component of social and political interaction. Marilyn Strathern (1979:249; see also Gewertz, this volume, on the Chambri) notes that when large exchanges take place public statements are being made through objects about secret matters such as wealth, the well-being of the clan, and the presence of ancestral ghosts. In daily life what is hidden is the inner self, within the skin, a person's basic capacities. in the process of decorating .... it is his inside which is brought outside.... Disguise is here the mechanism of revelation. The inner self is visible only to the extent that it makes invisible·the outer body.(249)

In the Trobriands, one's physical beauty, health, shining skin, and decorations are statements of one's power, potential, and desires. Beauty and the decoration of young people are attended to by their elders from just this perspective (see Weiner 1976:121 – 36). After one marries, however, one enters the major activities of adult life, which are grounded in exchange. Now the locus of the presentation of power shifts from the body to objects that contain the same statements of inner ability, power, desire, intention, fear, and love. One's physical strength and beauty diminish with age, but the objects one produces and acquires disguise the outer body and make the "inner self visible." Possession of a large *kula* shell must be seen from this perspective. One says notl ˙ng when the shell is given, for the shell itself speaks to the fame, renown, beauty, and ability of its new owner. One's name becomes synonymous with the ability to obtain the shell (see Weiner 1983a on *kula*).

Objects say things in situations that allow an individual's personal space not to be violated when the truth is being stated publicly. Therefore, they have the ability to displace the effects of "hard words." If two individuals who are not related to each other confront each other and "hard words" are spoken and fighting is about to occur, the situation may be resolved through the measurement of yams (*buritilulo*) by each party.[8] Quickly, the relatives of both individuals must prepare their yams. Both sides confront each other with the largest yams they own. Once the confrontation with yams has begun, fighting is averted. An object has mediated "hard words."

Exchange relationships are about production, labor, ritual, and even travel, as well as about the histories of relationships, making the object involved weighty with meanings. These meanings give autonomy to both partners because they address the implications of future loss and past histories. Objects extend the boundaries of personal space, exposing one's thoughts about someone else. Negotiation with objects may, in time, precipitate covert retaliation such as sorcery, but stating the Negative with objects will not elicit the immediacy of aggressive behavior. With objects, unlike "hard words," the danger in exposure for both parties is displaced. Objects represent the societal constraints in the regeneration of social relations. The constraints are the tensions between autonomy and domination. These tensions give to objects the power of displacement.

The Seductive Power of Tropes

A range of circumstances exists in which material transactions alone cannot accomplish the kinds of controls or strategies that one may desire. Trobrianders consider tropes (*biqa viseki*), which include metaphor, metonymy, analogy, simile, and riddles, to be appropriate for another significant mode of disguise (see J.D. Sapir 1977 on a general analysis of tropes; A. Strathern 1975b on Melpa "veiled" speech; Basso 1979 on "wise words"; Evans-Pritchard 1962 on *sanza*). Everyone understands the meaning in the figure of speech, but the words that explicitly state what is meant are not used. William Empson (1964: 341) has discussed an aspect of metaphor that is important to consider.

It seems to me that what we start from, in a metaphor ... is a recognition that "false identity" is being used, a feeling of "resistance" to it, rather like going into higher gear, because the machinery of interpretation must be brought into play, and then a feeling of richness about the possible interpretations of the word, *which has now become a source of advice on how to think about the matter*. (emphasis mine)

Following Empson, we can understand the way feeling is generated through the use of metaphor, and we then can see the way thinking about the matter will entice the listener. In this way, metaphor is not merely a substitution of one word for a similar word. Rather, the use of metaphor widens the range of possible associations that, when taken as Empson's "source of advice on how to think about the matter," becomes the production of meaning in a stronger, more persuasive way than the original word itself.[9] By demanding attention, thought, and evaluation, tropes, if interesting and effective, become weighty and may seductively enter the listener's mind. The ability to invent powerful tropes not only shows cleverness but indicates one's expertise at penetrating personal space as well.

The situation in which Trobriand tropes are used differs from the Zande *sanza* where the person in question should not know the true intent. The range of interpretations, however, gives these words their power because their use is timed specifically so that one can deny their "true" meaning (see note 2). Trobriand tropes also differ from Melpa "veiled" speech where often the audience does not know the meaning, and therefore the speaker gives the explanation (A. Strathern 1975b:190). In the Melpa case, the power of the trope appears to be sustained by the ability of the speaker to create new interpretations for an audience.

In Kiriwina, the disguised truth in the trope is known by everyone, but the sense of the trope becomes important by the implication that disguise is necessary. The two most important situations where tropes are employed involve sex and politics. Tropes are central in these encounters because influence over a potential lover or ally is tenuous at best. It is no accident that verbal encounters during *kula* negotiations are talked about in the same way as seducing a lover is.

A lover's relationship must begin with words, and these words are disguised in tropes. Tropes allow for the desires of one's mind to become public without becoming "hard words." These desires, however, remain dangerous because they occur in situations where kinship ties are not fundamental. Therefore, the possibilities of rejection are more likely.

Figures of speech are used in soliciting the agreement of a potential lover. Questions such as "May I borrow your pillow?" "May I drink some water?" or "May I ride your bicycle?" will be answered with laughter and with a half-joking negative reply. But the message is explicitly acknowledged and must be reinforced with giving things such as betel nut or tobacco. These kinds of objects should not be confused with things such as yams or *kula* shells, which are marked in terms of the social relationships that underwrite the history of their attainment. Betel and tobacco are ingested or inhaled immediately. Unlike *kula* shells or yams, they cannot be recirculated. One must give something else again.[10] I will return to the importance of betel and tobacco in my discussion of magic spells.

In much the same circumstances, political encounters precipitate such fears and dangers. In large intervillage meetings, for example, men

face other men with whom they have no direct kin or affinal relationship. Yet a man may need to influence and persuade these men to join
his side. In a public meeting, one has only verbal dexterity to use as
persuasion, and success is directly related to the weightiness of one's
tropes. An orator to be effective and strong should make his most
meaningful points through figures of speech: metaphor, metonymy,
analogy, simile, or litotes (see also A. Strathern 1975b; Bloch 1975;
Fernandez 1977; Howe 1977; Keenan 1975; Salmond 1975).

For example, a large public meeting, attended by over 200 men, was
held at the site of a cooperative store, which had been closed down.
During the meeting, M was asked to speak. M was a chief, and his
kinsman had been accused of taking funds from the store. M was sitting
on a chair, and when he started to speak he remained seated. "I do
not like to stand up to talk to you people. Something is stuck on my
leg. I have a sore on my leg and I do not like to stand up." Everyone
assembled knew that the sore referred to M's shame about his kin.
When M got up to speak, many men were frightened that he would
use "hard words" because of his shame. In having the courage to take
up the incident publicly, M promoted his own power and ability. He
used a strong trope about a difficult matter, avoiding the confrontation
that "hard words" would have produced.

In 1972 a tense meeting was held with *kula* men from the neighboring
island of Kitava. When Kiriwina men had gone to Kitava several months
before, the Kitava men told them that they had no *kula* shells. The
Kitava men lied because they had already given the shells to men from
Vakuta Island. At this meeting, X spoke for Kiriwina and said, "I have
the lock and you have the key, but you must find the right key to open
the lock." This speech meant that now Kiriwina men would not give
Kitava men any *kula* shells until they received the shells they were
owed. By using this trope, X made explicit "hard" demands using "good
words."

An example that comes closest to illustrating Empson's point involves a meeting where the discussion focused on two alternatives for
local governance. One villager said, "I give you an example. I have two
bowls; one bowl contains coconuts and the other contains chicken.
Which bowl do you want?" Everyone on the opposition side called out
"Chicken!" The speaker then aswered, "Ah, you are all very clever. You

explained everything in your own minds. Now you understand and you think for yourselves, and you accept my example."

At another meeting concerning the local government council, W, as council president, was in jeopardy; his position was being undermined by an opposition movement (see Weiner 1982b). In a dramatic speech he said:

I know two kinds of fibers for binding canoes. One is called *mumulukwausi* and one is *monuyobikwa*. You people are going to vote for which one you like. *Momulukwausi* is my fiber. If it goes bad, I can change it and put on a new one and then retie it. Other people who live near the lagoon have *monuyobikwa*. They tie it for a long time on the canoe and only then can they change it. But for me, I tie my fiber maybe for two weeks and then I change it. Come on, vote, and then we will find out which fiber is stronger.

References to the fiber concern knowledge of magic for the control of weather. The lagoon people (a major part of the opposition) knew magic for the wind, but W knew the most powerful sun and rain magic. He was challenging anyone to surpass his ability to reverse the weather at will. He stated his power to use his magic in the most destructive way, to destroy garden crops. W was issuing a threat made more intense because of his charge to vote (see Weiner 1976:223–26 for ethnographic details). In this speech, W combined the two most dangerous elements in verbal interaction: the allusion to his knowledge of magic and, in calling for a vote, a demand that "hard words" be spoken, which meant a demand to fight.

Voting is a Western introduction that is anathema to the fundamental principles of Trobriand social and political interaction. Although at some point in a meeting, a demand or suggestion for a vote might be made, the actual taking of a vote is averted. Even in the adjudication of land claims, chiefs who judge the cases never make an immediate decision. The moment someone calls for a vote, other men whisper, "If we vote, we will fight." Voting establishes winning and losing sides. To regain autonomy, losers must fight.[11] In the foregoing example, W condensed the most powerful political tactics into words describing strings for lashing canoes, pushing the tense situation to the brink of fighting. Speaking with tropes made exceedingly weighty, he avoided the use of "hard words." At the same time, he issued a warning to everyone present about his ability to use the most powerful magic in the Trobriands. Finally, he asked for a vote, demanding and warning that "hard words" would result, as he, himself, touched at their edge.

In political contexts, the use of figurative speech makes others think about the words spoken and decide, "Is that man talking about true things?" "Should I believe his words?" "Do his words sound good?" The condensation of desire into the disguise offered by tropes is itself an act of acumen; a person must be strong to be able to use words in this way to convince others to believe and follow. Not everyone has such ability, and in political situations many men are afraid to speak.

The Relation between Tropes and Objects

Like objects of exchange, tropes operate at a public level in addressing influence and desire. Like objects, the use of tropes exhibits an extension of one's personal space into the public domain. Tropes provide the disguise that allows for the emergence of desire and intent. Like the display of important objects, dexterity in the use of tropes is available only for the very strong.[12]

Tropes refer to past or present events and demand that attention be given to "how to think about the matter." One person directs others to think about experience from his or her own viewpoint and to assess past experience for future decisions. In this way, tropes are inherently idiosyncratic, even when everyone understands their meaning. The tension created through the use of tropes is situated in the very individuality of the operation, because basically one is saying that "my way is the only way." The film *Trobriand Cricket* (Leach and Kildea 1975) makes this point clear as each team taunts the opposing side in chants created to assert metaphorically each player's sexual power and ability to win in a game where the winner must be the home team (see note 11).

Objects are associated with other characteristics in relation to persuasion. Objects are not idiosyncratic. They necessitate labor tied to the priorities and needs of others. The difficulty in the creation and attainment of objects is in the attention and care that underlie reciprocity. The achievement of a return is not automatic. Economic exchanges say no as well as yes. The presentation of objects, either in acts of exchange or in display, states visually all the Negatives and Positives that went into the attainment of the object. Objects are heavily weighted with the social implications of past relationships and obligations, prior to the statements they make concerning individual desire in the present.

In the final analysis, objects outweigh the use of tropes and "hard words" in social interaction. Their weightiness includes more than physical qualities. Objects are produced by the singularity of individual creation, but their value is created and sustained through the societal implications of history and the contexts in which social relations are regenerated (see Weiner 1982a, 1983b on objects and their relation to history). The limitation inherent in the use of objects as the mode of social interaction is not their heaviness, from Gulliver's perspective, but rather their scarcity, their state of being rare things that represent the history of ownership and control.

In the society where "hard words" lead to disaster, where objects are about obligations that stretch through generations, and where the use of tropes gives no absolute certainty of success, social interactions, at best, are fraught with tensions and unrequitable desires. Only the use of magic is believed to have the power to enable a person to extend her or his will over others and to be protected from the desires of others. An understanding of the force of magic demonstrates that the kinds of power found in the use of "hard words," tropes, and objects are similar to those that give force and credence to the practice of magic.

The Force of Magic

Magic is thought to have the power to interfere with the will of others at the most direct level possible. Villagers' perceptions of each other are guided by the fears triggered through their beliefs in the constant suspicions and practices of magic.[13] The potential consequences of magic rooted in the framework of social encounters not only accentuate the danger in social interaction but, simultaneously, strengthen the need to protect one's personal space from the willfulness of others. Although the constant concern with magic produces wariness and fear of what others may do, it also produces a strength in one's own mind that one can defy the intentions of others. Thus, the perceived autonomy of personal space is heightened.

The privacy of one's thoughts and the power attributed to the exposure of one's thoughts, as in the use of "hard words," contribute to the perceived efficacy of magic. If words of "truth" disrupt and destroy, then the words of magic based on the "truth" of ancestors also have the ability to disrupt and destroy. If one's thoughts must be guarded carefully, lest they emerge and destroy, then thought is always potentially powerful and can be used in contexts that no one can control. The processes through which magic action is thought to occur are the heightened, focused counterpart of the processes involved in the most important situations of social interaction.

Success in magic provides each person with an autonomous connection with sources of potential help located in a dimension of time and space free from the dangers that exist in the domain of social interaction. By no means, however, am I imposing the traditional analytical distinction between magic as private and religion as public (see also Beidelman 1974; Douglas 1966; Evans-Pritchard 1967; J. Goody 1977). One's own thoughts and words are powerful resources that enable a person to displace all forms of social interaction while using the techniques of such interaction.[14]

Trobriand magic has been the subject of extensive debate since Malinowski's original work. Malinowski (see esp. 1935) emphasized that the words of spells are the most significant part of Trobriand magic (see Evans-Pritchard 1967 on verbal differences between Trobriand magic and Zande magic; see also Tambiah 1968, 1973). Malinowski also noted that, in the full performance of magic, the words usually are impregnated into an object that itself operates as a "medium" by transferring the words to the final object. As Nadel pointed out, "Yet whence this power ascribed to gestures and media' or, for that matter, to the words themselves?" (1957:197).

S. J. Tambiah (1968) reanalyzed the magic spells originally published by Malinowski. Tambiah noted the importance of metaphor and especially the significance of metonymy in the spells (as was also demonstrated by Munn n.d.) as the means by which "Objects and substances are used as agents and vehicles of transfer through contagious action." Further, Tambiah argued that use of metonymy "has several implications for lending realism to the rite, for transmitting a message through redundancy, for storing vital technological knowledge in an oral culture, and for the construction of the spell itself as a lengthy verbal form" (1968:190). From the totality of Trobriand language, however, the power of spells is grounded in more than realism, redundancy, and the storage of knowledge.

In the chanting of spells, words and the objects that absorb them must become powerful enough to activate a range of agents (Malinowski's medium) in the physical environment; e.g., birds, animals, plants, insects, and even the deceased former owners of the spells (ancestors), all of whom exist outside the daily life of social interaction.[15] For example, the whiteness of the cockatoo must be transmitted to a person's skin, or the guinea hen's knowledge of molding dirt underground must be transferred to a yam. The transmission in the former case enables a person to become beautiful. In the latter case, a yam gains knowledge of how to continue to grow underground when a stone blocks its path by moving dirt aside as a guinea hen does when it builds its nest. In spells, it is the stoniness of a stone, the whiteness of birds' feathers, the crunching sound of dry leaves that must be transferred from wildlife or ancestral referents through an agent to a patient, such as a person, a yam, a canoe, or the sun. Then the patient, i.e., the person, yam, canoe, weather, now having gained the desired attributes, such as beauty, size, speed, or dryness that will elicit desire or fear in other individuals, may accomplish the goals of the individual who solicited or performed the persuasive actions of magic.

The transference of attributes, selected for their precise physical characteristics, is believed to be accomplished through the recitation of the spell and the impregnation of the words into objects, such as leaves, coral, stones, betel, and even tobacco. These objects actually are as important as the spell because, without the appropriate object, the action of the spell would be ineffective. Words must be spoken into a material form that will transfer knowledge from one domain to another. Appropriate objects and words are perceived to be necessary to mobilize the specificity of thoughts into actual events. One's desires and intentions are enacted through a route that draws on the powers of tropes and "hard words" and applies these powers to objects that become agents.

In the production of magic the use of figurative speech found in tropes is intensified and exaggerated. Just as tropes in everyday discourse gain power through the disguise of direct desire for "advice on how to think about the matter," in the use of metaphor and metonymy in spells, the listener is seduced with interesting thoughts. In magic a person must persuade the agents outside the social domain to transmit these interesting ideas to a patient. The intensification of form and the specialization in figurative speech are the necessary beginnings of the long and demanding process through which a chain of information and control is passed on. The semantic specialization of spells and the forms in which they are used are testimony to the difficult task that one faces.

The verbal action of magic is so demanding that greater force is required than in the use of public tropes. Repetition, shifts in rhythm, specialized vocabulary, and changes in pronunciation (the very things Malinowski identified as the irrational aspects of magical language) are believed to be necessary to achieve successful results. Changes in pronunciation are employed to make the words "sound good," so that they will be attractive to think about for patients and agents. Specialized vocabulary contains archaic words believed to have been used by ancestors. These words give historical validation to the spell. Genealogies of those ancestors who formerly owned the spell are recited at the beginnings of the spell. Not only does the genealogy call on the assistance of the former owners, but it gives weight to the spell by demonstrating the successful history that the spell has had in effecting persuasion.[16]

Repetition of the spell, accompanied by changes in rhythm, is believed to be the effective force in causing the words to enter the appropriate object. Through the object the agents addressed in the spell are activated into conveying the necessary information to the patient of the spell, i.e., the lover, the canoe, the rain. This technique is especially important in assuring success for the most difficult and most valued magical action, such as sorcery, love, changes in weather, success in *kula*, or yam growing. In order for Z to control the rain, he must stay awake all night, chanting the spell over and over into a piece of black coral. The repetition acts as verbal persuasion. Such skill and stamina become the measure of one's strength and power to control. Within this physical and verbal tour de force, the power generated by the spell increases until finally the desired information has been absorbed by the agent and the patient.

While these physical actions and mental abilities are effecting persuasion, one's personal space takes on unprecedented energy and autonomy. Everything is possible in the moment of recitation, where such power generates the strongest sense that one's desires can be secured. The production of magic begins within the domain of a person's mind, but one's thoughts must be exposed in words and transferred to objects. With magic, the fear of exposure is inconsequential.

The language of magic is elevated to a poetic form (see Friedrich 1978). In the chanting of the spells, the autonomy of personal space is one's imagination. Through verbal intensification, one's relationship to the domain of the social becomes totally ego-centered. Unlike the imaginative construction of tropes in social and political discourse, however, the words of spells are historical records of past successes and achievements, through past owners. The use of tropes in magical language is formalized into a poetics that cannot be altered. The imaginative power of the spells occurs during recitation in a process similar to Shklovsky's definition of art as "defamiliarization": "a making strange [*ostranenie*] of objects, a renewal of perception" (Jameson 1972:51). The recitation of spells cannot be thought of as mere rote, for the words and the actions of saying the words elicit "a sudden awareness of the very textures and surfaces of the world and of language" (Jameson 1972:50; see also Empson 1964). Such poetic language in magic attracts attention to itself and to the physical and mental powers of the owner of the spell, thereby resulting in a renewed perception of a world that, even momentarily, one may create and control.

Even within this moment of perceived autonomy, however, one's verbal abilities, thoughts, and knowledge still cannot totally effect one's desires. The mediation of the agent, the object that carries the verbal messages to the patient, is necessary. Given the semantic complexity in both the composition of the spells and their recitation, it is the object, rather than the spell, that is the active carrier of intention and desire. Even with magic, the object is weightier than words.

The most telling example that sets into sharp relief the relation between object and word and the conflict between domination and autonomy is found in magic spells where the "poetics" of figurative speech include "hard words." In situations where the desire to destroy the autonomy of someone else is paramount, such as the most powerful kinds of love magic, "hard words" directly call upon the body and the mind of the other person to move and think in totally controlled ways. For example, in the most powerful spell for love magic, the "hard words" explicitly describe all the detailed physical actions of sexual intercourse. In another spell, "hard words" define the person's state of mind in that she or he will not listen to the advice of others, will refuse to eat any food, will long only to see and sleep with her or his lover. These spells are said to "spoil one's mind," causing the person to come under someone else's control, destroying his or her autonomy. The "hard words" must be spoken into a betel nut or tobacco, which must be chewed or smoked by the patient in order for the spell to work. Similarly, the spells for sorcery, spoken into betel or tobacco, contain "hard words" that explicitly describe the destruction of the body. Thus, through magic a person is thought to be able to destroy another's autonomy without the risk of exposure. In order to achieve this ultimate domination, one must, quite literally, enter the body and violate the autonomous space of the victim. But the entrance is achieved through the object that is the container and carrier of the message. Without the object, words alone have no effect.

Conversely, in everyday interaction, "hard words" alone are perceived to have the power to destroy the realities under which individuals tend to go about their lives by exposing another reality — the "truth." Similarly, "hard words" in magic spells expose the reality in the perceived "truth" of one person's desire for complete domination over another person. In both cases, one dramatically effects one's will over others. In the former circumstances, the danger in the exposure of "truth" is that the speech act is executed directly, leading to rejection, fighting, and even death, with the initiator as vulnerable to the same results as the subject. In the latter case, the person's desires are not executed in face-to-face interaction. Everyone may know what has happened when suddenly two individuals are in love, and many villagers assume that they know the identity of the person who caused the love or a death to occur. In usual circumstances, no one makes these claims public.[17]

As "hard words" in magic spells demand control over others, "hard words" also contain limitations in terms of their actual accomplishments. To be effective, "hard words" must be embedded in an object that enters the body of the victim. Only this object has the power to produce the desired state. Yet this critical stage in the production of magic allows for the reversal of all that went before, as the object may be rejected by the very person for whom it is intended.[18] Therein lies the dilemma of maintaining autonomy while achieving domination. The object must transfer the word, and in that capacity, the object exposes one's thoughts. The process of exposure protects one's personal space, but only at the cost of giving protection to the very person one wants to control.

Conclusion

The force of magic stretches the boundaries of one's own mind as it penetrates and may diminish or destroy the boundaries of someone else's mind. The potential control and danger manifested in the use of "hard words" in everyday discourse is displaced into the action of magic, where success is demonstrated publicly in the visibility of successful action, rather than in public statements of demands. Belief in the force and the perceived efficacy of magic is rooted in the perception that speech acts have power to disrupt and destroy, or to persuade, influence, and convince others in social interaction. To play out even the seemingly mundane, everyday situations of social interaction necessitates constant awareness and protection of one's own thoughts and desires. To take these thoughts and desires and give them a spatial field in which they can be transformed into actions describes the basic processes that occur in the use of magic. Personal intention is turned away from the confines of social morality, and at the same time intention is allowed to escape from the confines of one's own mind.

Words, both tropes and "hard words," are the formal elements that create the potential power to enable speech to shift or recreate perceived realities. In magical action, the words must enter a physical property in order to generate the necessary chain of events between agent and patient. As agent, the object absorbs the words and becomes the material extension of all the power brought to bear in the supreme ego-centered moments of the repetitious chanting of the spell. Once, however, thoughts held within one's personal space are given expression in a material form, intention is given its own disguise. It is a disguise more powerful than tropes and far safer than "hard words," but the creation of such individual autonomous safety and power is weakened by the very fact that it must be transferred into a material object. At this most autonomous moment, a person becomes dependent on a object to provide the result. To accept and not repay is the underlying dilemma in all exchange events. To accept a betel nut impregnated with a magic spell and not chew it underscores the same limitation in persuasiveness and domination.

Because objects, either in magic or in exchange, express ranges of emotions such as anger, fear, love, and distrust, they are given and returned with the same intent: to influence, seduce, convince, or destroy. Therefore, objects, whether they are necessary for the production of magic or for cycles of exchange, must be understood within the contexts of their own visual discourse. Objects become more than their physical weight either through the tropes and "hard words" they absorb in the performance of magic or through the histories of social relations as they move through time and space in exchange. This culturally imposed weightiness makes objects rare things that have the ability to displace tensions between autonomy and domination.

The processes of social interaction involve an awareness of the boundaries between a person's own personal space and the personal space of all others. How permeable these boundaries may be depends upon a person's ability to express desire and intention without exposure that is dangerous. The impact of danger occurs in the moment when domination, expressed by saying "hard words," destroys the boundaries and exposes the truth of autonomous intention. In the Trobriands, domination, in some degree, exists as part of all relationships, but the extent of domination remains muted through the mediation of exchange that allows intention and desire on both sides to be expressed without violation of personal space. A person's labor needs to be attended to carefully by those who are or hope to be the recipients of the productive results. The strategies in exchange relations apply not only to one time or one year; they stretch out through decades and connect generations to each other. In this way, the future and its possibilities, which must be constantly negotiated, serve as an ever present template for the presence of some degree of autonomy in all social relations. Objects, the result of labor and production, have the power to displace the dangers in exposure, not only because they are made weighty by history, but because they represent the weight of the future.

Moving from thoughts to words, or to objects, or to magic demands an extension of personal space that takes on an external form. Each transition is an attempt to rearrange or recreate one's own lived experiences. Equally, each transition necessitates a disguise that will allow the expression of thought while at the same time providing a measure of safety. Only "hard words," spoken directly to another person as "truth," confront and confound experience. The tension between autonomy and domination and between desire and demand can never be resolved without entering into a dangerous confrontation where disguise has been thrown off and security and retreat are no longer possible.

There are certain circumstances, however, when these situations still remain hierarchical. The aggressor is not in jeopardy and has only added the danger of the moment to his own powerful position of autonomy. A high-ranked chief may use "hard words" and announce without using tropes that he performed the actions necessary to cause someone's death. These acts are not employed indiscriminately; the tension and danger are formidable. Truth is exposed, but the truth is about more than the individual. The drama unambiguously testifies to the societal nature of all relationships. There are those who do dominate. Their domination does not release them from the fear of others, and it is this fear that makes these moments rare. The fear of exposure is surmounted, however, by the stronger need to claim full transcendence. In these moments, the true dilemma between domination and autonomy is exposed and resolved.

Notes

An earlier version of this chapter was presented as a paper at the symposium, "Communication in Ritual and Everyday Life: The interpretation of Ways of Speaking," American Anthropological Association, 78th Annual Meeting, Cincinnati, 1979.

Grateful acknowledgment is made to the Royal Anthropological Institute of Great Britain and Ireland for permission to reprint this chapter (expanded in this volume), which appeared in *Man* 18 (1983).

Research on which this paper is based was done in Kiriwina, Trobriand Islands, Papua New Guinea, periodically over the past eleven years. I am grateful to the following institutions for their support: National Institute of Mental Health, National Endowment for the Humanities, American Council for Learned Societies, University of Texas Research Institute, John Simon Guggenheim Foundation, and Wenner-Gren Foundation for Anthropological Research. I sincerely thank the National Government of Papua New Guinea, the Milne Bay Provincial Government, and the Institute for Papua New Guinea Studies for their assistance in facilitating my research plans. Above all, I am indebted to the many Trobrianders who educated me and who tried to teach me to behave appropriately.

1. Interest in the relationship between words and things has not been totally ignored, although the main thrust has been with the use of language to make reference to things. See, for example, the work of Brown 1958; Quine 1960.

2. The expertise in using *sanza* demands that the speaker says something nasty to someone "in the presence of others without his [the person] seeing the point of what is said while the others see it and go home and joke about it." If a man says something about his "stupid dog," he will be talking about his "stupid wife." If his wife understood his remarks, "her husband would feign innocence, saying that he was speaking only of his dog. ... He is careful, when making the remark, to look towards his dog" (Evans-Pritchard 1962:222).

3. The "truth" may be discussed in very private conversations that occur with close kin or special friends and take place inside one's house, usually at night, or in the bush, or at the beach. But, even in these instances, there is always danger associated with telling someone about serious, secret matters, for the person may tell others at some later time.

4. I had this encounter in 1972, and I remained close friends with the person over the past eleven years. He has never mentioned this incident to me. During my last visit to the Trobriands in 1982, someone who was present when the incident occurred reminded me about it during a private conversation. Thus, it still has not been forgotten.

5. All Trobriand deaths are believed to be caused by others through the use of traditional magic or chemical poisons, except for those individuals who live to be very old and who die without any prolonged illness. "Their time was up" is the way these latter deaths are perceived.

6. Andrew Strathern (1975a) presents an account of Melpa feelings concerning shame and anger that overlaps in certain respects with Kiriwina ideas. He reports an informant's statement concerning *popokl* (anger and frustration): "When we are *popokl* about something we hide it, we keep it to ourselves and don't tell people. We preserve a good

exterior" (105). But in Mount Hagen, *popokl* eventually becomes public, revealing itself through time by causing sickness: "Either the person harmed falls sick in protest against the wrongdoing, or the wrongdoer himself falls sick as a result of the wronged person's anger" (106 – 7). Shame, however, is always "on the skin," and everyone is immediately aware of the public disgrace. In the Trobriands, shame is expressed by the person hiding away, either living in the bush or at the beach. Traditionally, shame, in certain cases, would have led to suicide.

7. Even chiefs may not receive yams from others during a harvest. The meaning is quite clear to everyone that one person or many are expressing their disapproval about something.

8. Malinowski gives a detailed description of this event (1935:181 – 87, 473). My information differs in a few essential areas. (1) Malinowski writes of "community A" against "community B," but the opposition is always between the members of one *dala* (lineage) against those of another *dala*. (2) The yams are never perceived as "gifts." They are the statement of one *dala's* ability and power over another. (3) Warfare does not follow (Malinowski [see 1935:473] was uncertain about this), but everyone believes that the losing side will at some future time attempt to poison the members of the winning side so that finally the *dala* will be finished. A *buritilaulo* produces more fear and anxiety than any other public event I witnessed. See also Michael Young's (1971) description and analysis of the use of yams as the expression of anger and hostile relations on Goodenough Island, Papua New Guinea.

9. See Paul Ricoeur's important essay that addresses these issues from "the boundary between a *semantic* theory of metaphor and a *psychological* theory of imagination and feeling" (1978:141). Although I do not explore Ricoeur's attention to the psychological dimension of metaphor here, I believe that his approach holds out much that would be relevant to the analysis I present.

10. T. O. Beidelman pointed out to me that gifts of seduction in all societies have an element of the ephemeral. If we discount money and jewelry as addressing more than seduction, then we note that, in polite society, gifts such as perfume, alcohol, food, and flowers are perceived as appropriate.

11. During cricket matches, a winning side is never publicly announced. Rather, the host team should always win, but the visiting team, among themselves and their friends, will always say they "truly" won. This is well demonstrated in the film *Trobriand Cricket* (Leach and Kildea 1975).

12. For a range of essays on the subject of metaphor see Bauman and Sherzer 1974; Becker and Yengoyan 1979; Gumperz and Hymes 1972; Sacks 1978; Sapir and Crocker 1977.

13. Although there are specialists in terms of knowledge for certain kinds of spells, especially the most important and feared spells, Malinowski's (see esp. 1925) notion of the Trobriand "magician" tends to ignore the viability in the circulation and ownership of spells and the fact that individuals during their lives obtain access to some kinds of spells. Even if a person does not own knowledge of a spell, she or he may pay for the practices of someone who does.

14. Ideas concerning these processes are not unique to the Trobriands. Levy (1973) presents similar examples from Tahiti. His informants said, "Magical thinking 'blurs fantasy and reality,' 'makes thought and wish omnipotent,' is 'free of the constraints of space and time,' is 'egocentric,'" (256). Further, a basic precept of magical thinking is that "words affect social processes and are therefore assumed to affect natural processes"

(257). In a totally different context, Becker (1979) describes the use of ancient languages in Javanese shadow theater, when the Javanese ancestors are addressed at the beginning of each scene. "Like Vedic hymns, they invoke the character in his own language by a kind of word magic, in which to state a thing properly and effectively, even without intent ... is to effect power in the world, bridging time and space" (232).

15. Among the Melpa (A. and M. Strathern 1968), magic texts refer to creatures and plants classified as "wild" as opposed to domestic, and as in Kiriwina, these creatures and plants are called upon to transfer certain qualities they possess to the desired patient.

16. See Weiner (1976:70–72) on the performance of magic spells immediately following a person's death and burial, when the name of the deceased is added to the beginning part of the spell, thereby continuing the genealogy of ownership. Because spells are inherited through individual instruction, entire spells or parts of a spell may be lost because the owner did not transmit it. Spells are often obtained, however, from individuals who live in other parts of Papua New Guinea.

17. An exception that proves the rule is the situation when an important chief has caused the death of someone and decides to announce publicly that he is the one responsible. While everyone else is in mourning attire, he will walk through the village of the deceased dressed in his most elaborate clothes.

18. A Kiriwina chief told me that Kiriwina sorcery (bwaqau) was much better than the practices in Dobu. In Kiriwina, a bwaqau must perform the spell on three different occasions, and therefore, the person must be induced to chew or smoke three times. (This is usually accomplished through an intermediary.) Only the third time is believed to be fatal. If someone applied counterspells at the first or second sign of sickness, the person could be saved. But in Dobu, he said, "People are really bad, one chance and you are finished. In Kiriwina we are better, because we give three chances."

7. Of Symbolic Anchors and Sago Soup: The Rhetoric of Exchange among the Chambri of Papua New Guinea

Deborah Gewertz
Amherst College

Ever since Marcel Mauss's seminal *Essai Sur le Don*, it has been possible to regard prestations as objects that encompass specific meanings and intentions. Generalizing from Maori ethnography, Mauss postulated the existence of a "spirit of the gift," identifying it as a "force....in the thing given which compels a recipient to make a return" (1967: 1). Subsequent ethnography has made us aware, however, that the meanings and intentions contained in objects of exchange are far more varied than the homogeneous reciprocal compulsion that Mauss suggested.

There seem to be at least three variables that must be taken into account in order to adequately interpret any exchange. The first is the identity of the exchange item itself. Cultural objects contain a symbolic dimension that is meaningful to both giver and receiver. Among the Mae Enga, for example, pigs are "the hearts" of patriclans. Hence, the giving of a pig conveys a meaning quite different from that conveyed by a gift of sweet potatoes, which are in no way repositories of patrilineal substance (see Meggitt 1974). The second variable is the identity of the giver and receiver. Salt among the Baruya, for example, changes from a gift into a commodity, depending upon whether the recipient is a member of the donor's group (see Godelier 1977: 127 – 51). Finally, the meaning of a gift may vary according to the context in which it is given. Among the Chambri, a gift of food from wife-giver to wife-taker compels the return of ceremonial valuables. Under different circumstances, however, the same two individuals may exchange as members of initiation moieties, in which case the gift of food from one requires the return of the identical commodity from the other.

Depending upon the arrangement of each of the three variables, different messages are conveyed from donor to recipient, from recipient to donor, and from both to others taking part in the exchange. Participants may consciously manipulate the variables in order to make statements relevant to political contingencies. Thus, a language of exchange is created whose semantic complexity is exponentially related to the particular exchange situation.

Like any organized symbol system, the language of exchange can be used either with eloquence or with ineptitude, according to how well the "speakers" observe culturally accepted rules of persuasion. These rules constitute a rhetoric of exchange, with which the ethnographer must be familiar in order to understand any exchange situation.

I do not mean to suggest that gaining familiarity with these rules is a simple matter. The polysemic or multivocal nature of cultural signs, including items of exchange, necessitates that the messages conveyed through them be somewhat ambiguous (V. Turner 1967: 48 – 48). Thus, in order to understand these messages we must interpret them, a task that is hard enough for those engaged directly in the discourse. For the socially disengaged and culturally maladept ethnograper the task is even more problematic. Misunderstanding is rarely life threatening, while Western cultural categories continually distort meaning. One can have little assurance that she or he has internalized the native point of view but, at very best, can provide a translation that is internally consistent while it incorporates whatever data has been gathered (Geertz 1974, 1977).

In this chapter I provide such a translation, focusing on a confrontation between members of the Chambri tribe of the East Sepik Province of Papua New Guinea and representatives of the Mensuat, their neighbors and former barter partners. This confrontation was temporarily resolved by an exchange. My aim is to explicate the language used in resolving the incident, considering the implications of the changing political context in which it took place. My method is to move between native understandings of the event, its broader political context, and my own observations and explanations of both in order to achieve a higher-level interpretation that communicates them all.

Background

The 1,300 Chambri live in the East Sepik Province of Papua New Guinea, on an island-mountain some 500 feet in height. The mountain rises from the middle of Chambri Lake, a large shallow floodplain south of the Sepik River. Their three villages, Indingai, Kilimbit, and Wombun, are located along the shore of their island. Each village contains between nine and thirteen patriclans. The Chambri consider all patriclans to be essentially equal, distinguished only by the ownership of distinct ancestral names. Each clan owns hundreds of names that refer to the ancestors who once held them; to the ancestral spirits and the magical powers invoked by their recitation; and to the natural objects, territories, and resources owned and lived in by ancestral spirits. The headman of the clan, Mangemeri, for example, owns the name *yangor*, which means "white water." His ownership of this name gives him the power to bring this "white water" back into Chambri Lake after every dry season. Although patriclan members claim common descent, it is the inheritance of totemic names, not the transmission of blood, that links them together.

The patriclans are also landowning groups, but the Chambri do not value cultivable land, as do the people of the Highlands of New Guinea, for they are not horticulturalists. They subsist primarily upon fish, which Chambri women net and trap in Chambri Lake, and sago, a carbohydrate prepared by women of the Sepik Hills from the pith of the sago palm, *Metroxylum rumphii*. Traditionally, Chambri women took their fish to barter markets in the Sepik Hills where they traded for chunks of sago, each about six inches in diameter. One fresh or smoked fish was traded for one chunk of sago, for supply and demand did not affect the relationship between fish suppliers and sago producers. In fact, the Chambri associated barter markets with weddings, where "male" fish were married to "female" sago, and the barter relationship was extremely stable until the mid-1960s when the sago suppliers resettled on the shores of Chambri Lake and began charging money for their produce (see Gewertz 1977). Now Chambri women sell their fish to migrant laborers in the towns of Pagwi, Maprik, and Wewak, and they purchase sago either at a modern money market at Indingai village or at a sago store operated by the Mensuat people on Peliagwi Island.

The transformation of the barter system was not the only change experienced by the Chambri during the 1960s. They also became members of an Australian-imposed political division, the Gaui Local Government Council. Now, together with representatives of the Sepik River Iatmul, and of the natives from the Sepik Hills and from the Burui-Kunai, Chambri Council representatives allocated tax and other revenues to local projects such as road improvement, health-post maintenance, water tank construction, and so on. An Indingai has held the prestigious and powerful position of council president ever since Gaui's inception, and he relies upon political support from Sepik Hills natives, particularly from the Mensuat and the Changriman, in order to maintain his control. The Chambri did not traditionally rely upon Sepik Hills natives for political support. They formerly regarded their sago suppliers as little better than women — weak, dirty, and inherently unequal. It was the president of Gaui who encouraged the sago suppliers to move from their hamlets in the Hills to the shores of Chambri Lake, for he required a constituency within the council. It is nonetheless with ambivalence and trepidation that he and the Chambri accept those they called "children of dogs" as political equals and crucial council allies.

The Depth of Truth

On July 18, 1974,[1] Baga, a Mensuat from Peliagwi Island, arrived at Chambri to explain why members of his clan killed a crocodile belonging to the clan led by Mabkan, the second-wealthiest man of Kilimbit Village.[2] Mabkan told me that, to appease his anger over the dead crocodile, he intended to serve Baga a bowl of soup. I was confused by what I took to be his gesture toward conciliation, for I assumed that Mabkan was the injured party. His crocodile had been killed by Baga's kin. Mabkan assured me that Baga would learn to respect Chambri power by eating the soup, but I remained puzzled. Indeed, I became completely bewildered when, shortly after Baga's arrival, Mabkan and other Chambri from Indingai and Kilimbit decided to postpone serving the soup and unite in a curious enterprise whose relation to the crocodile I was to fully understand only after analyzing my data upon returning from the field.

Near the largest men's house of Indingai Village there stands a conical hole filled with muddy water, about twenty feet in diameter and fifteen feet deep. This hole is where the Chambri believe their apical ancestor, Emosue Apanke, together with his Iatmul comrade, Kwolimbank, anchored Chambri Island to the spot on which it now stands. The island, it seems used to float throughout Chambri Lake until the pig-man, Emosue, and the dog-man, Kwolimbank, anchored it with a stone slab and a piece of palm, respectively. Moreover, the Chambri argue, "if you think we're lying, we can remove the water from the hole and show you the stone and the palm." And this is what they did for Baga's benefit.

I was permitted to see the two anchors only after they had been decorated with colorful and aromatic leaves, and perhaps artfully disposed in other ways, as well. Emosue's anchor was a small, flat, triangular slab of stone, while Kwolimbank's was a rectangular piece of palm bark; each was about two feet in height. They were positioned at the bottom of the hole, which was slowly refilling from three small underground springs that the Chambri believe carry the white man's water from the east, Iatmul water from the north, and Sepik Hills water from the south, to mingle with Chambri water in the hole. The palm bark was closer to the center of the hole than was the slab of stone, a fact that seemed to upset my Chambri informants, and that I heard Mabkan reiterate to Baga four different times with great passion. He told Baga that at the last water-removing ceremony — which occurred, as far as I can tell, about five years before[3] the stone and the palm stood side by side, and that the time before, the stone was closer to the center than the palm. Baga nodded his recognition of the change and entered the men's house with Mabkan for the second half of the day's events, the serving of the soup.

All the "beds," raised platforms that flank the long sides of the men's house, were filled with Indingai, Kilimbit, and Mensuat men. Mabkan began to speak. He is the tallest man in the three Chambri villages, about six feet tall, and his voice is resonant and trumpeting.[4]

"Although it is true," he said, "that I am the father of the dead crocodile, I do not wish to speak of it now, but wish to talk about the soup which is now cooking in the ancestral saucepan of Woliwopan."

All the men nodded in agreement with Mabkan's largesse, and my neighbor leaned over to tell me that Mabkan is truly a big-man.

Mabkan continued, "I also wish to say a few words about the market at Indingai. It is supposed to help women who have no husbands. But people buy from everyone, and this is not right. You people from Mensuat should help widowed women and pass by women with husbands."

Baga stood up, walked to the center of the men's house, and replied, "I thank you for your good words, but I do not think Mensuat will sell their sago at Indingai anymore, for we have no friends among the Chambri."

The men's house hummed with whispered comments until Sapi, an old and respected Indingai, shouted at Baga, "What, aren't I enough?"

Baga replied, "No, truly you are not enough. In the past, when my grandfather knew your grandfather, Mensuat women did not paddle their canoes to Indingai. No, they truly did not, for Chambri women come to our market. Now, we need more, and you are truly not enough!"

"Enough of this talk," a young man from Indingai stood up and shouted. "This is rubbish talk. Sago is something to buy and sell. If you Mensuat want money, you will send your wives to Indingai. If you care nothing for money, well, never mind, then. You old men are talking about rubbish."

At this point, a very old man from Kilimbit began to relate early Chambri history, beginning with Emosue's ascent from a hole atop Chambri Mountain, but he was interrupted by Mabkan, who announced that the soup was ready. It was a pink, gelatinous liquid, made of sago flour, coconut meat, and coconut milk, and it hung in strands from the stirring spoon like melted mozzarella cheese. Mabkan dished out the soup into aluminum bowls that had been collected from various women's houses, and his clan comembers distributed the full bowls to the seated men.

While the bowls of soup were being distributed, Baga announced that he was going home to Peliagwi. He promised to return to Chambri on the following Sunday to complete the crocodile negotiations but did not want to partake of the soup, for, he said, "my stomach is sick and I do not wish to eat." Mabkan acted the perfect host and wished Baga a safe journey, saying, "the soup is nothing anyway, so never mind."

After Baga left the men's house, several Chambri stood up to tell about their totemic ownership of the soup's ingredients, but they were interrupted by others who, in falsetto voices, began to describe, and then mimic, the sexual act. Their mimicry became increasingly licentious, until it subsumed the talk about the ownership of totems.

It was at this point that I was given a large bowl of soup. I ate it very slowly, for my taste for sago was not well developed. Men kept walking by me to see how much of the soup I had eaten and to tell me to hurry up, for I was getting old, and the soup was going to give me many children, "maybe ten, or five," they said.

Shortly after I finished my soup, the men began to disperse. They were disappointed because, as Mabkan explained, "Baga saw Emosue and Kwolimbank, [the anchors in the dredged hole,] but still would not eat the soup."

Clearly, Mabkan and his fellow Chambri had been trying to convince Baga of something by showing him the anchors and offering him the soup. Before describing their arguments and explain the rhetoric of both ceremonies, I must relate more background. In particular, I must introduce the Kandingai Nyaula, descendants of Kwolimbank, the dog-man.

Failed Communions: The Nyaula Intrusion and Mensuat in the Middle

Nyaula is a dialect and political division of the Iatmul people of the Middle Sepik. There are seven Nyaula villages on the Sepik River. Their members distinguish themselves from the Parambei Iatmul, who live in another seven villages, downriver, to the east.

Traditionally, the Nyaula were Chambri allies, while the Parambei were their enemies.[5] In fact, the Chambri used to call Kandingai "the fourth Chambri village," because its inhabitants trace their descent from "our ancestor's comrade, Kwolimbank." More recently, however, relations between Nyaula and Chambri have soured as a result of Nyaula incursions into Chambri territory.

When the Kandingai were deprived of sago after a war with the Yentchamangua, around 1943, a Chambri leader invited his friends and allies to seek temporary shelter on Timbunmeri Island in Chambri Lake. The Chambri assumed, it seems, that the Kandingai would return to their natal village after their hostilities with Yentchamangua had been forgotten. Many Kandingai, however, decided to stay on Timbunmeri, and now claim ownership. They argue that they bought the island from its original owners, the Garamambu, Changriman, and Mali peoples of the Sepik Hills.[6]

Moreover, other Nyaula, initially from the Sepik River village of Japandai, have recently settled on Arinjone and Luk Luk, two small islands also in Chambri Lake. The Chambri bitterly resent what they consider far more of an intrusion than the coming of the Europeans but they have been unsuccessful in their attempts to evict the Nyaula from their new homes legally.

Thus, the Chambri think of the Nyaula as dangerous intruders, and as I was told by Mabkan and other Chambri after Baga's departure, they wished to convince Baga and his fellow Mensuat of this fact by removing the water from the conical hole.

Their argument took the form of an enthymeme (Aristotle 1954: 26 – 30), whose items were:

(1) The anchor that is located at the center of the hole represents the people who will dominate Chambri Lake.
(2) The Nyaula anchor has moved closer to the center of the hole than the Chambri anchor.
(3) The Nyaula are closer than the Chambri to dominating Chambri Lake.

Clearly, this argument is logically valid, regardless of what we think of its premise. However, it also seems a red herring; it dodges the main issue of whether the Mensuat owe continued allegiance to the Chambri. The Mensuat's behavior resulted, Mabkan told me, from their recognition of their significant position as constituents within the Gaui Local Government Council. Were they, in fact, beginning to recognize that the Chambri were dependent upon them? Clearly, Baga's threatened withdrawal from the Indingai market reflected this new sense of autonomy, for both the barter and the sale of sago had always been as much of a political as an economic relationship.

The Sepik Hills peoples had never been economically dependent upon the Chambri for fish or for any other commodity. They lived in small, semimigratory bands and always had sufficient access to the rich fish resources of Chambri Lake. They were, however, vulnerable to Chambri attack and lived in hard-to-reach mountain hamlets for defense. They also protected themselves by catering to the Chambri need for sago. Barter, to the Mensuat, had always been a means of securing political autonomy, and when Baga threatened to withdraw from the Indingai market, he meant the Chambri to know that he no longer feared their domination.

Thus, while the Chambri were arguing that they—and not the Nyaula —belonged in the "center" of Chambri Lake, a more significant issue was at stake: whether the Sepik Hills peoples would continue to help maintain Chambri dominance within the Gaui Council. The bark anchor may have moved closer to the center of the hole, and the Nyaula may have settled on islands within Chambri Lake, but the actual middlemen — those who had a central position in deciding between the claims of the Chambri and those of the Nyaula within the council — were the Sepik Hills peoples, with Baga, perhaps, their temporary advocate.[7]

I do not wish to suggest that the Hills peoples have any real decision making power within the Gaui Council. The truth is quite to the contrary, in fact, for their villages are small (see Table 7.1), and they are entitled to very few council votes. The Hills people do, however, have the ability to withdraw their support from the Chambri and to transform the balance of power within the council (see Table 7.2).[8] Thus, they can subvert the desires of their allies, a fact that Baga may clearly have wished the Chambri to appreciate when he acknowledged responsibility for killing Mabkan's crocodile and threatened to withdraw from the market.

Mabkan told me that he did, most definitely, appreciate this fact and expressed his appreciation by offering Baga the soup from Woliwopan. As I shall indicate later, however, the soup he offered was unacceptable because it carried the message of Sepik Hills subservience with every spoonful — precisely the message least acceptable to Baga at the time.

Baga never returned to Chambri to complete the crocodile negotiations. Indeed, the incident was never again mentioned by any Chambri unless I provoked him with questions. I traveled to Peliagwi two weeks after the event to interview Baga, who was loquacious but uninformative. He insisted that he refused the soup because he felt sick and because the soup was "no good." He would not or could not convey

Table 7.1
Population of Iatmul and Chambri Villages in 1974

Nyaula Iatmul	2,595	*Chambri*	1,308
Japandai	216	Indingai	368
Yamanambu	226	Wombun	468
Japanaut	379	Kilimbit	472
Nyaurengai	195		
Kandingai	483		
Yentchamangua	282		
Korogo	814		
Parambei Iatmul	3,025	*Sepik Hills*	569
Suapmeri	308	Changriman	130
Indabu	280	Mali	84
Yentchan	394	Mensuat	156
Parambei	728	Yambi Yambi	148
Malingai	401	Milae	51
Kanganaman	725		
Tegowi	189		

NOTE: All figures include migrant laborers. The Iatmul and Sepik Hills data were collected by D. B. Robertson and compiled in *Ambunti Patrol Report* No. 3 (1974). The Chambri data were collected by the author.

Table 7.2
Voting Members of the Gaui Local Government Council

Linguistic Division	Sawos[a]	Nyaula	Parambei	Chambri	Sepik Hills
Village	Mainga	Kandingai	Parambei	Indingai	Mensuat
	Jama	Timbunmeri	Malingai	Kilimbit	Changriman
	Burui	Nyaurengai	Tegowi	Wombun	
	Kumpupu	Korogo	Yentchan		
	Kwimba	Yentchamangua	Indabu		
	Kosimbi	Japanaut	Suapmeri		
	Aurimbit	Japandai	Kanganaman		
	Wereman	Yamanambu	Aibom[b]		
	Yangit				
	Jinginimbu				
	Torembi				
	Slei				
	Yakiap/Miambei				
	Yamuk				
	Marap				
	Sengo				
	Gaikeropi				
	Nogosop				

[a]The Sawos-speaking peoples are sago suppliers to the Iatmul. They were never allied to the Chambri, and now see their development needs as different from those of the water peoples. I have been told that they rarely vote en bloc, for they suffer from intervillage animosities.

[b]Aibom generally votes with Chambri. Its original inhabitants were probably Sepik Hills speakers who temporarily camped there in caves. These were decimated by disease and war, and now Aibom is primarily inhabited by Parambei and Chambri migrants.

to me why he thought the soup inferior, and I cannot, therefore, incorporate his point of view within my explanation of his behavior. I will speculate, however, that when Baga refused to eat the Woliwopan soup, he was refusing to participate with Mabkan in communion — both in its general sense of sharing and in its specific sense of receiving sacrament. The Woliwopan soup was made from the elements essential to traditional barter relations, and Mabkan wished both Chambri and Mensuat to incorporate these essentials. As he put it, "the soup is half Mensuat and half Chambri." Sago, the food of mothers' blood, is considered to be female by the Chambri,[9] whereas coconut milk and meat, which they associate with semen, or "fathers' milk," is considered quintessentially male. The Woliwopan soup, thus, mingled male and female elements, much as male fish were "married to" female sago at barter markets. The soup, however, did not symbolize the sociological aspects of marriage, as do barter markets, but rather represented its sexual and procreative elements. (The sexual mimicry during the ceremony coupled with the promise that the sago soup would cause me to have "ten, or five" children lend credence to this interpretation.)[10]

Mabkan's insistence that the Woliwopan soup would convince Baga of Chambri power indicates that it was meant to communicate more than his desire for commensalism — more than his hope that they would share in a stable and productive future through their mutually beneficial union. I believe that, on another level, Mabkan was trying to seduce Baga — offering to consume with him the child of their union and thus become themselves united.

The saucepan of Woliwopan had no exceptional ceremonial significance apart from the fact that Woliwopan is one of the hundred or so names of the founder of Mabkan's clan. The saucepan was not a native artifact; it was made of aluminum and could have been no more than a few years old. Its importance was in the name that had been given to it. Because the saucepan possessed Woliwopan's name, it also possessed his power. Baga recognized that the saucepan of Woliwopan represented the strength of Mabkan's clan through the generations; it stood, in effect, for the womb that produced Mabkan's ancestors and that will produce his descendants. Baga admitted as much when he told me that the saucepan was "the same as Mabkan's mother." More to the point, it carried the sago and coconut child-soup with which, I believe, Mabkan wished to insure Baga's allegiance.

Baga, I suspect, was thinking of divorcing the Chambri, not of solidifying his relationship with them. He certainly could not accept Mabkan's "child-soup," since Mabkan had, in effect, depicted Baga's essential inequality by showing him the anchors in the conical hole and serving him the soup from Woliwopan's saucepan.

The conical hole suggests two related images. First, and most obviously, the hole is a microcosm. The Chambri say that in it are mingled the waters from the north, south, east, and west, from the River, Hills, White Man's land, and the Lake itself. It is thus a representation of the Chambri world, which they explicitly use to predict the future and explain the past.

The hole also represents a vaginal canal that contains the anchors of Emosue Apanke and Kwolimbank embedded in its cervix. Indeed, the Chambri refer to the hole as "our mother." The anchors, then, are forever impregnating the world with their Chambri and Iatmul descendants. It is important to recognize that only representatives from water villages — only Emosue Apanke and Kwolimbank — provide the world with procreative anchorage. The Chambri perceive themselves and the Iatmul as assertively masculine, in contrast to the submissive and feminine Hills peoples, and thus depict a world made stable and continuous by their ancestors' phalli.

There is another dimension to this sexual image that may have been significant to Baga, that Emosue Apanke and Kwolimbank were "wedded" to the same "woman," i.e., their anchors were embedded in the same hole. Although the peoples of the Middle Sepik do not, as far as I know, share women, they live in exogamous, patrivirilocal clans, practice the levirate, and espouse specific (although various) prescriptive marriage rules.[11] To be wedded to the same woman would thus mean sharing clan comembership. Or, as Baga may have perceived it, Kwolimbank and Emosue Apanke, as comembers of the "water-village group," were married to the same woman who must, by extension, be a subservient and sago-supplying "bushwoman." Why, then, should it be relevant to Baga, himself a member of the "bushwomen group," whether the Nyaula or the Chambri became "the number one man"?

Mabkan, let us assume, wished to convince Baga that the choice mattered very much and that the Chambri deserved to "win" the Nyaula. What, then, did his argument consist of? He demonstrated to Baga that the bush people had been excluded from "the cervix of the world" and then offered him soup from Woliwopan's saucepan. But for Baga to drink this soup would have been an acceptance of the Chambri view of the bush people as passive, feminine, and submissive. And this is precisely the conception that Baga was fighting against by killing a Chambri crocodile and threatening to withdraw from the Indingai market.[12]

Mabkan's Mistake

How could Mabkan have miscalculated so disastrously? It seems to me that one possible explanation of Mabkan's mistake could begin with a look at the gap between modern political contingencies and traditional modes of symbolic formulation. I could argue, for example, that traditional symbolic formulas — e.g., the sexually oriented symbols of dominance and submission that in the past had always been successfully used to verify bush-water relations — now conflicted with the sociopolitical fact of political equality within the Gaui Council. To put it more simply, Mabkan failed to acquire Mensuat support because his most general cultural orientations could no longer provide an adequate image of the political process; he simply did not have the vocabulary with which to win Baga's identification and allegiance (Geertz 1973: 142 – 69).

I cannot accept this argument, however, because Mabkan chose to communicate with Baga through the sago soup. Whatever meanings were contained in the soup were conveyed through Mabkan's design. Although his use of the symbolic soup may have been inept, we cannot argue that he was encumbered by a lack of appropriate symbolic meanings. We must assume, instead, that the Chambri—who explicitly sought Baga's allegiance — had the vocabulary with which to win this allegiance and that Mabkan chose not to speak the necessary words, either because he had other things on his mind, or because he did not care for their implications.

He had, after all, been insulted by Baga. If a Chambri had killed the crocodile, Mabkan would have immediately demanded monetary compensation. It would then have been clear that Mabkan had been offended, that his status had been lowered, and that he had the right to attempt to reestablish his reputation by publicly confronting his antagonist. If Mabkan had not confronted this hypothetical Chambri crocodile killer, he would have implicitly accepted the killer's superiority.

This flexible tit-for-tat system of alternating asymmetries characterized the essentially equal relationship between individual men and groups throughout Melanesia. At any point in time an individual or group achieves temporary ascendancy in the eyes of equals through, for example, killing a rival's crocodile, generously compensating wifegivers, or donating a treasured necklace to an exchange partner. For equality to be reestablished the owner of the crocodile demands over-remuneration; the compensated affines more generously repay their own wife-givers; the exchange partner reciprocates with an even more valuable arm shell; and so the system goes, promising to balance itself out through time.

To reachieve equality, then, Mabkan would have had to publicly diminish the offending crocodile killer. He would have held a public fit by screaming accusations throughout the three Chambri villages, and confronting the killer with threats to destroy property, rape clanswomen, and otherwise wreak havoc until duly compensated for the crocodile. He would, in fact, have enjoyed the opportunity to display himself, and he and the crocodile killer may well have become fast friends over the inevitable compensatory ceremony. Or so I had seen it happen before, for inappropriate crocodile killing, while certainly a potential threat to the true owner's ascendancy, is not a serious offense. In fact, it happens rather frequently, since the creatures are apt to entangle themselves and drown in the fishing nets of owners and nonowners alike.[13]

Baga understood what Mabkan's reactions would be and wished to make the most of the fortuitous crocodile killing. He told me that he was pleased when he learned that Mabkan's crocodile had drowned while entangled in his sister-in-law's fishing net, for Mabkan was an important Chambri who would be forced to mount a major ceremony (literally, "perform a big play") in order to overcome his shame at a Mensuat's power to attract and destroy his property.

If Baga had not challenged Mabkan by publicly announcing his responsibility for the crocodile killing, Mabkan would have ignored the event. Mabkan admitted that he wished he had journeyed to the town of Wewak during the week of July 18, and thereby avoided the entire affair. As it was, he was forced to accept Baga's challenge but was unsure of how to respond appropriately. How could he respond to Baga — a man who had been considered an unequal, a child of dogs and bush spirits — but who was being wooed into equality by Gaui's president and other Chambri leaders? How could he save face without jeopardizing relations with a people who were potentially crucial allies?

Symbolic Encodings: The Dilemma Resolved

By ignoring Baga's challenge, Mabkan would have lost face within the three Chambri villages, particularly because the challenge had come from an inferior. By accepting Baga's challenge, however, he would have alienated those upon whom the Chambri were dependent for support within the Gaui Council. Mabkan could not easily resolve this conflict. He was, in fact, in a classic double bind, "a situation where no matter what a person does he can't win" (Bateson 1972:201).

Bateson identifies three characteristics of the double-bind situation:

(1) When the individual is involved in an intense relationship; that is, a relationship in which he feels it is vitally important that he discriminate accurately what sort of message is being communicated so that he may respond appropriately.
(2) And, the individual is caught in a situation in which the other person in the relationship is expressing two orders of message and one of these denies the other.
(3) And, the individual is unable to comment on the messages being expressed to correct his discrimination of what order of message to respond, i.e., he cannot make a metacommunicative statement (1972: 208)

Mabkan was involved in an intense relationship, one in which he felt it vitally important to distinguish between Baga as an individual and

Baga as a representative of a crucially significant political group. On the one hand, Baga was inviting Mabkan to reply to the challenge he had made by assuming responsibility for killing the crocodile. On the other hand, he was warning Mabkan that if he did respond in a manner appropriate to relations between equals it would jeopardize the allegiance between Mabkan's people and his own.

There is only one way out of most double-bind situations, and that is to shift to a metaphorical level of communication and thereby become someone else, to insist that one is somewhere else, or to change the very nature of the situation into something else. "Then the double bind cannot work on the victim, because he isn't he and besides he is in a different place" (Bateson 1972: 210).

This switch to a metaphorical level of communication is precisely what Mabkan accomplished within the water-removing and soup ceremonies. Throughout both ceremonies he overlooked the fact that he was an affronted man, whose crocodile had been slaughtered, and whose integrity had been challenged. Rather, he acted the perfect host, ostensibly welcoming Baga, an equal council ally, to participate in commensalism. The Mensuat, therefore, could have no complaint, for Mabkan was clearly admitting their temporary ascendancy by refusing to call Baga's bluff. Yet, through the symbols of the anchors and the soup, Mabkan communicated the essential superiority of the Chambri and of himself. Since political contingencies made it necessary for Mabkan to ignore the crocodile challenge, he would metaphorically reveal Baga to be an unequal bushman whom the Chambri had always controlled and who was, therefore, essentially unworthy of Mabkan's wrath.

Thus, even though Baga refused the soup, Mabkan had, indeed, resolved his personal conflict. By mounting the water-removing ceremony and soup exchange, he proved his ability to conjoin resources and mobilize his covillagers, thus demonstrating that he was an equal among equals. Simultaneously, by serving Baga the soup and by showing him the anchors, Mabkan communicated his conception of bush people without seriously threatening the Mensuat-Chambri Council alliance. So he had not made a mistake after all but had successfully stalemated Baga by adeptly, and without warning, changing his level of discourse. Baga could not, after all, change the soup's ingredients, rearrange the anchors' positions, or transform the meanings invested by the Chambri in the soup and the anchors as easily as he had killed Mabkan's crocodile.

I wish to emphasize, however, that while Mabkan's metaphoric coup had no significant negative effects upon bush-water relations, it also had no positive effects. The Chambri are still insecurely allied to the bush villagers; they fear the loss of their sago supply; and they have not been able to stop the Nyaula intrusion into their lake. In this sense, the water-removing ceremony and soup exchange did not regulate the ecosystem in the manner of the great ceremonial exchange systems of Papua New Guinea, the *kaiko, te, moka*, and *kula* (see Rappaport 1968; Meggitt 1974; A. Strathern 1971; Weiner 1976). Apart from their role in the creative resolution of Mabkan's specific conflict, is there any general significance to such minor ceremonial and exchange events? Let me recapitulate somewhat before answering this question.

Although the Chambri had always been economically dependent upon their sago suppliers, they countered their dependence by posing a military threat to the small, vulnerable Sepik Hills' hamlets. In fact, the bush people were afraid not to supply the Chambri with sago. But today this military threat no longer exists, for the Pax Australia and the growth in significance of the Gaui Local Government Council have eliminated whatever coercive power the Chambri once held over their sago suppliers. They can no longer openly treat the bush people as inferiors, for they now depend upon bush support within the council. Moreover, the Chambri also now fear lest their council allies refuse to continue supplying them with sago. In fact, it may be that they fear loss of their carbohydrate more than loss of Sepik Hills support within the Gaui Council.

It seems, therefore, that Mabkan certified Chambri dominance by revealing the anchors and offering the soup to Baga. He could not express his dominance explicitly for fear of alienating the Mensuat. Therefore, he communicated his message through propositions that, because they were both symbolic and sanctified, could be neither denied nor ignored. The ceremonies' message was this: "You, Baga, will continue supplying me, Mabkan, with sago, for it is written in the anchors and in the soup that we Chambri are essentially in control of you Mensuat, regardless of the contingencies of the extant sociopolitical situation."

This restatement of Mabkan's solution to his double bind is reminiscent of Rappaport's (1971:69 – 70) analysis of the role of ritual in regulating ecosystems. He states that:

to sanctify statements is to certify them, and ritual, therefore, . . . not only invokes in the participants private religious experiences, it provides a mechanism for translating these private experiences into messages of social import; it also provides a means for certifying these messages. . . . People are more likely to accept sanctified than unsanctified messages as true. Insofar as they do, their responses to these messages will be non-random, and therefore predictable. . . . What is necessary for the survival of populations is that the social interactions of its members be in some minimum degree orderly.

Clearly, the anchor and soup ceremonies certified propositions that alleviated the Chambri insecurity about the continuity of their sago supply and of their political status. But these sanctified propositions called for no responses on the part of either the Mensuat or the Chambri. They informed no behavior whatsoever. I would argue, in fact, that the ceremonies prevented responses from occurring by translating the dominance of the Chambri over the Mensuat from the sociopolitical to the sacred domain, from secular to sacred propositions.

As Rappaport points out, sacred propositions contain no material terms to bind them to any particular social form. They are also cryptic and essentially reinterpretable (1971:71). They may either remain on the "sacred shelf," never informing, or rather, never disturbing orderly social relations again much as the major political party of Mexico has stored its revolutionary heritage in its self-designation as "the part of the institutionalized revolution." Or they may be revitalized and transformed to cog more neatly into extant socio-political situations. This is what I suspect happened after Melanesians were forced by European unresponsiveness to translate their ideas about the formation of reciprocal relationships from the secular domain of marriage and exchange to the sacred domain of ancestral control during the early stages in the formation of cargo cults.[14]

What I am suggesting, in effect, is that under certain circumstances people make unnecessary the secular enactment of what seem to them to be crucial relations by storing these relations in the sacred domain. These circumstances may involve double-bind situations that trigger the performance of ceremonies whose purpose is to resolve the double binds while they translate the relations from secular to sacred propositions. Finally, I would argue that these sacred propositions are likely to be conveyed through exchange. Items of exchange, as elements of discourse, have the advantage of tangibility. Unlike words, they cannot be easily qualified, contradicted, or disavowed. Relationships established and maintained through conversations are open-ended. They can develop in any number of ways, many often threatening to the status quo. Exchanges, on the other hand, can only be accepted or refused. If accepted, the terms of the relationship remain substantially the same. If rejected, the relationship as presently defined is terminated.

For all their tangibility, however, items of exchange are characterized by a special ambiguity. There is always the possibility of their being willfully shorn of meaning. Baga can alway declare the soup to be just soup, and his reason for refusing it an upset stomach. Baga's stonewalling does not change the way the event has been publicly perceived, but it does contribute to the elimination of the matter from public discourse. The crocodile incident, and the painful and perplexing political transformation of which it is a symptom, have become matters not open to discussion and, as such, have been temporarily resolved, or at least "tabled."

Notes

Reprinted, with some changes, from the *Journal of the Polynesian Society* (September 1980) 89 (3): 309 – 28. By kind permission of the publisher.

Many of the ideas in this chapter were delivered in another form at the 77th Annual Meeting of the American Anthropological Association in the symposium, "Symbolic Aspects of Melanesian Exchange," and at the 1980 Meetings of the Association for Social Anthropology in Oceania in the symposium, "Language and Politics."

My research from 1974 through 1975 was sponsored by the East-West Center Population Institute, the National Geographic Society, and the Graduate School of the City University uf NEW YORK. I returned to the field during the summer of 1979, sponsored by a summer stipend from the National Endowment for the Humanities and a Miner D. Crary fellowship. Although I lived among the Chambri during both field trips, I made prolonged visits to the neighboring Mensuat and Iatmul peoples.

1. The incident occurred nearly six months after I entered the field. I have changed the names of the individuals I describe.

2. The Chambri believe that their ancestors reincarnate in the form of crocodiles. They are therefore very cognizant of those inhabiting their lake, the largest of which they call by name. There was no doubt in any Chambri's mind that Mabkan owned the dead crocodile, for it had been seen and identified before, and it was killed near a rivulet owned by Mabkan's family. The crocodile had been found dead by Baga's younger brother's wife. It had become entangled and drowned in her fishing net. Baga publicly acknowledged responsibility for the deed, and all concerned, Mensuat and Chambri alike, allowed him to do so.

3. The Catholic priest stationed at St. Mary's Mission had seen the water-removing ceremony some two years after he arrived at Indingai, nearly seven years before I arrived.

4. The Chambri and Mensuat speak different languages. When interacting in the past they used the Chambri language. Today, Neo-Melanesian (Pidgin English) is understood and spoken throughout the Middle Sepik, and was used by all Chambri and Mensuat discussing the crocodile killing. I am fluent in Neo-Melanesian and had no difficulty understanding their conversations, which I taped as a check against my notes.

5. Simbuksuan, a migrant from Parambei village to Indingai village, killed his former neighbor, thereby severing relations with his natal village, displaying his courage and prowess as a member of his Chambri clan of adoption, and beginning a long series of skirmishes between the Parambei and the Chambri (see Gewertz 1981).

6. Traditionally, Timbunmeri Island served as a temporary campsite for the semimigratory Sepik Hills peoples from Garamambu, Changriman, and Mali. The Chambri argue that the Kandingai gave shell valuables to these peoples to verify the establishment of a temporary barter relationship. The Kandingai insist that they, indeed, purchased the island.

7. The situation within the Gaui Council can become very complex, with tensions apparent between the "intrusive" subset of the Nyaula Iatmul and other Nyaula villages, between Nyaula and Parambei villages, and so on. Complementary opposition does tend to prevail, however, and no Nyaula or Parambei councillor can side with a Chambri councillor about an issue of significance and expect to maintain his constituency.

8. It is impossible to predict whether the Chambri would be unable to form a new coalition within the Gaui Council if the Sepik Hills' councillors withdrew their support. Perhaps they could. They are not sure of their capacity to establish a new power base, however, and feel particularly insecure about losing the Hills peoples' support because they have for so long been dominant over these sago suppliers.

9. Ruddle et al. support my contention when they write, "it seems possible to make the general statement that where sago work is women's work, sago is a symbol of female sexuality in myth and ritual" (1978:92).

10. I was the only woman present at the soup ceremony. Chambri women are generally not permitted to enter men's houes.

11. See Korn 1971 and Fortune 1933.

12. I doubt whether Baga and the other Mensuat subscribe to the Chambri conception of all bush people as weak and dirty "children of dogs." I am, however, certain that all the Sepik Hills peoples are familiar enough with the Chambri symbol system to under-

stand the meanings encoded within it. This is clearly indicated by the fact that at barter markets bushwomen allow Chambri fishwives to treat them as inferior sago suppliers. They understand that the Chambri view them as ineffectual *because* they are sago suppliers, regardless of how they rationalize this Chambri belief to themselves.

13. It would be interesting to compare the incident I have described with an earlier example of a Mensuat killing a Chambri crocodile. Unfortunately, I am unaware of any other example. I would expect, however, that prior to the 1964 descent of the Sepik Hills peoples to the shores of Chambri Lake, all such incidents would have been ignored by the Chambri. As I have already indicated, confrontation is necessary and possible only between equals, and it is only recently that the Chambri have been forced to view the Hills people in this manner.

14. I am indebted to Krystyna Starker for suggesting the relationship between cargo cults and double-bind relationships.

III.
Hierarchy: Speech and the "Taken-for-Granted" Polity

8. Lāuga and Talanoaga: Two Speech Genres in a Samoan Political Event

Alessandro Duranti

University of California, Los Angeles

Introduction

In this chapter I will discuss several ways in which a social event constitutes a "frame," in Bateson's terms,[1] within and through which particular speech genres are performed and interpreted. I will show that two speech genres recognized by Samoans, *lāuga* [la: 'uŋa] and *talanoaga*, differ in their internal organization, form, and content according to the context in which they are performed. My discussion will also demonstrate that native distinctions are sometimes context-sensitive, that is, they do not equally apply across different sociocultural contexts.

The scene of this study is a particular type of meeting of titled people (*matai*) — both chiefs and orators — in a traditional Samoan village.[2] I will refer to this kind of meeting throughout this chapter as the *fono*. Although this is the term also used by Samoans, the word *fono* has quite a variety of possible interpretations, which must be specific in each context (cf. Duranti 1981; Mead 1930; Shore 1982). The *fono* discussed here are special meetings that are called for discussing some particularly important "case" that threatens the established political alliances, the respectability of some community leaders, or the alleged "mutual love" (*fealofani*) of the village or district members. A *fono* works as a "high court" and as a political arena for the kind of antagonistic interaction that Victor Turner (1974) describes as typical of social dramas. It is within a *fono* that the leading members of the community try to overcome crises in the social life of the village, struggle for power, and challenge the existing alliances and hierarchies. In this context, language is the most important medium and is an essential element for defining what goes on. At the same time, the use of speech within a *fono* can be understood and related to the use of speech in other social contexts only if we take the entire social event as an interpretive frame, which "gives the participants instructions or aids in [their] attempt[s] to understand the message" (Bateson 1972: 182).

Both the organization of talk and the language of a *fono* are different, in many respects, from conversation. In the next section, I discuss the distinctive features of the talk in a *fono* as a whole. In the last section, I show that, despite similarities among all *fono* speeches (illustrated in the next section), native speakers make a distinction between two different types of speeches: *lāuga* and *talanoaga*.

In the spirit of the approach proposed within the ethnography of speaking (cf. Bauman and Sherzer 1974, 1975; Frake 1972), I will first illustrate the basic native criteria for the distinction in question: a topic constraint and a sequential constraint. On the basis of my own observations, I will also illustrate some further differences between the two genres in the last section. Finally, I will compare the *lāuga* in a *fono* with the *lāuga* delivered in an exchange of dowry and bridewealth and a *lāuga* at the installation of a chief. I will argue that the differences must be related to a different focus of interaction and to the social function of speech in the social event. A *lāuga* in a ceremony is the climax of that event, the most important domain for display and evaluation of verbal art, in which the performer assumes a commitment toward the audience and the audience toward the performer. However, a *lāuga* in a *fono* is perceived as a transition point, a necessary introduction to the forthcoming discussion, which is the climax of the political event.

Data Sources and Research Methods

The data for this study were collected during a one-year period of fieldwork in the village of Falefā on the Island of Upolu, in Western

Samoa. The data consist of direct (participant) observation and audio recording of *fono* in the village. Informal conversations and ceremonial speeches were also recorded for comparative purposes, and several informal interviews were conducted with chiefs and orators from the village who could provide insights and evaluations of the events from a Samoan perspective. A large number of the interviews and discussions with chiefs and orators in the village were also recorded (for more discussion on data sources and methods cf. Duranti 1981).

Definition of the Event: What Is a Fono?

I am particularly interested here in addressing two issues with respect to the definition of a *fono*: (1) Is it possible to define a *fono* as distinct from other events in the society (that may share with the *fono* several important or minor features)? (2) Can we establish the event's boundaries and other characteristics in a way that would be consistent with the native view?

These are important questions, not only with respect to the *fono*, but, more generally, for any ethnographic account of speech events in a given society. In what follows I will provide a list and a description of what I judge to be characteristics of the *fono* consistent with these questions, although I will not always specify with respect to which other event a particular feature becomes relevant.

Accounts of other types of *fono* in other villages and with other foci of attention and goals can also be found in Mead (1930), Freeman (1978), and Shore (1982).

Features of the Event

Boundaries. In talking about "boundaries" we must distinguish along two dimensions: *spatial boundaries* and *temporal boundaries*. The spatial boundaries define the "space" in which the event is taking place. The *fono* discussed here takes place inside one house. There are other social events in which participants (also) act in an open space (usually in front of a house), and there are other *fono* (*fono tauati*) that take place in several different houses at the same time (see Shore 1982 for a description of a *fono tauati* in the village of Sala'ilua on the island of Savai'i).

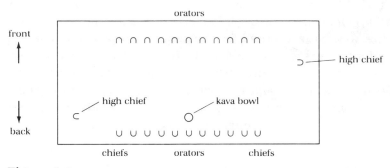

Figure 8.1
Seating arrangement of *matai* in a *fono*.
The symbol ∪, which is taken from child language transcription procedures (cf. Ochs 1979), indicates the direction of the pelvis (bird's-eye view) and, therefore, of people's positions with respect to each other and the possible reach of their eye gaze.

The way people seat themselves inside the house is also significant and is done according to an ideal plan structured on the basis of statuses (chiefs vs. orators), ranks (high vs. low-ranking titles), and extent of active participation in the event. Variations and "violations" of the ideal plan are common and must be understood as having the abstract plan as a key. Very roughly, the two senior orators[3] of the village and the orators who are going to speak sit in what is considered the "front" of the house.[4] High-ranking chiefs sit in either one of the two shorter sides (*tala*); other chiefs and those orators who are in charge of the kava ceremony sit in the "back." Figures 8.1 provides an example of an actuaal seating arrangement in one of the *fono* I recorded.

Temporal boundaries refer, for instance, to the beginning and to the end of thee event. The beginning of a *fono* is always signaled by a kava ceremony. Almost anytime *matai* get together for some official reason, kava is served. However, the way kava is distributed varies. In the *fono* I am describing, the order of kava serving at the beginning is different from any other gathering of *matai* in that orators drink first and according to a particular sequence principle (cf. Duranti 1981). The order of drinking kava also parallels the order of speakers in the *fono*, at least up to a certain (predictable) number. Right after the kava an orator

Figure 8.2.
Temporal Boundaries of a *Fono*.

from a particular subvillage[5] will deliver the first speech of the day, a *lāuga*. After this speech, either other *lāuga* follow (one for each of the subvillages represented at the meeting) or the discussion (*talanoaga*) starts.

The end of a *fono* is sometimes marked by another kava ceremony. At other times, though, the end is less clear-cut, and one may perceive a gradual change in the form and content of verbal and nonverbal behavior going from more "formal" to less "formal" features. (I am thinking here of the various characteristics of "formality" discussed by Irvine 1979.) A different kind of end marker from the official kava ceremony is *laughter*. A person will make a joke — and the laughter that follows it, with public recognition of that particular speech act as a "joke" — signals that the tension is (or, at least, "should" be) over and people should relax. After this, the verbal interaction resembles conversation, with several people speaking at the same time and in a less homogeneous and restricted register. Figure 8.2 illustrates the temporal organization of a *fono*.

Time. Fono take place in the morning, usually on a Saturday (but other days may also be chosen), probably to allow people who work in the capital to participate. These *fono* do not take place regularly but are instead called only if some important matter must be discussed. (Other types of *fono*, as, for instance, the *fono o le pulenu'u*, take place every other week, on Mondays, regardless of the particular issues to be discussed.)

Norms of etiquette. Several norms must be followed by the participants in both their verbal and nonverbal behavior. Since I will discuss the verbal behavior at length in the rest of the chapter, I will mention here only three nonverbal norms: (1) Everyone sits on mats and cross-legged (chiefs, but not orators, are allowed to put one foot on the other leg's thigh [*napevae*], and only while they are not delivering a speech). (2) A person may walk across the internal "circle" of *matai* for a ceremonial reason only (e.g., in the distribution of kava). (3) If someone who is sitting in the front row wants to give something to someone else of those present, he must call upon some untitled man from outside the house or a *matai* of low rank from the back row to deliver the object from one *matai* to the other.

Reasons for a fono. A *fono* is called when a breach of some social norm has taken place or is about to take place, such a breach involving some social relation between individuals or groups (e.g., families, sub-villages). A crisis or a conflict makes the village "weak" according to the Samoan world view, and it ruins the "beauty" of the village. The "love for each other" (*fealofani*) must be restored. This process, among other ways, takes the form of a *fono*, in which the trouble sources are discussed and certain measures are taken by the *matai*, who represent all the families and people of the village, to remedy the misconduct of those who violated the social rules and alliances.

Goals and outcomes. Following Hymes's suggestion (cf. Hymes 1972: 61), a distinction must be made between the goals of (some of) the individuals engaged in the interaction within a *fono* and the outcomes of that interaction from the point of view of the community. Personal ambition or rivalry among powerful members of the community may be in the background of the convocation of a *fono*; however, what the society as a whole gets out of these meetings may be independent of and beyond the particular goals of some individuals. From the society's point of view, the *fono* is the place for restating secular alliances and values; it is also the time in which the social structure and the ties with the tradition are challenged, and changes of more or less importance may take place.

Verbal interaction in the Fono: An Overall View

In this section I will describe some of the main features that distinguish verbal interaction in the *fono* from verbal interaction among the same individuals before the event starts (or in other, less planned types of activity). All the characteristics of speech listed must be understood as belonging to both *lāuga* and *talanoaga*, the two types of speech I will discuss in the last section. (For an example of interaction among *matai* before the *fono* starts, see the Appendix.)

Turn-Taking Rules[6]

In a *fono*, speakers' turns are preallocated up to a number that is predictable from the situation (cf. Duranti 1981). I am using the term "turn" in a different way from what is meant in "conversation analysis" (cf. Sacks, Schegloff, and Jefferson 1974), and more in the way the term has been used by Duncan (1972). Turn organization and turn management in a *fono* are in many ways different from conversation. I propose thus to use the term "macroturn" to characterize the difference from, and, at the same time, maintain the relationship with, "turns in conversation."

Within one's speech (macroturn), predictable responses are elicited from the audience (all of which convey agreement, e.g., *mālie!*, "nicely [said]"). This is the most common environment for brief overlap.

It is always the case that, after the audience has given the requested feedback (cf. the use of *mālie!*), the one who is delivering the speech will reselect himself, unless his last utterance conveys the message "end of my speech." (The most common formula is *manuia le aofia ma le fono!* which may be translated as "best wishes to the assembly and the council!" or "long life ... "). If the person has terminated his speech, the audience will not answer *mālie!* but, instead, *mālō fetalai!* (for an orator); *mālō saunoa!* for a chief); or *mālō vagana!* (for one of the two senior orators). They could all be translated as "congratulations for [your] speech!"

Gaps between macroturns are generally longer than between turns in conversation (this may be a characteristic of macroturns).

Overwhelmingly, parties self-select in starting to talk.[7]

Once a party has started, there are no "second starters." This means that nobody else will compete with the current speaker for the floor if he has the right to speak at that particular time. Thus, for instance, at the beginning of the *fono* people must speak in a prearranged order. If one person violates that order by self-selecting himself at an inappropriate time (as happened once in a *fono* I recorded), another person (who has the authority to do so) may interrupt the current speaker to

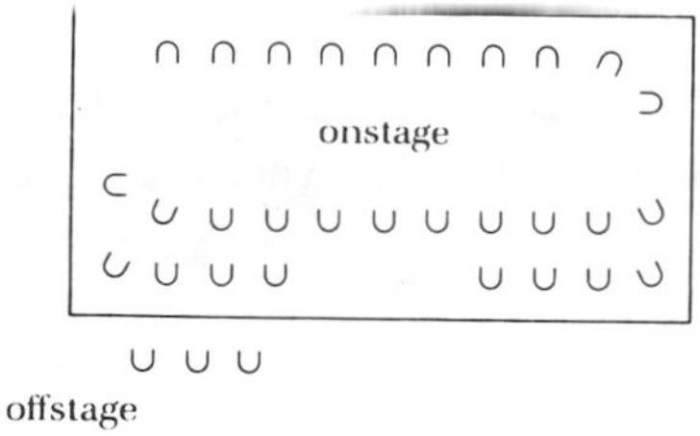

Figure 8.3
Onstage/offstage participants

reestablish the proper procedure. Furthermore, there are cases in which someone else may begin to talk after a person has started to deliver his speech, but this would not be sensed as "competitive" with the ongoing speech, although it might be competitive in terms of focus of the interaction. Here a distinction may be drawn between "onstage" and "offstage" participants, a feature of the event that can also be captured by referring to what I call the *spatial boundaries*. When someone talks while another person is giving a speech, it is more likely to happen among those *matai* who sit in the back of the house than among those who are sitting in the front. Among those who sit in the back of the house, there is more a tendency to do this among those sitting in a second back row, if there is one (see Fig. 8.3). Such "offstage" or "backstage" interaction would not be immediately perceived as competitive with the ongoing speech. This backstage talk is in a much lower volume than the official speaker's voice, and it usually lasts a relatively short time. It also tends to occur toward the beginning and the end of the meeting, not in the middle of it, when the discussion is more lively and less predictable. One could suggest, then, the following generalization: talk that overlaps with the official speeches tends to occur at the external spatial and temporal boundaries of the event.

Linguistic Characteristics of a Fono

I will now describe certain linguistic features of a *fono* that characterize *fono* speeches as a whole, regardless of the distinction between *lāuga* and *talanoaga*.

Lexicon. In Samoan, there is a special set of words that are used for talking about *matai*, their actions, feelings, relatives, belongings (Milner

1961). Thus, whereas the common word for "to see" is *va'ai*, the word for a chief or an orator is *silasila*; whereas an untitled person is said to be *ma'i* to say that he is sick, a titled person is said to be *gasegase*. In some cases, two different terms are used according to whether the referent is (related to) a chief or an orator. Thus, a common house is a *fale*, but a chief's house is a *maota*, and an orator's house is a *laoa*. A chief's wife is a *faletua*, but an orator's wife is a *tausi*. Instead of the common word *sau*, "come, arrive," the expression *afio mai* can be used in talking about a chief and the expression *maliu mai* in talking about an orator. In some cases, even subtler distinctions can be made between, say, a high-ranking and a low-ranking or medium-ranking chief or between a common orator and a senior orator.

The selection of one term (e.g., common word) over another (e.g., respect word), however, is not simply a function of the referent. That is, it is not simply due to whether one is talking about an untitled person or a *matai*, but it is to a large extent related to the particular kind of social event or speech act that one is involved in. Thus, for instance, whereas in an exchange of greetings or in a request for a favor the respect vocabulary terms are common, in informal household interaction among relatives or friends, common words are preferred instead. To a large extent, it seems that respectful words are used in those interactions in which it is the social identity associated with the title that matters or is highlighted, for whatever purpose. In this sense, it is clear that a *fono* is among the most typical environments for the use of respect vocabulary, given not only that someone's title is extremely important in a *fono* but also that the very fact of being a title holder is defined by the participation in the village *fono* (cf. Mead 1930). Some examples will illustrate the way in which the fact of being in a *fono* explains the use of a respect vocabulary term. The first case is in example (1) below, in which, before the meeting has started, the senior orator, Moe'ono, asks Taofiuailoa (shortened "Loa") whether the orator, Mata'afa (pronounced Maka'afa), has come from the two nearby sub-villages (Falelua). Here we find the common word *sau*, "come," in the line indicated by an arrow. In example (2), when Mata'afa's presence is acknowledged within the *fono* interaction, a respectful term, *maliu mai*, is used in the line indicated by an arrow.

(1) (Transcript I, p.10; *Fono*, April 7, 1978; before meeting starts)

Moe'ono: *'A fea fo'i lo kou pikogu'u (a) li'i, (0.3) Loa?*
             "Where is the rest of your subvillage, Mr. ... Loa?

Taofiuailoa: *(Se) ka'ilo ā iai. (0.2) Savalivali mai ā kaika ke le (iloa).*
             "Poor me, how do I know? ... I walked here. I don't know."

→   Moe'ono: *Ga'o Maka'afa a le Falelua ga sau?*
             "Only Mata'afa of [the people from] the two subvillages
             has come?"

Taofiuailoa: *Ia ai a ga'o // Maka'afa.*
             "There is indeed only // Mata'afa."

(2) (Transcript I, p.47; *Fono* April 7, 1978; after the discussion of the first topic on the agenda of the meeting, the chief Tevaseu and the orator Mata'afa are called to participate. Their arrival is recognized by the senior orator, Moe'ono, chairman of the council.)

Moe'ono: (...) *Ia. 'O lea 'ua lua afio mai Kevaseu*
             "So, now you [chief] Tevaseu have come"

→   *maliu mai fo'i Maka'afa.*
             "[you] have come too [orator] Mata'afa."

Another interesting example is found in a speech by a titled woman, who has gone to the meeting to speak in favor of her brother, Savea, a young chief. Normally, as reported by Milner (1961), one does not use respect vocabulary terms in talking about oneself or close relatives. In the woman's speech, however, we find the word *finagalo*, "wish, opinion," used to refer to her brother's decision, example:

(3) (Transcript III, p.49; *Fono* April 7; Savea's sister, who holds the orator title "Tafili," is delivering her second speech of the day.)

Tafili: *'A 'o legei kaimi, lelei ā le malamalama.*
           "But at this point, it is better to understand."
           Uā 'o le maka'upu, 'o le maka'upu o lea 'ua-
           "Because the discussion, the discussion is about the fact that"
           'ua lafo kaofi iai le kalosaga iā Savea
           "Savea has already filed a request [to the court]"

→   *iga ia kakala loga- [Pause] figagalo i laga kagi.*
           "so that [he] would change his ... mind about his petition."

There is a brief pause before the speaker utters the respectful term *finagalo* (pronounced *figagalo*) for her brother's decision, but she finally chooses to treat him as a chief rather than as a brother. This choice makes sense within the *fono* context, in which Tafili must speak as an orator who respects a chief's opinion rather than as a woman who wants to protect her brother.

Another typical aspect of *fono* speeches is the extensive use of parallelism (cf. Jakobson 1968).[8] We find, that is, different words, phrases, or sentences used to convey the same concept but referring to different statuses or ranks. An example can be seen in example (2), where the speaker uses the verb *afio mai*, "come," in talking about a chief (Tevaseu) and the verb *maliu mai*, also meaning "come," in talking about an orator (Mata'afa). Parallelism often seems to be employed for restating the basic traditional distinctions that are made in the social structure of the village — e.g., between chiefs and orators, between common orators and senior high-ranking orators (*matua*), and so forth. In some cases, the choice of a different word or expression for different statuses reflects a difference in decision power. Thus, orators often talk about chiefs' "decision, will" (*tōfā*, *finagalo*) but about their own "hope" (*fa'amoemoe*) or "humble opinion" (*tāofi vaivai*).

Morphosyntax. I will present here a few examples of the kind of morphosyntactic variation that one finds between the language used in conversation and the language used in a *fono* speech.

In the *fono* speeches there are more sentences with "full constituents" than in conversation. By considering only main declarative sentences with transitive verbs we find that out of 17 sentences in conversation before the *fono* had started only 3 (17.6%) have (in addition to the verb) both Agent NP and Object NP superficially expressed by nouns or full pronouns. Once the *fono* has started and speeches are delivered, we find, instead, that out of 58 transitive sentences 17 (29.3%) have full Agent and Object NPs in them.

In *fono* speeches there is a greater tendency for verbs to appear with tense/aspect markers than in conversation.

The so-called transitive suffix -*C(i)a* appears in a wider range of forms and contexts during a *fono* than in conversation. Several linguists have tried to capture the syntactic or discourse function of the various verbal suffixes known under the label -Cia (e.g., -a, -ia, -mia, -tia, -ina) (cf. Chung 1978; Cook 1978; Milner 1962, 1973). When we look at the *fono* speeches, however, we realize that the grammatical or informational context alone cannot explain the use of -Cia in this context. Generally, in the language of a *fono* we find a broader spectrum of -Cia environments and a higher percentage of -Cia suffixes than in conversation. This suggests that -Cia is also a stylistic marker — a point also made by Tuitele, Sāpolu, and Kneubuhl (1978).

Sentence subordination and coordination is more clearly marked in *fono* speeches than in conversation, which is in turn characterized by what Givón (1979) calls "loose subordination."

In a *fono*, speakers sometimes use the particle *'i* before a full pronoun (e.g., *iā 'i kākou* "to us [inclusive]"). This feature, very common in the language of the Bible, is usually absent in conversational Samoan.

Phonology. Samoan exhibits the possibility of two phonological registers, one in which there is an opposition between /t/ and /k/, and between /n/ and /ŋ/ (written "g"), and another register in which the contrast is neutralized and only the two velar segments, /k/ and /ŋ/, are realized. The first register has been characterized as associated with Western-oriented activities or institutions, (school, church, radio, government documentation, etc.) (cf. Shore 1982) or with literacy (cf. Duranti and Ochs 1984). The *k*/*g*-pronunciation is instead typical of traditional activities or of activities that are not associated with Western values or institutions. This includes both informal conversation and formal speeches in traditional ceremonies and in *fono* of the kind discussed here.[9]

Generally speaking, *fono* speeches are characterized by more careful pronunciation than conversation among *matai* before the meeting starts or in other contexts. This is clearly tied to a slower speed of the *fono* language in general.

Lāuga and Talanoaga: A Native Distinction

In the previous section I presented several features of *fono* speeches and pointed out which ones distinguish the language of a *fono* from the language used by the same individuals in a different context (e.g., conversation before the meeting). In this section, I will show that, despite the many similarities among all the speeches in a *fono*, native speakers,[10] in fact, make a distinction between two genres *lāuga* and *talanoaga* .

In the following subsection, I will provide the native criteria for such a distinction. Futhermore, I will discuss the role of the sociocultural context in defining the particular genre and its features.

The term *lāuga* has a general, nonspecialized meaning and a context-specific, specialized one. Generally speaking, a *lāuga* is any kind of ceremonial speech, which follows certain patterns of internal organization (with different "parts") and makes great use of respect vocabulary and figurative language. In this sense, a speech performed at a funeral, as well as any of the speeches delivered in a *fono* is a *lāuga*. In a more specific, technical use of the term, *lāuga* refers only to certain speeches delivered by certain orators at a particular point in a given social context. In this more specialized sense, only some of the speeches delivered in a *fono* are *lāuga*. Other speeches are *talanoaga*, a term that outside a *fono* means "chat, conversation" and that in a *fono* means "discussion."

The Native Criteria for the Distinction

What are the criteria by which *lāuga* and *talanoaga* in a *fono* can be distinguished? As in the case of the Yakan litigation discussed by Frake (1972), the physical setting could not indicate the difference or the passage from one type to the other.

The basic criteria[11] by which native speakers distinguish the two types of speech are the following: (1) topic choice and (2) sequential ordering.

Topic choice. In a *lāuga* the agenda of the meeting is mentioned, but it cannot be discussed. Speakers cannot express their opinion on the matter. This can be done only in the *talanoaga*, or discussion, part of the *fono*; and *talanoaga* is also the term used for a speech given in this part of the meeting.

Sequential ordering. Once a *fono* starts, first there are one or more *lāuga*,[12] then *talanoaga* follow. Once the "discussion" has started there can be no more *lāuga*.

The end of *lāuga* and the beginning of *talanoaga* is announced by one of the two senior orators with a special formula (*fa'auso le fono*); cf. (2) in the Appendix. Furthermore, at the beginning of a speech that is not a *lāuga*, a speaker may remind the audience of the fact that he is going just to discuss, talk, and not perform a *lāuga*. He would then use expressions such as *tātou talatalanoa*, "let's talk," or *ou te tautala atu*, "I am [going to] talk; I am [just] talking." This is a way of "keying" (cf. Goffman 1974) his performance, that is, of suggesting how the audience should interpret his words. By saying "I am just talking," the speaker is saying "do not take my speech as a *lāuga*, that is, do not expect me to respect the format and rules of *lāuga*; instead, expect me to tell you my position on the issue."

On the basis of the native distinction, I have reexamined the transcripts of the *fono* speeches looking for further differences.

Further Differences between Lāuga and Talanoaga. I will describe the differences between *lāuga* and *talanoaga* along the same lines as I described their similarities in the previous section.

Turn-Taking. The set of potential speakers varies from *lāuga* to *talanoaga*. Only orators who are sitting in the front row can give a *lāuga*. Anyone (chiefs and orators sitting in the front or in the back) can participate in the discussion.

With respect to overlaps and competition for the floor, in the *talanoaga* part of the *fono* overlaps are more likely to occur along with some competition for the floor. For instance, if someone gets "carried away" with his speech and is too harsh, another *matai* may interrupt him and take over the floor.

With respect to question-answer pairs, these occur only in a *talanoaga*. They may fall in either one of the following two categories: (1) a momentary "side sequence" (cf. Jefferson 1972) (e.g., before going on with the discussion, the senior orator who is chairing the meeting may interrupt his *talanoaga* to ask someone in the audience whether so-and-so hs been officially informed of the meeting, who was in charge of delivering a certain message, etc.); (2) within a *talanoaga* speech, a person may ask a question involving one of the *matai* present. In this case, the latter may subsequently answer in his speech, or ask permission, during a pause, to answer immediately.

In addition to the use of the word *mālie!* (see the previous section) as an elicited response within one's speech, which is common in *lāuga*, the word *mo'i*, "true," "right," is also found during a *talanoaga* as an expression of agreement with the content of the speech. This fact reflects a difference in focus between the two genres. It marks a shift from *form* to *content*.

When more than one *lāuga* is performed in a *fono*, each speaker must thank and/or acknowledge all the previous speakers. This is usually done by starting from the last one and then going back to the first one, followed by the second, and so on. When giving a *talanoaga*, instead, the speaker may thank the speaker immediately before him and some important *matai* who had spoken before, but there is no predictable norm.

Lexicon. In terms of the register being used, some "slips" into ordinary language, "vulgar" expressions, may occur in the *talanoaga*, but not in a *lāuga* (e.g., *okaoka!*, an expression of surprise).

In the *talanoaga* more proverbs are used to picture a situation or to express a concern. They are associated with "opinions" or "viewpoints."

Morphosyntax. Along with recognition as well as denunciation of actions accomplished (or intended) by some of the powerful figures of the community, more constructions with agents appear in the *talanoaga* (as in a trial, it seems important in a *fono* to specify "who did what").

Oratory style. From mostly *homiletic* ("reinforcement of what is already known"; cf. Firth 1975: 42) in the *lāuga*, the oratory becomes also *persuasive* and *manipulative* in the *talanoaga* (see Firth 1975 for these categories).

Forms of reference. Whereas in a *lāuga* only titles are used to refer to people who are *matai*, in a *talanoaga* it is also possible to hear, at times, somebody's untitled name being used next to his title. This fact probably relates to a shift from *lāuga* to *talanoaga* with respect to the opposition "title: individual." In the introductory, ceremonial speeches, reference is made to titles as historical mythical figures that have a life of their own, independent from the specific persons who hold those titles at any given time. In the *talanoaga*, instead, along with the recall of some more recent, specific event, people show an interest in other people's actions, and in their individual identities.

Talanoaga in and out of the Fono

The differences between *talanoaga* in a *fono* and outside the *fono* are more or less captured by the description of the *fono* verbal interaction given in the previous section. Despite the fact that the *talanoaga* in a *fono* shares some features with more informal verbal interaction (e.g., a few expressions typical of casual talk, question-answer pairs, some "stories"), it is still very different from what is usually considered a conversation, a chat. Thus, we could say that the *talanoaga* in a *fono* is a type of speech that shares many features with the *lāuga*, but it tends toward more colloquial Samoan — without, however, ever completely coinciding with the way people would interact in casual conversation.

Lāuga in the Fono and Lāuga in Ceremonies

Despite the fact that the *lāuga* in the *fono* and the *lāuga* performed in ceremonies share some very basic common features, they are also different in some respects. The common features of *lāuga* in the two contexts have to do mostly with the structure of the speech, its lexicon, and sequential organization.

There is a basic structure that a *lāuga* must qualify for. Some variations are allowed (either personal or contextual). A *lāuga* has a certain number of "parts" (*vaega*): (1) *folasaga* or "introduction"; (2) *'ava*, "kava'" (3) *fa'afetai*, "thanksgiving"; (4) *pa'ia*, "dignity of the chiefs"; (5) *taeao* (literally, "morning"), "recount of important events in the history of Samoa"; (6) *'auga o le aso*, "reason for gathering"; (7) *fa'amatafi lagi* (lit., "clearing of the sky"), "wishes of good and long life." Despite some variations across different speechmakers and on different occasions, some parts are mandatory and follow the order given here (e.g., the *pa'ia* may come after the *taeao*, but a speech must end with the *fa'amatafi lagi*; the *folasaga* may be left out, but every *lāuga* must contain the *fa'afetai*, or "thanksgiving to God").

Each of the above-mentioned parts is made out of an arbitrary number of expressions, mostly metaphors, taken from a very rich corpus transmitted orally over the centuries from one generation of *matai* to the next.

Differences between Lāuga in Ceremonies and Lāuga in Fono. Eleven major differences between *lāuga* performed in a ceremony and *lāuga* performed in a *fono* are described in the accompanying list. The data on the *lāuga* in ceremonies consist of transcripts of two different kinds of ceremonies (an exchange of dowry and bridewealth and an installation of new *matai*), participant observation of several other ceremonial encounters, and interviews with speechmakers in the village on the content and significance of the speeches.

(CEREMONY):

1. Before the *lāuga*, there is a debate (called *fa'atau*) among the orators present, in order to decide who will give the speech. This discussion may be a pure formality lasting only a few minutes, or a very long and complex negotiation.

2. The number of *lāuga* is known beforehand (usually the two parties, e.g., hosts and guests, deliver one speech each).

3. The one who delivers the *lāuga* must be a recognized, skillful (*poto*) speechmaker (this is guaranteed by the fact that he was good enough to win the debate at the beginning — see item 1).

4. People later evaluate the "beauty" of the speech, its form (see Keenan 1974 for a compatible Malagasy example).

5. The speech performance usually represents an agreement of some sort.

6. The speech is usually addressed to a subgroup of the village's *matai* and families.

(FONO):

1. There is no debate. Orators who wish to speak sit in the front row, usually one orator for each subvillage.

2. The number of *lāuga* may vary, according to two factors: (a) how many subvillages are represented in the *fono*; (b) whether the chairperson decides to start the discussion immediately after the first *lāuga*.

3. The one who delivered the *lāuga* for a given subvillage may not be a particularly skillful speechmaker. He must be powerful enough to be allowed to sit in the front row with the higher-ranking orators.

4. The *lāuga* is not talked about subsequently. There is much less emphasis on the act as a display of oratorical skills.

5. The *lāuga* is a prelude to a possible confrontation. Agreement among the different parties may or may not be reached.

6. The speech is addressed to the entire village, or even to the entire district. This is symbolized by the enunciation of the full version of the ceremonial address (*fa'alupega*), which mentions all the important titles.

7. The speechmaker may be formally interrupted (*seu*) at a certain (relatively predictable) point, and he may have to shorten his speech (e.g., to stop the speechmaker from mentioning genealogies (*gafa*), which should not be recited publicly).[13]

7. The speechmaker cannot be formally interrupted, although he may actually be stopped for a number of reasons.

8. Once the speech is over, no parts are added or repeated. It is assumed that speechmakers do not make mistakes, or that his mistakes cannot be repaired by others.

8. If the speechmaker has not mentioned the agenda of the day (or has not done so properly), the chair of the meeting may ask him, after the speech is over, to "repair" by announcing the agenda (or doing it in more precise terms.

9. No specific part of the speech is dedicated entirely to the fuller version of the ceremonial address to the village.

9. A specific and fundamental part of the speech is dedicated to the ceremonial greeting to the village (see item 6).

10. The speech is usually delivered in a very distinct voice quality and in high volume.

10. The voice quality is similar only at times to that of the *lāuga* delivered in a ceremony. The pitch and the volume are not as high.

11. There is compensation for the speechmaker (e.g., money, a fine mat).

11. There is no compensation for the speechmaker.

All these differences can be accounted for by considering two factors: (1) the focus of the event in which the *lāuga* is being delivered and (2) the role of the *lāuga* in the event. In fact, not only are the speeches different in different social events, but speakers'/participants' expectations with respect to the speech also vary from one event to another.

A ceremony marks a change in somebody's status; it is a rite de passage, e.g., from unmarried to married, from untitled to titled (*matai*), from alive to dead (a funeral ceremony). The ceremony both represents and *is* that change of status.[14] Someone in the community enters in the event with one status and emerges with another. In the case of an exchange of dowry and bridewealth, or in the case of an investiture of a new chief, the ceremony is the public announcement of an agreement that has been reached by two or more parties (e.g., two families, different lines in the descent groups). Such an announcement takes its verbal form in the *lāuga* that will be delivered. The village will know from that speech that those two families are now related or that a certain man has become a chief, a "sacred" person. A ceremonial *lāuga* says all of these things, and more. It goes back in time to the eternal values of the community, to the names of the sacred and mythical figures of the ancestors who founded the village or the whole country.

The ceremonial *lāuga* is the most sophisticated form of verbal art in Samoa. It is the time for the best speechmakers to display their eloquence, their knowledge, their skills. The *lāuga* in a ceremony is the socially recognized domain of "performance" par excellence, in the sense in which this dimension has been defined by Bauman (1977: 11):

performance as a mode of spoken verbal communication consists in the assumption of responsibility to an audience for a display of communicative competence....Performance involves on the part of the performer an assumption of accountability to an audience for the way in which communication is carried out, above and beyond its referential content. From the point of view of the audience, the act of expression on the part of the performer is thus marked as subject to evaluation for the way it is done, for the relative skill and effectiveness of the performer's display of competence.

With respect to these characteristics, the *lāuga* in a *fono* differs from a ceremonial *lāuga*. There is no real competition over who should deliver the speech; people do not usually comment on the speech after the event is over; there is no immediate compensation for the speechmaker. *Lāuga* in the *fono* do not stand on their own. They are a prelude to something else. Their role is to define the event as a political one, to greet the assembly, and to prepare the atmosphere for the more important and difficult moments to come, namely, the debate and confrontation among the *matai* about some particularly important issue. The *lāuga* itself, in a *fono*, is not the focus not the climax of the social event. While the speechmaker routinely enunciates those very same expressions that are characteristic of a *lāuga* in a ceremony, people around him are hardly listening; they cannot enjoy his performance, because they are concentrating on what will come next, preparing themselves psychologically for the discussion, thinking of their speech (*talanoaga*), of the position that they should take, and the consequences of leaning more on one side or the other.

It is then the nature of the speech event, its social and cultural significance, that determines the form, meaning, and the connotations of a *lāuga*. Within the same genre, namely the *lāuga*, variation is not only possible, but expected, to fit the needs of the participants in the event.

Conclusions

In this chapter, I have discussed several ways in which the speech event may constitute a "frame" for performing and interpreting a particular speech genre. In the *fono*, the meetings of chiefs and orators in a Samoan village, both the organization of verbal interaction and the particular kind of language that is used by the participants are very distinct from what goes on in conversation among the same individuals (before the *fono* starts, and even more different in other social situations). The turn-taking rules are different, the lexicon is specially suited for talking "about" *matai* and "to" *matai*. Different terms and expressions are used for differentiating among statuses and ranks of the people addressed or referred to. Even the morphology and syntax of the language exhibit some distinctive characteristics. All these facts make the event and the people who participate in it very special, different from other events and from other individuals in the community. Within the event itself, however, native (competent) speakers differentiate between two speech genres: *lāuga* and *talanoaga*. Early in this section I discussed the native criteria for such a distinction; I also pointed out some other differences that can be found once the native distinction has been clarified.

In the rest of the chapter, I show that the terms used for this important distinction in the *fono* speeches (*lāuga* and *talanoaga*) also refer to speech genres found outside the *fono*. However, a *lāuga* in a *fono* differs from a casual conversation or discussion outside a *fono*. We need, then, the event as a "frame" to interpret these genres in each case. Finally, I provided a list of several important differences between a *lāuga* in a *fono* and a *lāuga* in a ceremony. I also discussed those differences and explained them on the basis of the different nature of the social event in which they are performed. In so doing, I employed the notion of "verbal art as performance" in the sense suggested by Bauman (1977). I showed that, despite their structural similarities, the *fono lāuga* and the ceremony *lāuga* are performed by the speechmaker and perceived by the audience in a different way. The social and cultural significance of the event (*fono* vs. ceremony) was used to explain the differences. The social event is thus a "frame" for performing and interpreting speech.

Appendix: Transcripts of verbal interaction among *matai* (1) before and (2) during a *fono*. Figures in parentheses indicate length of pauses in seconds.

(1)   (Transcript of April 7, 1978. Before starting the *fono,* senior orator M (Moe'ono)
      inquires about where the other senior orator (Iuli) is.)

M: *'A fea le makua //* (o le   )?
      Where is the matua //(   )?
                          ((*Finishing his greetings to the assembly*)) *makua*
                                                                   (to the) *matua*
      ma kagaka o le Kui Akuua.
      and the people of the King of Atua.
      (0.3)

M: *'O fea Iuli?*
      Where (is) Iuli?
      (1.2)

C: *'E ma ke le'i feiloa'i a a'u ga usu mai ā le loku.*
      We didn't meet. I got up early (to) go to church.
      Sau ai a.
      (Then) I came here.
      (1.8)

M: *'A'o i (ai) ō?*
      But is (he) over there?

C: *Ke lē iloa fo'i?*
      (I) don't know (about that) either.
      (2.0)

D: *Le iai.*
      (He) is there.
      (1.0)

D: *A loku gei.*
      (He's) at church now.
      (0.5)

M: *Mm.*

E: *I ai, Iuli?*
      who: Iuli?

D: *Mm.*

F: *Sa loku.*
      (He went to) church.

(2)   (Second speech on January 25, 1979. One orator has just given a *lāuga*, and the
      senior orator, Moe'ono, who is chairing the meeting, opens the discussion).
      ((*Long pause*)

M: *Ia fa'amālō fekalai Kaofiuailoa. (3.0) Ua 'e fa'amakagi le*
    Congratulations for your speech K. (3.0) You have opened
    aofia ma le fono. (2.0) ma ua 'e momoli fo'i le kākou
    the meeting. (2.0) and expressed also our
    fa'afekai i le oga le malosi 'uma lava.
    thanksgiving to the One who has all the powers [= God].
(2.0) (Unidentified speaker)
?: *Mālie!*
?: *Mālie!*
M: *Kau ia iga ia fa'afofoga lo kākou Makai, (1.2) fesoasoagi*
    May our Lord listen to us (1.2) (and) help
    mai iā 'i kākou 'o Akua fa'alelalolagi ma kākou vaivaiga.
    us, the gods on the Earth [= matai] and our weaknesses.
    (3.0) A 'o legei kaeao ma le aofia ma le fogo, (1.5) ia ua ala
    But this morning (in) this meeting (1.5) (we) express
    fo'i mai i le lagi mamā ma le soifua maua 'Āiga ma Aloali'i
    also our wishes for a healthy life to the chiefs
?: *Mālie!*
?: *Mālie!*
M: *Ala mai fo'i i fagugalelei le kōfā i le Makua legā ma*
    (we) also express the same to the senior orator here and
    le kākou 'a'ai.
    to the orators of our village.
    (1.5)
I: *Mālie!*
M: *Kākou vi'ia le Akua i mea aupiko aluga.*
    We praise God for the highest accomplishments.
?: *Mālie!*
?: *Mālie! lava!*
?: *Mālie!*
M: *'O sā ma faiga o Moamoa ((the name of the village malae)) o legā*
    The sacred names of Moamoa, your highness K, has
    Ua pa'i i ai lau kōfā Kafiloa.
    already mentioned.
T: *Mālie!*
M: *'Ae o le kakou aofia ma le fogo, (0.8)*
    But as for our meeting (0.8)
    (0.8)
M: *O le 'ā fa'auso loa.*
    The discussion will be started now.
?: *Mā//lie!*
M: *Auā e lē 'o se fogo o le kī ma le kolo.*
    Because this is not a *fono* with an extremely serious matter.
?: *Mālie!*
M: *Leai o le fogo- (2.0) o lo kākou kofi faipule o lo kākou*
    No. It's a *fono* about our representative (to the Parliament)
    ikū ma Lufilufi.
    for our district.

Notes

An earlier version of this paper was presented at the 1979 Annual Meeting of the Linguistic Society of America and was published as Sociolinguistic Working Paper Number 72 by the Southwest Educational Development Laboratory, Austin, Texas. I wish to thank Richard Bauman, Edward Finegan, Professor G. B. Milner, and Bradd Shore for some very helpful comments on the earlier drafts.

The research on which this paper is based was partially supported by a National Science Foundation Grant (No. 53-482-2480 – Elinor Ochs, principal investigator) and by the Consiglio Nazionale delle Ricerche in Rome, Italy. While writing this paper I was supported by the Linguistics Department of the University of Southern California.

I would like to thank my wife Elinor Ochs for her constant support and constructive criticism during our fieldwork and thereafter. Many people in the village where we were living and conducting our research project helped us in may different ways and made our work and our participation in the village life possible. In particular, I wish to thank Rev. Fa'atau'oloa Mauala and his wife, Sauiluma, who accepted our research group as part of their family and helped us throughout our whole experience. I also learned a great deal about Samoan language and culture from several chiefs and orators in the village, who shared with me their knowledge and experience of the *fa'a Sāmoa*. In particular, I would like to thank Iuli Sefo, Lua Veni, Savea Savelio, and Tula'i Tino.

Transcription conventions: I have used standard Samoan orthography, in which the letter "g" stands for a velar nasal (/ŋ/), the apostrophe (') for a velar stop (/?/), and the macron on a vowel (as in ā, ē, ī, etc.) for "long vowel." Samoan exhibits two phonological registers, one in which there is an opposition between /t/ and /k/, and /n/ and /ŋ/, and one in which only /k/ and /ŋ/ are used (cf. Duranti 1981; Duranti and Ochs 1984; Shore 1982, Milner 1966). I have used the standard convention of adopting the first register (with "t" and "n") for words out of context, in their citation form. Transcripts of actual verbal interaction are instead done according to the actual pronunciation adopted by the speakers.

In the transcripts I have used mostly the conventions of "conversation analysis" (see Appendix in Sacks, Schegloff, and Jefferson 1974). The double solidus (//) indicates the point at which the speaker's talk is overlapped by another participant's. This convention is usually accompanied by a long single bracket at the point of overlap, with the utterance of the intervening party placed beneath. Words between parentheses indicate that I was not sure of the transcription. Empty parentheses indicate that no reasonable guess was possible. Some information about the context is put within double parentheses (( )). I have also used parentheses in the English translation to mark linguistic information that is not overtly available in the Samoan utterance. Brackets are used, at times, for conveying some extra information on some of the terms used by the speakers, if they need a particularly "rich" interpretation.

1. Bateson says that "a frame is metacommunicative. Any message, which either explicitly or implicitly defines a frame, *ipso facto* gives the receiver instructions or aids in his attempt to understand the messages included within the frame" (Bateson 1972: 188; cf. also Goffman 1974).

2. The characteristics of the *fono* that I will describe are the ones that I have observed in *one* village (Falefā). I am aware of the fact that a certain degree of variation should be expected from one village to another or from one island to another. Only further research in other locations in the country (in addition to the literature already available, cf. Freeman 1978; Shore 1982) will provide the necessary basis for a detailed comparative analysis of *fono* in Samoan society.

3. In Falefā, there are two special titles, called *matua* (translated by Samoans themselves as "parents," although the word for "parents" has a long *a*, *mātua*), which give their holders some special status "in between" or "beyond" the traditional distinction between orator (*tulāfale*) and chief (*ali'i*). Although they are referred to as *tōfā*, the term used for orators, they share several of the chiefs' privileges. In a *fono* one of the two *matua* chairs the meeting, and they both seem to have enough prestige and authority to publicly order or scold high-ranking chiefs (cf. Duranti 1981; Shore 1982; Keesing and Keesing 1956).

4. The "front" of the house is established on the basis of an external point of reference, namely the road or the *malae*, depending on the way the house is built and the place in the village where it is located.

5. The first round of speeches in the *fono* is always the same, and it follows a rule that says something like "one speech from each subvillage, in the following order, first..." The number of subvillages may vary, from four (the minimal number) to seven, or even more if the entire district gets together.

6. I am using here the pioneer work by Sacks, Schegloff, and Jefferson (1974; Schegloff, Jefferson and Sacks 1977) as a fundamental point of reference in my account of Samoan turn-taking. The points I am illustrating here are only a few, and a more detailed analysis of Samoan turn-taking across social situations is in progress.

7. Before starting to talk, speakers may signal their intention to talk by a readjustment of their body posture and a clearing of their voices. They may also look at any other potential speaker for the next turn, trying to spot any signs that would indicate that person's intention to speak next. There is also a verbal cue that signals a person's decision to speak and affirms his intention to hold the "vacant" floor (i.e., *ua*, "so, well," followed by a brief pause).

8. Cf. Bauman (1977) for further references to several works on parallelism in different contexts and across different cultures.

9. In different kinds of meetings, it may be possible to find t/n-pronunciation.

10. The category "native speaker" is, in fact, too broad here, given that many native speakers in the community may not be able to make such a distinction. It would be more accurate to say "a subgroup of the adult population, roughly coinciding with the *matai* of the village."

11. In reading a transcript of a *fono*, a native speaker (e.g., an orator) may spend some time analyzing a certain speech before being able to say whether it was or was not a *lāuga* "strictly speaking." The identity of the speechmaker can sometimes be a cue. Only the holders of certain titles can actually perform a *lāuga* in a *fono*; others cannot. The first group roughly corresponds to orators (*tulāfale*), the second to chiefs (*ali'i*) and the two senior orators (*matua*).

12. If the senior orator who chairs the meeting speaks as a second, he will open the discussion (*talanoaga*), and therefore there will be no more *lāuga*. If he lets another orator from his subvillage speak after the first speech, then all the subvillages that are

represented in the *fono* must give a *lauga* before his turn will come again to open the discussion.

13. On the taboo against mentioning genealogies in Samoa cf. Freeman 1964.

14. As suggested to me by Edward Finegan (personal communication), a distinction may have to be drawn here between ceremonies that are "performatives" (in Austin's sense) and ceremonies that are public recognitions of something that has actually already happened. The installation of a chief may be an example of the first kind and a funeral of the second.

9. Three Perspectives on Role Distance in Conversations between Tongan Nobles and Their "People"

George E. Marcus
Rice University

And we must be prepared to see that in societies with settled inequalitarian status systems and strong religious orientations, individuals are sometimes less earnest about the whole civic drama than we are, and will cross social barriers with brief gestures that give more recognition to the men behind the mask than we might find permissible.

Erving Goffman
The Presentation of Self in Everyday Life (1959: 245)

In Tonga, as in other Polynesian societies with kingships and elaborate chiefly hierarchies, certain tensions in the cultural definition of chieftainship as a societal institution are variously registered at the situational level in the negotiation of a chief's identity among different constituencies. The structural phenomenon of hierarchy is contingently produced in the way that the dual character of any chief as title holder and being of inherent, extraordinary quality is situationally recognized by others. Part of any chief's status derives from his mystified place in a hierarchy, the content of which is an elaboration of kingly glory at its pinnacle. But, there is also a populist dimension to a chief's position — especially middle-level chiefs away from king and court and "out there," so to speak, among his people — that depends on his ability to "pass" as one of them. He is both "of the people" — an exemplar of the most widely shared qualities of personhood in the society — and "for the people — a living symbol of chiefly title and substance through which the stature of his people is condensed and displayed but that originates in the kingship that has alien and mystified associations for them. The negotiation of the chief's identity as both an ordinary and an extraordinary being among his people in the immediacy of casual social situations and the unintended consequences of such microlevel politics of the situation for societal political structure is the concern of this chapter.

Contrary to my impressions from a prefieldwork reading of the early literature on Tonga — historically, one of the most stratified of Polynesian societies — I repeatedly observed instances in which contemporary nobles attempted with varying degrees of success to hold their nobility apart, as it were, and to engage unselfconsciously in ordinary conversation with commoners. These instances occurred most typically in the context of informal kava-drinking sessions on a noble's estate or at his town residence in which he and members of his *kāinga*, "estate population,"[1] were present. In comparison with Maurice Bloch's focus on political oratory in chiefdoms (1975), I am concerned with a kind of backstage arena in a society noted for its chiefly ceremonials.[2] Bloch distinguishes formalized speech events from informal ones (1975: 24), but he does not mention situations where persons whose high status is normally marked in ceremonial contexts are outside their element, as it were, and lack the same kinds of support for their performances in the presence of social inferiors that they enjoy on formal occasions. On formal occasions, physical avoidance, oratorical language, mediating attendants, strict rules of protocol, preexisting ideological mystification of high status, and the possibility of substantive sanctions for inappropriate behavior are all devices that make ritual peformances conform to the fiction of a predictable game, the limits of which high-status persons believe they control or in which their status identity is unproblematic. As Bloch showed, flexibility and creativity, involving knowledge of protocol, define the restricted politics of such situations.

In contrast, on culturally unmarked, definitively casual occasions, in which spontaneous, ad hoc communication rather than avoidance or protocol is appropriate, the superordinate positions of high-status persons are often acknowledged by others present, but without the masking or mystification of their qualities as persons, which is otherwise redundantly achieved in formal contexts. Here, the politics of the situation concerns an ambiguity about the definition or attribution of high status itself, which precipitates a metalevel process of reassessing personal situational identities as conversations develop.

Goffman has provided a conceptual model of the general sociological phenomenon of role distance (1961: 85 – 152), which will help us to understand the dynamic in Tonga between chiefly status and personhood in situations of casual conversation. According to this model, the initiative in communication is with the high-status person, who typically stimulates a condition that Goffman calls role distance: "the individual is actually denying not the role but the virtual self that is implied in the role for all accepting performers ... for the special facts about self that can be conveyed by holding a role off a little are precisely the ones that cannot be conveyed by throwing the role over" (108). Often, role distance is triggered by a joking self-diminution by the superordinate person, that is, by a half-serious attempt to pass downward.

Goffman seems to overemphasize the control by the high-status person over what precisely is communicated in his initiated role distancing. In Tonga it is probably more appropriate to see role distancing on one level as a tentative, probing process involving the negotiation of an undetermined identity for the high-status person, the noble, in which he is interested in *new* information about where he stands and is uncertain of exactly to what extent his attempt to pass down will be successful. For Tongan nobles, the ability to chat unselfconsciously (*talanoa*, literally "no account talking") in kava-drinking sessions with commoners is the linguistic medium by which the relative discrepancy between a noble's chiefly person and office is mutually established and reestablished for himself and his *kāinga*.

In the epigraph to this chapter, Goffman suggests that the role concept of Western sociology (which his work innovatively transforms) may not be relevant as a means of describing relationships in some non-Western societies. Tonga is certainly one of these. Whereas role playing may be a comfortable way of viewing interactions for Western social scientists as well as for some Western natives, the notion of a self, disembodied from requirements of performance across contexts, is an understood but awkward distinction for Tongans to make. In contemporary Tonga — and to some degree in precontact Tonga — chiefs cum titled nobles have been among the few persons who have born a burden of role playing akin to the Western sense (ministers and some government officials are others in the modern context who saliently play roles). This does not apply to all chiefs but only to those below a certain threshold of status, the mystique of whose chiefly substance (sino'i 'eiki, "chiefly body," in the sense of a chief's blood or composition as a person) is ambiguous enough to contrast with chiefly conduct, that is, the formal aspects of playing a chiefly role. As will be discussed in the next section, this ambiguity applies to most contemporary nobles. For them, title holding is situational role playing; and being a chief, which entails a situationally marked difference between chiefly substance and conduct, imposes a considerable load on interaction in a society that, now more than ever, gives "more recognition to the man behind the mask than we might find permissible," as Goffman says. The experienced problems for Tongan nobles is to overcome situationally given chiefly separation and to become known unambiguously *in the context of the interaction* as "full-bodied" persons with some degree of chiefly substance by those on whom they depend for various kinds of instrumental support.

The remainder of this chapter views the phenomenon of role distance in conversations between nobles and their estate *kāinga* from three interrelated perspectives. First, on the most immediate level of psychocultural orientations to social relations, role distance is the behavioral manifestation of experienced discomfort for a noble in mediating situationally the fact of his a priori separation from whatever group of status inferiors among whom he moves and the fact that he is known intimately as a person by his *kāinga*, who, in their lifelong association with him, are thoroughly familiar with his biography.

Second, on the level of a more self-conscious, manipulative politics of the occasion, role distance may be seen as a set of metacommunications between the noble and others present, directed toward establishing the style and tone of the noble's participation in casual talk and, by so doing, indexing the mutually perceived composite standing of the noble as a chiefly person and title holder. For his part, the noble engages in a first hand, personal experiment, where, in a tentative manner, he probes to see how he will be perceived as a person. Beyond sensitivity to feedback, he may also actively attempt to persuade his *kāinga* audience to accept him as he wishes to be perceived from moment to moment and from occasion to occasion by manipulating the conditions of role distance that his presence initiates. However, such manipulation is risky to the noble's self-esteem, as is the entire phenomenon of role distance, since he has only partial control over how he will be assessed; *kāinga* members exercise perhaps the critical leverage in setting the tone of the noble's integration as a participant in their kava talk.

This perspective reduces the complexity of role distance as a process to an interpersonal politics, focused on a gamelike exchange of interests between noble and *kāinga* about how their situation of interaction should be defined. It assumes that their talk is motivated, to varying degrees of consciousness, by the actors' calculating self-interest. In this case, the definition of the situation is keyed to the noble's performance as conversationalist, in which a message about the perception of the noble's chiefly status and his authenticity as a person among his supporters is at stake.

Third, on the more abstract level of societal political organization — as distinct from the linguistically mediated situational politics of participants — role distance events are consequential for the continuing vitality of a vestigial, feudal-like system of nobility in Tonga, despite severe legal constraints and the considerable erosion of traditional supports for it. From this perspective, role distance can be seen as one process of legitimation, which facilitates the noble's use of his restrained position of privilege on his estates as a viable resource, sustaining a claim to elite status in contemporary Togan society.

These levels represent aspects of a situation that are interwoven and that operate simultaneously; here they are artifacts of analysis, distinguished for the convenience of exposition. However, before proceeding, I wish to amplify an argument that will run through the following discussions. The situational fixing of a genre style of casual speaking simultaneously indexes the noble's composite chiefly standing or reputation and establishes the conventionality of his person in role distance. The interpersonal politics of the situation arises from the negotiation of a level of collective recognition of the noble's reputation, but his reputation as a chief, relative to ideal criteria, is of less consequence for the vitality of societal hierarchy in Tonga than the political instrumentality accorded him merely by his ability to interact with ease among his constituency in appropriate contexts. The strength of the nobility as an elite is thus founded on the ability of title holders, who reflect a diversity of outcomes as to their perceived chiefly standings, to achieve a psychocultural integration as persons/conversationalists in face-to-face relations with their *kāinga*.

Psychocultural Factors in the Manifestation of Role Distance among the Contemporary Tongan Nobility

The Tongan nobility consists of thirty-three hereditary titles, including those of the royal family, which are passed from father to eldest son. These titles are all that were exempted from the late-nineteenth-century dismantling of the old chiefly order by Tupou I's legal and far-reaching substantive reformation of Tongan society. Formal privileges and landed estates are associated with each title, but with severe restrictions on the economic and administrative powers of nobles over their patrimonies. These restrictions were imposed in the interest of the secure political centralization that the Tupou monarchs had established under British protection (ending in 1970).

However much the body of noble titles became the most visible and permanent locus of chiefship in modern Tongan society, historic chiefly association, widespread among the population and traceable in origin before the new regime, did not disappear. Also, other traditional criteria of chiefship, more important than title holding, survived. These are based on a mystique of chiefly body or substance (expressed as *sino*, "body," or *toto*, "blood"), derived from demonstrable close personal kinship with the present kingly line or from important historic linkages to the now defunct line of sacred kings, the Tu'i Tonga. Most historic chiefly associations do not have much continuing substantive importance in contemporary Tonga. They are revived situationally and

on ceremonial occasions, which have little influence over events outside their bounds. However, the superior criterion of chiefly status by
substance or embodiment rather than by mere title holding is of critical
importance for nobles and how they are perceived as chiefs by different
audiences. I have discussed the complex permutations of chiefly status
in modern Tonga elsewhere (Marcus 1977, 1978b: 18 – 73), but it is
important to note here that only a few nobles embody sufficiently
unambiguous substance as chiefs such that their inherent differences
are in harmony with, or even overshadow, their holding of chiefly office.
A few others are clearly common men without chiefly substance who
happen to hold noble titles. The remainder, which is the majority and
the segment of the nobility of interest here, are formally separated from
the commoner population by their titles and offices but are of ambiguous chiefly substance, which is variantly perceived and evaluated by
the different constituencies among whom such nobles interact.[3]

While the aura of chiefship in the form of beliefs about the power of
chiefs as uncommon individuals with special license or capacities has
waned in modern Tonga, only those nobles above a certain threshold
can depend on their redundantly supported criteria of chiefship by
blood and title to make face-to-face encounters with status inferiors
unproblematic. Since such beings are more totally separated from
commoners, and since they are more completely masked by mystique
than other nobles, what they say and do on informal occasions is largely
irrelevant to defining them as persons. In a sense, their presence makes
an informal occasion effectively formal. Below this threshold of separation, experienced by high aristocrats and the kingship, nobles are
confronted with the situational negotiation and fixing of their identities
as persons in the shadow of chiefly roles that may or may not be seen
to fit the outcome of this process. They may be unsuccessful at unselfconscious *talanoa* and thus find themselves regarded near the
threshold of high aristocracy. Or, by settling into unselfconscious *talanoa* and being acknowledged as thoroughly ordinary beings, they may
establish themselves as common men among their *kāinga*, distinguished only by the holding of titles.

The central concern of a noble is not, however, how his chiefly status
is perceived but how well he can take part in smooth social interaction,
thereby identifying himself as a member of his community of origin.

Being unproblematically integrated into social relations is the sine qua non for the assignment of any situational or societal political significance to the noble's act of role distance. Unless a noble is one of those few persons in Tongan society conceived as a different manner of being, his good reputation and fund of personal credit among his people depend on their ease of interaction with him, regardless of the level at which his chiefly status, matched against ideal criteria, comes to be generally recognized by them.

There is a general relationship in Tonga between engaging unselfconsciously in ordinary conversation (*talanoa*) and a male's integration as a person into a community. Such integration depends upon his "mind/personality" (*anga*) being known with immediacy as well as upon a corresponding sense that he "fits with" (is *maheni* with) his living environment — both qualities realized, in part, through being an ordinary conversationalist. It is precisely chiefly role playing that makes such psychocultural integration a special problem, manifested in role distance, for a noble.

At the most basic phenomenological level, the noble is separated from interaction in the presence of status inferiors simply because his (titled) chiefliness must be acknowledged as elevated position, which is important in defining the situation for others, independent of his status as a person of more or less chiefly substance. When any noble appears on a scene, interactions among those present are notably restructured toward some degree of ritualization. This occurs most clearly in the activity of kava drinking, which is the common setting of sociality among men in Tonga. There are different levels of kava formality, the most ritualized being the royal kava and the least ritualized being the informal kava, where spontaneous conversation among status coequals occurs. Routinely, the appearance of a noble transforms an informal kava among commoners into a setting of ritual actions focused on him, which inhibit and frame the flow of conversation. Often, the noble's presence marks an occasion for others without any verbal participation on his part. Once I saw a noble abruptly leave a kava session, which disrupted the mood and flow of discussion keyed to the noble's presence; his silent, nonchalant exit noticeably bothered the others who remained, leaving them off balance and momentarily disoriented.

This effective isolation in the role of context maker for a situation can be a very uncomfortable and lonely circumstance, which limits a noble's rapport with commoners. He has no room to express himself freely or to maneuver as a full participant in such relationships. Role distancing and an attempt to engage in unselfconscious *talanoa* constituted a noble's claim, first and foremost, to personhood, that is, to having his person, separate from his title, acknowledged and then assessed as to its chiefly substance by different audiences. How chiefly role playing variantly affects the noble's smooth integration in social relations may be examined by brief discussion of two relevant, systematic dimensions of a noble's life: stages of his personal development and, as an adult title holder, his contexts of speech activity.

Before he succeeds to his title and during his later life the circumstances of a noble's personal separation are different from his mature, adult period as title holder. The youthful noble heir apparent more easily integrates with his fellows during the liminal *talavou*, "male adolescence" period (see Marcus 1978a: 256–59) than during any other time of life. Most status distinctions are suppressed during this period, and while consciousness of the heir's future title holding is clearly evident (his leadership and privileged position among *talavou* are perceptible), it is very much in the background. Like other *talavou*, he is relatively free to establish a conventional personal reputation that follows him into adulthood. Thus, by the time he succeeds to the title and becomes a formal context maker, a noble has already been known more intimately as a particular kind of person during his *talavou* career. Yet, he is now at a disadvantage among his *kāinga*, who are usually familiar with his past biography, in not being able to continue to express himself as a person. He is instead isolated by a context-transforming dimension of himself from which he can never be completely disassociated. It is in this sense that chiefly role playing is generally recognized among Tongans, but it is also seen as burdensome and an obstacle to communication for persons who play it. To what extent a noble's *talavou* reputation will reemerge during his adulthood of title holding depends on outcomes of role distancing and the noble's long-term reaction to such periodic feedback.

As an old man, the noble takes on the characteristics associated with male aging — weakness of body and mind — that, analogous to the earlier *talavou* period, integrates him once again with shared, common characteristics of being Tongan, irrespective of rank. Consequently, in aging, the extent of separation experienced in a noble's adulthood naturally tends to decline. In old age, title holding becomes an advantage in softening the embarrassment of declining competence as a person, but role distancing is no longer so much triggered or encouraged by the noble as being manifestly given. In fact, the one elderly noble whom I observed took every opportunity to close the given situational gap between his title and his presence as an aged person so that as an integrated chief and person he might be taken seriously, despite his age.

Separation for the title holder, who is neither definitively *talavou* nor *motu'a*, "old one," varies primarily with distinct contexts of speech activity on which his ability to validate his personhood depends. On one extreme, there are the most formal of contexts; for example, royal kava ceremonies, where the noble's participation is precisely defined, and if not programmed into the ritual, he avoids any ad hoc speaking. Instead, oratory is the task of *matāpule*, "ceremonial attendants," who represent nobles and sit at their sides. Each noble recruits his own *matāpule*, and although their titles are hereditary, *matāpule* serve actively at the pleasure of each succeeding noble.[4]

On the other extreme, there are the most informal and familiar of contexts — those of domesticity and close family relations in which the protocol of kinship takes priority over protocol keyed to distinctions of chiefly status. Tonga has an interesting kinship system that is uniform for all personal kindreds and family groups in the society, but it is a domain of indigenous conceptualization distinctly separate from matters of chiefly status. What is important is how a chief extends and withdraws recognition of membership within the sphere of his close kinsmen, an issue that it is not necessary to pursue here. A noble's verbal and nonverbal communication with his close kin in domestic settings is primarily affected by who they are in relation to him as a kinsman, rather than as a title holder.

Between these two extremes is the area with which we are concerned, and only with a single but important part of that area: the noble in relation to his estate *kāinga*. The noble normally escapes verbal communication in this middle range of interaction by a conscious strategy of physical avoidance. This is particulary true of his avoidance, outside ritual contexts, of other nobles of ambiguous relative chiefly rank to himself or of commoners with recognized high chiefly associations. Alternatively, a noble's interactions are situationally mediated by a third party, such as a *matāpule*, who speaks for himself. This is normally the case on marked ritual occasions, but also in the formality and etiquette that the noble precipitates wherever he is present.

Any failure of avoidance or mediation to protect a noble from unexpected public interactions leads to visible mutual discomfort and embarrassment among those interacting. Such accidents are even more common nowadays in the crowded conditions of Nuku'alofa and in the course of noble participation on government boards and committees. It is only in the presence of his estate *kāinga* in this middle range of speaking contexts that a noble cannot escape (nor for the sake of building support and control over his primary resource, his estates, does he wish to escape) frequent interaction with those in a fixed but inferior relation to himself. While he is the focus of formal occasions on his estate, and much of his conversation with his *kāinga* is mediated for him, he must nonetheless do considerable "public relations" work on his own, in which he attempts to integrate himself into casual group situations as an ordinary person. This exposes the discrepancy of his substance and formal position to face-to-face interaction and evaluation.

Role Distance as a Process of Establishing a Noble's Status Identity during Kava-drinking Sessions on Estate Visits

Most nobles live in the capital or regional towns of Tonga and visit their estates only periodically. I lived on two estates where their respective nobles were absentees, but periodically made visits, each lasting two to four weeks. These visits were carefully orchestrated affairs on both sides. A resident noble does have a different kind of relationship with his people than does a visiting one, merely by the fact of his residence and what it signifies — a difference I have discussed elsewhere (see Marcus 1978b: 83 – 85). The resident noble, who is usually retired from active participation in elite affairs, focused in the capital, or who suggests by his estate residence a marginal, socially backward position among the nobility, develops a less separated daily existence in relation to his *kāinga*. In contrast, the visiting noble, whatever his stature in town, can elaborate his office and personal status on visits with a good deal of prearranged pomp and circumstance. Because the visiting noble is the more typical case in contemporary Tonga, and because the problem of a visiting middle-range noble in defining his identity among his *kāinga* is more sharply elaborated and more episodic in occurrence than that of a resident noble, I develop the rest of this discussion with a non-resident noble on periodic estate visits in mind.

When a noble visits his estate, direct interactions with his people are mediated in different ways by middlemen, who represent him on his estate both when he is present and absent. These include the town officer, who handles general arrangements for a visit; the noble's *matāpule*, who speak for him during particular planned ritual events such as funerals, feasts, and welcoming kava ceremonies; and often, the local minister of the Wesleyan church, to which most nobles belong. Yet, often during a noble's visit, or reciprocally, when a group from his estate visits him in town, a noble is present in a setting where casual social intercourse is overwhelmingly appropriate and chiefly formalities are painfully awkward. These invariably occur in households, where men, seated in a circle, drink kava, prepared by unmarried women, especially invited to perform this task. Such sessions punctuate and parallel various routine village functions. For example, during village work days, older men spend the entire day drinking kava as they watch younger men labor and while women are involved in food preparation. Prior to Sunday church services, notables of the congregation regularly gather at the minister's house for a brief session of kava drinking. In addition, nightly kava-drinking sessions, often lasting until daylight, are the most common male pastime in Tonga. In all these kava settings, the process of kava preparation and distribution is unmannered, and conversation is unrestrained but low-key. Stories are told, news related, and controversies aired, but the latter rarely take the form of heated debates.

During his visits, out of goodwill and interest, a noble frequently appears at such kava sessions, and he often hosts nighttime gatherings wherever he is staying in the village. Moreover, any repeated avoidance by the noble of such settings would be criticized by his *kāinga*. It is during these occasions of casual kava *talanoa* that the noble deals with the challenge of role distancing as an index of his standing with his *kāinga*.

The noble's attempt to *talanoa* and pass downward goes beyond its immediate psychocultural circumstance to a much more motivated and self-conscious act in these settings. The noble is, in fact, probing the limits of his separation in all its dimensions on such occasions to gain maximum feedback concerning how he is perceived in his chiefly role. In doing so, he, at the same time, exposes and clarifies for his evaluating *kāinga* audience an identity as a being of some mix of chiefly substance and common personhood within the formality of office-holding. Sliding into self-conscious *talanoa*, playing at it, or being excluded from it totally are outcomes the consequences of which will be discussed in the next section.

On a more Machiavellian level, the capacity to pass smoothly in ordinary conversation on his estate has an additional benefit for a noble, which might make him view role distancing as a conscious technique of political craft. Not only does the relaxed kava reveal the noble as an integrated person/chief to his *kāinga*, which can only increase his credit among them, but it also gives the noble, who can thoroughly pass, firsthand inside information about what is happening on his estates, which he would otherwise learn only indirectly from his middlemen, or by reading signs through the formality that routinely defines situations of interaction with his *kāinga*. Despite the fact that some may be inhibited in a variety of ways in *talanoa* when the noble is present — as they might also be when he is not present — he nonetheless stands to gain a range of varied information about the people and events on his estate through the gossip and conversations of kava sessions. Once taken for a coequal conversationalist, the noble can spend long periods of silence as a passive, interested listener, without a focus of attention upon himself (incidentally, the fieldworker benefits from the same passive anonymity after an initial, more active period of at first polite, and then less self-conscious, speaking during a long kava session).

Two Ethnographic Examples

This section intersperses a discussion of role distance as situational process with two examples, drawn from my fieldwork data. Both concern nobles who attempt to immerse themselves in casual conversation, but only one of whom achieves this integration, while the other's efforts to pass downward are effectively rejected by his coconversationalists. The discussion and examples are focused upon the early part of the action in kava sessions, when the group sets the tone and resolves in some way the challenge to the definition of the situation by the presence of a noble and his role-distancing behavior. The discussion of the role distance events for each of the examples will be presented in composite form, summarizing what I perceived as the role distance style of each noble, after having observed them numerous times in kava sessions during their estate visits.[5]

Before proceeding, some background information on each example is necessary. Noble X holds a title of relatively little importance historically, but his genealogy on the maternal side links him peripherally to the royal kindred and endows his person with some measure of inherent chiefly substance. He has spent most of his life in the capital and is a relative stranger to his estate *kāinga*, on whom he nonetheless makes regular demands through intermediaries. On estate visits, he displays self-conscious generosity, in making feasts, in giving large church contributions, and in resolving land alloction disputes. During kava sessions, he practices a highly self-conscious role distancing, forgoing formalities, such as ranked seating and the order of serving kava, to an extent that embarrasses village middlemen, who derive their own prestige from their service to him.

Noble Y holds a title of historic importance but has no recent genealogical linkages to the dynastic line. He was born and raised among his estate *kāinga*, and succeeded to the title only because the previous holder, to whom he had a collateral tie, had no heir. He now lives in the capital but makes regular and lengthy visits to his estate, where he maintains a residence. On his estate, noble Y seems to expect a marked offering of deference in his everyday dealings with his *kāinga*, but he mercurially slips in and out of a chiefly role according to context and whim. In contrast to noble X, he does not seem so self-conscious about being consistently authoritative and generous in most relations with his *kāinga*. Likewise, in nightly veranda kava sessions during his visits, he clearly distances himself from chiefly formality, but makes no show of it, as does noble X.

Goffman (1967) notes that the superordinate person in a setting has the prerogative of both initiating and timing role distance and that the fundamental definition of the situation, in which the context-marking presence of the distanced role "remains in charge," is never overtly challenged in what happens within the frame of the situation itself. Verbal play, wit, and joking interjected at will by the superordinate participant is the mechanism, which Goffman notes as commonly triggering role distance. It also keeps role distance under the superordinate's control and pacing (Goffman's examples mostly concern medical contexts, involving doctors in the presence of patients and staff). Although a noble indulges in joking and self-effacement in the course of conversation, as a natural part of sustained participation in a kava session, the actual triggering of role distance is usually a more formal act. Such an act makes those present aware that however far the noble may be accepted as a person — and this remains to be established — the normal formalities of a noble's kava should be forgone. Thus, the ritualizing effects on a setting of his formal position must be overcome in some direct way as an opening gambit. Most often, the noble works with a *matāpule*, who is present with him, in achieving this initial explicit statement that the person of the noble is to be more exposed to interaction than is his office. The *matāpule* usually cues the gathering by means of a simple statement (more or less a command) that the special procedures of the noble's kava will be forgone or else will be done in a modified, relaxed form.

Following this opening, the noble is initially more vocal than others, and also more of a center of attention, but eventually, he finds himself in a position, if he wishes it, as listener and occasional speaker during a session that can last several hours. In the noble's initial remarks, there is often a noticeable element of "speaking down" to his audience. In telling a story, the noble seems to appear more animated and high-pitched in his voice than is usual either for himself or for others. However, it is difficult to distinguish patronization in this talk from a kind of uneasy probing to break the given formality, which is motivated by the noble's discomfort in role playing. Regardless, the politics of the situation is in the group's collective adjustment to the opening verbal presentation of self by the noble. It is critical whether the noble's stories go over smoothly, whether he is listened to without noticeable signs of deference, whether his comments about another person's remarks stimulate or suppress further comments, and whether those present are able to avoid status competition among themselves by mutually currying favor with the noble. These issues are sorted out in a give and take underlying initial kava talk, whereby it is determined to what degree the kava will be affected by the noble's presence.

Upon entering the kava circle, noble X takes the central position but instructs his *matāpule* to forgo the ritual commands by which kava is made and distributed in the presence of a chief. He urges a government civil servant, visiting his native village, to move and sit beside him, but the man refuses, and the noble ridicules him by asking if the center of the circle is not good enough for him. The civil servant remains silent and expressionless, his face turned to one side. Another man asks polite questions of the noble about conditions in the capital. The noble answers each question enthusiastically and at length. At the first long break in the conversation, the noble makes detailed comments, in storytelling form, about what he has seen in the village during his visit, but no one responds to his observations in any detail. The kava session lasts three hours, and the noble remains a center of attention or reference during the entire period. He initiates discussions; discussions are initiated with reference to him; or he offers what becomes the final comments on others' conversations. To me, the talk seemed less intimate, bawdy and wide-ranging in local subject matter when the noble was present than when most of the same men drank kava in the noble's absence. Yet, while marked politeness toward the noble, a hesitancy to get too involved in topics of local interest, and a constant marking of the noble's presence in the drift of the conversations were all apparent in the situation, no one seemed ill at ease or self-conscious about his participation. Following this session, I was told that noble X made onerous demands on his people, but he was a very suitable representative of them in the wider society. Although not considered very knowledgeable or poised by his people, he was nonetheless felt to be *maheni*, "in harmony with," them.

Noble Y holds frequent kava sessions at his estate residence, and there seems to be a tacit assumption of informality when *kāinga* members attend these sessions. Nonetheless, a newcomer to the circle waits shyly outside the noble's yard until he is directly invited by the noble or his *matāpule* to join the circle. The noble dominates the first part of the kava with intimate, half-ridiculing, half-affectionate stories about persons and happenings in the village. There is considerable laughter, and some variant interpretations to these stories are offered, some of which subtly contradict the noble's version or mildly ridicule him in return. When the noble tires of talking, he seems to depend on his *matāpule* or the town officer to shift attention away from him by their encouraging others to speak. During the five-hour session, the noble occasionally interjects a comment or a question; he leaves briefly on three occasions; he drifts off to sleep several times, as do others; and he conducts numerous low-voice side conversations. Noble Y does not again dominate the session until the very end, when he asks his *matāpule* to conclude the sessions with a formalized round of kava, prepared and served according to command. This noble customarily concludes kava sessions with such formality. While he was resident, no one really spoke of the noble as a distinctive personality, separate from his office. Only when the noble was absent did people discuss his chiefly demeanor—how well he represented them (about which there was much disagreement). During his residence, people were aware of the presence of his office and how it rearranged their activities, but he was a conventionalized person in the daily life of the village—one with whom they could be at ease.

Most nobles are never completely and unselfconsciously able to immerse themselves in *talanoa*. Achieving such absolute distance might be disconcerting to a noble if he did not expect it, since it would signal that he is perceived as a completely ordinary person who happens to hold a chiefly office. The advantage of such an extreme outcome is the minimal effect of a noble's presence on the information that he might gain as a full participant in the kava — he achieves maximum relative anonymity and benefits from knowing at first hand what goes on among his *kāinga*.

At the other extreme, complete failure of the noble to *talanoa* unselfconsciously and to achieve anonymity as a participant — that is, to experience a constant frustration of his attempt to distance himself from the role by exorcising deferential speech from the situation — may indicate the *kāinga's* perception of a noble as of high chiefly substance, signaled by the strict limits on his capacity to be an ordinary person among them. The cost of such chiefly elevation is a decline in the richness and detail of inside information that the noble could otherwise gain as a situationally defined coequal.

The efforts of noble X to engage conventionally in ordinary conversation were largely frustrated. This is not because he tried too hard, which he did, or because he was in fact a stranger to his *kāinga*, but rather because such a level of integration was just not perceived as appropriate by those with whom he conversed. He was very clearly perceived to be someone of chiefly substance behind his title. Nonetheless, it is just as important to understand that, despite his separation both as person and title holder, the mere initiation of role distance did serve to authenticate noble X as a person, with whom his *kāinga* could be at ease situationally, however chiefly his person was perceived to be.

Noble Y engages with relative ease in ordinary conversations with his *kāinga*, partly because of his familiarity with their lives (and vice versa), and partly because he had no obvious genealogical criterion qualifying him as a person of chiefly substance — so much so that, while not marking the initiation of role distance as much as assuming it, noble Y insisted on a ritual closing of kava sessions that reaffirmed his chiefly separation, insuring that role distancing would never go too far.

Most occasions that I witnessed were between the extremes of the noble's complete relative success and failure to distance himself by participating in *talanoa*. The regard in which a noble is held and the corresponding quality of his relationship with his *kāinga* can subtly change over time. While it is difficult to know precisely why such cumulative changes occur, role distancing is the most revealing experiment by which the noble can periodically register the state of his integrated person among his *kāinga* and, at the same time, actualize it for all present (including the fieldworker).

Finally, the noble's role distancing can be viewed as similar to a classic case of the double bind but that does not remain a dilemma, governing a situation, because a choice between conflicting options is not being forced. Rather, the double bind is in the constitution of the situation itself. The inherent contradiction of a noble among status inferiors who are not quite kin but with whom he is intimately associated precipitates a level of interaction and conversation that informs the noble who is among his *kāinga*, and strengthens their mutual relationship as the basis for giving a chiefly vestige political and economic substance in contemporary Tonga.

Consequences of Role Distance for the Substantive Position of the Nobility as an Elite in Tongan Society

Quite apart from the quality of relationship that a noble is able to sustain with his *kāinga* through a history of face-to-face encounters, nonetheless they both have an a priori relationship, defined mutually by the fact that a noble title and its estates are an immense personal resource of the individual possessing them. Ideally, the noble's person and title should be one — a mutually reinforcing source of honor and prestige, which collectively represents a people in the society at large through the noble's performance of ritual tasks in relation to the kingship. When the noble is viewed as their symbolic representative, there is usually a total cooperation with him as well as a careful evaluation of conduct by his *kāinga*. However, when a noble attempts to exploit his estates as a personal resource, in which he makes various decisions and requests affecting life on his estates, his *kāinga* is much more circumspect and tentative in offering support. Also, it is when the noble is most clearly acting in his own interests that his *kāinga* are likely to be most sensitive to any discrepancy between the status of his title and the status of his person.

The noble is limited in his prerogatives, with his major local leverage being the power to distribute any unclaimed land on his estates. To maneuver beyond this leverage, a noble must have established considerable credit with his people. This is accomplished, not through any continuing leadership function, but rather through the identity the noble is able to establish as person in casual interaction with members of his *kāinga*.

The broader political significance of the situations discussed in this chapter concerns the manner in which what political theorists label legitimacy is created for a noble among his hereditary constituency. The political and economic force of chiefship in modern Tonga—filling the anemic shell of nobility that is restrained by law, by the greater importance of church organization, and by a centralized monarchy— depends on the creation of such legitimacy. The fact that a mild form of feudal relationship continues to be a substantive resource for modern nobles is a puzzle that can be suggestively addressed by an understanding of how the quality of relationship between a noble and his people is defined through settings such as the kava sessions previously discussed.

As has been demonstrated, role distance derives neither from a patronizing hubris nor from a sense of humility by the noble; rather, it is the noble's reflexive way of clarifying in terms appropriate to Tongan psychocultural organization the blocking of immediacy in relationships, caused by the burden of playing a role. This immediacy is an indispensable dimension of any relationship that also might have instrumental, practical dimensions.

Regardless of the relative degree of his success at immersing himself in the kava session — whether he is perceived as a man of high chiefly substance or just an ordinary person—the noble achieves an authentic personal relationship with his *kāinga* on which a long-term, mutually self-interested relationship is sustained. As long as middle-range nobles are able to define themselves personally to their people in such kava sessions, even the most demanding and exploitative nobles in modern Tonga have a fund of credit, which brings submission. Once the noble's personal limits in relation to his people are known by them, he is *at those limits* an integrated chief for them. This intimate knowledge gives a certain predictability to a noble's actions, which permits a *kāinga* to develop a high tolerance in complying with demands that nonetheless may be felt to be exploitative.

There is a great variety of reputations among contemporary Tongan nobles, but I have not been concerned with why one noble is considered excessive and another kindly, both of which are judgments based, not on a noble as an isolated individual, but as a known person in relation to his *kāinga*. Rather, I have been concerned with the contexts in which a noble could be known sufficiently well by status inferiors to have a defined personal reputation at all. Also, I have been equally concerned with why, given restraints on the office, middle-range nobles have remained political factors in modern Tonga. The development of hereditary advantages as actual resources, based on the exploitation of people and land, requires the repeated exploration by a noble of the contours of his identity in a society where chiefship has been considerably demystified during the twentieth century. This exploration occurs most routinely as a function of the noble's being present at informal kava sessions during estate visits.

In any such session, what is simultaneously at stake is the noble's psychocultural integration as a conventional person in the flow of Tongan social relations and a collective expression or register of his aura as a chiefly person among his people. As an unintended consequence or cumulative outcome of the situational micropolitics that arises from the immediacy of negotiating the trade-off between the noble's conventional presentation of self and his degree of chiefly aura, an aspect of societal macro politics also becomes established. The effective interactional balance of communal identity and aura helps provide nobles the social resources for public display and legitimation of the nationwide hierarchy with the king at its apex. It is this third level of societal consequence that distinguishes situational politics in Oceanian societies with elaborate chiefly hierarchies from those in societies that can be characterized as egalitarian, where the politics of the situation is more transparently the politics of the society.

Notes

Reprinted, with some changes, from the *Journal of the Polynesian Society*, 1980. 89(4) : 435–453. By kind permission of the publisher.

1. *Kāinga* for any ego is a loose category of reference, encompassing all those related to one by attribution of kinship; that is, one's kindred. The special use of the term in

connection with a noble refers to his people, that is, the population resident on his estate. In this usage, the term is generally considered to mean the population of the estate from which the noble himself originates and only those among the population who are themselves considered to be natives of the estate. In practice, the term is used flexibly to cover all populations of a noble's estates and all residents of them, however long-standing. The important point for this chapter is that whereas a noble is clearly separate from his *kāinga* in its special sense, the term also carries with it a connotation of common descent, by which the noble is a member of his estate *kāinga* as a generalized, elevated kinsman. Nobles who are not sufficiently mystified by a high status as chiefly persons (i.e., sharing blood and substance with royal descent line) in the eyes of their *kāinga* experience most acutely the ambiguity of simultaneous separation from, and commonality with, their *kāinga*.

2. There are ceremonial occasions in Tonga—even rites of inversion superficially akin to role distancing — for which Bloch's remarks about formalized communication are relevant, but it is important to distinguish the everyday life scenarios, discussed in this chapter, from them. During the course of fieldwork, I was impressed with a lack of fit between ritual and everyday life, recurrent scenarios. Nobles carry the ritual marking of events with them, but the negotiation fo the noble's personal identity, intruded upon the casual activities of his estate *kāinga*, is quite different from ritual repertoires and what they mean in contemporary Tongan society. One can retrieve an elegant structuralist account of Tongan culture merely by focusing on the complex rituals that are still performed or by manipulating cultural categories out of their historical context, but such an account would be a poor guide, for example, to gauging what chiefship means in a society where it has been thoroughly demystified over the past century. The historically sensitive understanding by contemporary Tongans of their traditional institutions is perhaps most difficult to grasp in the analysis of cultural productions, which are ossified repertoires. Rather, it is most easily investigated on the margins or in the interstices of such productions — in Goffman's terms, in the backstage region of performance, such as the noble's attempt to *talanoa* in the shadow of his title.

3. This chapter presumes to deal only with contemporary Tonga—what I observed of nobles as a fieldworker. During the past century, there has been a clear demystification of the qualities associated with chiefly status, and it is in terms of this historical development that the frequent occurrence of role distancing is so interesting. However, my impression is that the literature on Tonga, which has been predominantly concerned with aboriginal conditions, highly overrates the mystique of chiefs as a pervasive and widespread routine phenomenon. Much of the early contact literature, which is the primary source of later scholarly work, dwells on chiefs at the apex of society or with chiefs on marked ritual occasions. These are both foci where evidence of situational chiefly mystique, at least judging by modern traces, would have been the greatest. This is not to say that Tongan chiefship in general did not have more substance and therefore more mystique in the old order but only that, if present conditions are any indication of past ones, "middle-range" chiefs, like most modern nobles, experienced the same status bind between their formal separation as titled chiefs and their ambiguous personal chiefly status, which required them to step away from their roles and conform in speech and act to more generally shared standards of personal behavior.

4. A note is in order here on the relative development of oratorical skills among the nobility and others. Nobles themselves are rarely called upon to speak publicly, and what oratory of nobles I was able to observe (mostly at funerals and feasts during estate

visits) was rather undistinguished and forced. Especially on royal occasions, strikingly creative, if not poetic, oratory is displayed by *mātapule* rather than by middle-range nobles, who receive little or no training in traditional skills as young men. In contrast to nobles, commoners typically have the opportunity to develop modest oratorical skills in the course of church participation, where speech-making has been most routinely developed in modern Tonga. Men participate regularly as *malanga* "lay preachers," in local congregations and have occasions to speak formally at feasts and other church-related functions. Not as rich as classic oratory in chiefly defined contexts, church-related oratory constitutes basic training that prepares Tongans for their speaking per-formances associated with life-stage events such as births, marriages, and deaths. On two estates where I resided, nobles rather uncharacteristically served as *malanga*. Their sermons were undistinguished compared with those of other members of the congre-gations. Here, as elsewhere, chiefly separation hinders the noble's social competence, rather than marking a role with special performance requirements through which ora-torical skills might be developed.

5. In this chapter I refrain from extreme microanalysis, which has been one of the strengths of sociolinguistic research. Rather, I remain analytically one level above a focus on the content of in-context speech acts, with a focus instead on the conditions that precipitate and encompass a particular genre of speaking—*talanoa*—in special circum-stances. Candidly, I would be hard pressed to do a fine-grained analysis of the many ordinary conversations between nobles and commoners that I heard, since I recorded no actual conversations, nor can I reconstruct them in a way that would make com-mentary on specific utterances a critical support for my arguments. Still, the important point for our purpose here is the extent to which the tacit definition of the situation becomes one of ordinary conversation in kava settings where a noble is present as a speaker/participant.

Bibliography

Abrahams, R. D., and R. Bauman
    1977   "Sense and Nonsense in St. Vincent: Speech Behavior and Decorum in a Caribbean Community." *American Anthropologist,* 73 : 762–72.

Abrams, M. H.
    1957   *A Glossary of Literary Terms.* New York: Holt, Rinehart & Winston.

Adriani, N., and A. C. Kruyt
    1950   *De Bare'e-sprekende Torajas van Midden-Celebes.* 2d ed. rev. Amsterdam: Noord-Hollandsche Uitgevers Maatschappij.

Albert, E. M.
    1972   "Cultural Patterning of Speech Behavior in Burundi." In J. Gumperz and D. Hymes, eds., *Directions in Sociolinguistics: The Ethnography of Communication.* New York: Holt, Rinehart & Winston.

Aristotle
    1954   *Rhetoric and Politics.* New York: Modern Library.

Arno, Andrew
    1976   "Joking, Avoidance and Authority: Verbal Performance as an Object of Exchange in Fiji." *Journal of the Polynesian Society* 85 : 71–86.
    n.d.   "Impressive Speeches and Persuasive Talk: Traditional Patterns of Political Communication in Fiji's Lau Group from the Perspective of Pacific Ideal Types." Paper presented at the ASAO Symposium on Language and Politics in Oceania, 1980.

Atkinson, Jane Monnig
    1979   "Paths of the Spirit Familiars: A Study of Wana Shamanism." Ph.D. diss., Stanford University.
    1983   "Taking Tucks in the Sacred Canopy: The Construction of an Indonesian Minority Religion." *American Ethnologist* 10(4).

Aufenanger, H.
    1962   "Sayings with a Hidden Meaning." *Anthropos* 57 : 325–35.

Basso, Keith H.
    1979   "'Wise Words' of the Western Apache: Metaphor and Semantic Theory." In K. Basso and H. Selby, eds., *Meaning in Anthropology.* Albuquerque: University of New Mexico Press.

Bateson, Gregory
    1972   *Steps to an Ecology of Mind.* New York: Ballantine Books.

Bauman, Richard
    1977   *Verbal Art as Performance.* Prospect Heights, IL: Waveland Press, Inc.
Bauman, Richard, and Joel Sherzer, eds.
    1974   *Explorations in the Ethnography of Speaking.* London: Cambridge University Press.
Bauman, Richard, and Joel Sherzer
    1975   "Ethnography of Speaking." *Annual Review of Anthropology.* Vol. 4. B. J. Siegel, ed. Palo Alto: Annual Reviews.
Becker, A. L.
    1979   "Text-Building, Epistemology, and Aesthetics in Javanese Shadow Theatre." In A. Becker and A. Yengoyan, eds., *The Imagination of Reality.*
Becker, A. L., and A. Yengoyan, eds.
    1979   *The Imagination of Reality.* Norwood, N.J.: Ablex.
Beidelman, Thomas O.
    1963   "Terms of Address as Clues to Social Relationships." In A. W. Gouldner and H. P. Gouldner, eds., *Modern Sociology.* New York: Harcourt, Brace & World.
    1974   *W. Robertson Smith and the Sociological Study of Religion.* Chicago and London: University of Chicago Press.
Bernstein, Basil
    1971   *Class, Codes and Control.* Vol. 1. London: Routledge & Kegan Paul.
Black, Peter W.
    1982   "Conflict, Morality and Power in a Western Caroline Society." *Journal of the Polynesian Society* 91.
Bloch, Maurice
    1971   "Decision Making in Councils among the Merina of Madagascar." In A. Kuper and A. Richards, eds., *Councils in Action.* Cambridge: Cambridge University Press.
    1975   "Introduction." In M. Bloch, ed., *Political Language and Oratory in Traditional Society.* New York: Academic Press
    1977   "The Past and the Present in the Present." *Man* 12 : 278–92.
Bloch, Maurice, ed.
    1975   *Political Language and Oratory in Traditional Society.* New York: Academic Press.
Bloch, Maurice, and Jean Bloch
    1980   "Women and the Dialectic of Nature in Eighteenth-Century French Thought." In C. MacCormack and M. Strathern, eds., *Nature, Culture and Gender.* Cambridge: Cambridge University Press.

Blom, Jan-Petter, and John Gumperz
    1972   "Social Meaning in Linguistic Structures: Code-Switching in Nor-
           way." In J. Gumperz and D. Hymes, eds.

Borker, Ruth
    1980   "Anthropology: Social and Cultural Perspectives." In S. Mc-
           Connell-Ginet, R. Borker, and N. Furman, eds., *Women and Lan
           guage in Literature and Society*. New York: Praeger.

Bourdieu, Pierre
    1976   *Outline of a Theory of Practice*. Cambridge: Cambridge Univer-
           sity Press.

Brash, E. T.
    1971   "Toki Pilai, Tok Piksa Na Tok Bokis: Imaginative Dimensions in
           Melanesian Pidgin." *Kivung* 4 (1) : 12 – 20.

Brennan, P.
    1970   "Enga Referential Symbolism: Verbal and Visual." In P. Brennan,
           ed., *Exploring Enga Culture*. Wapenamanda: Kristen Press.

Brenneis, Donald
    1974   "Conflict and Communication in a Fiji Indian Community." Ph.D.
           diss., Harvard University.
    1978   "The Matter of Talk: Political Performances in Bhatgaon." *Lan-
           guage in Society* 7 : 159 – 70.
    1979   "Conflict in Bhatgaon: The Search for a Third Party." In Subra-
           mani, ed., *The Indo-Fijan Experience*. St. Lucia: University of
           Queensland Press.
    1980   "Strategies of Offence Choice: Malice and Mischief in Bhatgaon."
           Canberra Anthropology 3 (2) : 28 – 42.

Brenneis, Donald, and R. Padarath
    1975   "'About Those Scoundrels I'll Let Everyone Know': Challenge
           Singing in a Fiji Indian Community." *Journal of American Folk-
           lore* 88 : 283 – 91.

Brown, P., and G. Buchbinder, eds.
    1976   *Man and Woman in the New Guinea Highlands*. Washington:
           American Anthropological Association.

Brown, Penny, and S. Levinson
    1978   "Universals in Language: Politeness Phenomena." In E. N. Goody,
           ed., *Questions and Politeness: Strategies in Social Interaction*.
           Cambridge: Cambridge University Press.

Brown, Roger
    1958   *Words and Things*. Glencoe, New York: The Free Press.

Burke, Kenneth
    1966   *Language as Symbolic Action*. Berkeley: University of California
           Press.

Cavell, Stanley
    1966   "The Availability of Wittgenstein's Later Philosophy." In G.
           Pitcher, ed., *Wittgenstein*. New York: Anchor Books.
Chung, Sandra
    1978   *Case Marking and Grammatical Relations in Polynesian*. Austin:
           University of Texas Press.
Clastres, Pierre
    1974   *Society against the State*. New York: Urizen Books.
Cohn, B. S.
    1967   "Some Notes on Law and Change in North India." In P. Bohannan,
           ed., *Law and Warfare*. Austin: University of Texas Press.
Collier, Jane
    n.d.   "Marriage, Women's Work and Social Stratification among Plains
           Indians" (MS).
Collier, Jane, and Michelle Rosaldo
    1981   "Politics and Gender in Simple Societies." In S. Ortner and H.
           Whitehead, eds., *Sexual Meanings*. Cambridge: Cambridge Uni-
           versity Press.
Comaroff, John
    1975   "Talking Politics: Oratory and Authority in a Tswana Chiefdom."
           In M. Bloch, ed.
Conley, J., W. O'Barr, and E. Lind
    1978   "The Power of Language: Presentational Style in the Courtroom."
           Duke Law Journal: 1375 – 99.
Cook, Kenneth
    1978   "The Mysterious Samoan Transitive Suffix." Proceedings of the
           Fourth Annual Meeting of the Berkeley Linguistic Society.
Crocker, J. Christopher
    1977   "The Social Function of Rhetorical Forms." In J. D. Sapir and
           J. C. Crocker, eds.
Douglas, Mary
    1966   *Purity and Danger*. London: Routledge & Kegan Paul.
    1983   Talk presented at Stanford University, Graduate School of Busi-
           ness.
Duncan, Starkey
    1972   "Some Signals and Rules for Taking Speaking Turns in Conver-
           sation." *Journal of Personality and Social Psychology* 23 : 283 –
           92.
Dundes, Alan, Jerry Leach and Bora Özkök
    1972   "The Strategy of Turkish Boys" Verbal Dueling Rhymes." In J.
           Gumperz and D. Hymes, eds.
Duranti, Alessandro
    1981   *The Samoan Fono: A Sociolinguistic Study*. Pacific Linguistic
           Series B, vol. 80. Canberra: Australian National University.

Duranti, Alessandro, and Elinor Ochs
  1984   "Literacy Instruction in a Samoan Village." In B. B. Schieffelin,
          ed., *Acquisition of Literacy: Ethnographic Perspectives.* Nor-
          wood, N.J.: Ablex.
Empson, W.
  1964   *The Structure of Complex Words.* London: Chatto & Windus.
Evans-Pritchard, E. E.
  1940   *The Nuer.* Oxford: Clarendon.
  1962   *Essays in Social Anthropology.* London: Faber & Faber.
  1967   "The Morphology and Function of Magic: A Comparative Study
          of Trobriand and Zande Ritual and Spells." In J. Middleton, ed.,
          Magic, Witchcraft, and Curing. Garden City, N.Y.: Natural History
          Press.
Evens, T. M. S.
  1977   "The Predication of the Individual in Anthropological Interac-
          tionism." *American Anthropologist* 79 : 579–97.
Ferguson, C. A.
  1959   "Diglossia." *Word* 15 : 325–40.
Fernandez, James
  1977   "The Performance of Ritual Metaphors." In J. D. Sapir and J. C.
          Crocker, eds.
Firth, Raymond
  1975   "Speech-Making and Authority in Tikopia." In M. Bloch, ed.
Fisher, L.
  1976   "Dropping Remarks and the Barbadian Audience." *American
          Ethnologist*, 3 : 227–42.
Fortune, Reo
  1933   "A Note on Some Forms of Kinship Structures." *Oceania* 2 : 1–9.
Foster, G.
  1972   "The Anatomy of Envy: A Study in Symbolic Behavior." *Current
          Anthropology* 13 : 165–86.
Frake, Charles O.
  1963   "Litigation in Lipay: A Study of Subanun Law." Proceedings of
          the Ninth Pacific Science Congress. Vol. 3. Bangkok.
  1972   "'Struck by Speech': The Yakan Concept of Litigation." In J. Gum-
          perz and D. Hymes, eds.
  1977   "Plying Frames Can Be Dangerous: Some Reflections on Meth-
          odology in Cognitive Anthropology." *Quarterly Newsletter of the
          Institute for Comparative Human Development* 1(3) : 1–7.
Freeman, Derek
  1964   "Some Observations on Kinship and Political Authority in Sa-
          moa." *American Anthropologist* 66 (no. 3, pt. 1): 553–68.
  1978   "A Happening Frightening to Both Ghosts and Men: A Case Study
          from Western Samoa." In N. Gunson, ed., *The Changing Pacific:*

Essays in Honour of H. E. Maude. Melbourne: Oxford University Press.

Fried, Morton
 1967 *The Evolution of Political Society.* New York: Random House.
Friedrich, Paul
 1979 *Language, Context, and the Imagination.* Stanford: Stanford University Press.
Garfinkel, Harold
 1967 *Studies in Ethnomethodology.* Englewood Cliffs, N.J.: Prentice-Hall.
Geertz, Clifford
 1973 "Thick Description: Toward an Interpretive Theory of Culture." *The Interpretation of Cultures.* New York: Basic Books.
 1974 "From the Native's Point of View." *Bulletin of the American Academy of Arts and Sciences* 28 : 221–37.
 1977 "Found in Translation." *Georgia Review* 4 : 788–810.
 1980 *Negara: The Theatre State in Nineteenth-Century Bali.* Princeton: Princeton University Press.
Gell, Alfred
 1975 *Metamorphosis of the Cassowaries.* University of London: Athlone Press.
Gewertz, Deborah
 1977 "From Sago-Suppliers to Entrepreneurs: Marketing and Migration in the Middle Sepik." *Oceania* 48 : 126–40.
 1981 "An Historical Consideration of Female Dominance among the Chambri of Papua New Guinea." *American Ethnologist* 8 : 94–106.
Gibbs, J.
 1967 "The Kpelle Moot." In P. Bohannan, ed., *Law and Warfare.* Austin: University of Texas Press.
Giddens, Anthony
 1976 *New Rules of Sociological Method.* New York: Basic Books.
 1979 *Central Problems in Social Theory.* Cambridge: Cambridge University Press.
Gilsenan, Michael
 1976 "Lying, Honor, and Contradiction." In B. Kapferer, ed., *Transaction and Meaning.* Philadelphia: ISHI.
Givón, Talmy
 1979 "From Discourse to Syntax: Grammar as a Processing Strategy." In T. Givón, ed., *Syntax and Semantics.* Vol. 12: *Discourse and Syntax.* New York: Academic Press.
Gluckman, Max
 1962 "Gossip and Scandal." *Current Anthropology* 4 : 307–15.

Godelier, Maurice
    1977   *Perspectives in Marxist Anthropology.* Cambridge: Cambridge
            University Press.
Goffman, Erving
    1959   *The Presentation of Self in Everyday Life.* New York: Doubleday.
    1961   "Role Distance." In E. Goffman, *Encounters.* New York: Bobbs-
            Merrill.
    1967   *Interaction Ritual.* Garden City, N.Y.: Doubleday.
    1969   *Strategic Interaction.* New York: Ballantine Books.
    1974   *Frame Analysis.* New York: Harper & Row.
Goody, Esther
    1978   "Towards a Theory of Questions." In E. Goody, ed., *Questions
            and Politeness.* Cambridge: Cambridge University Press.
Goody, Jack
    1977   *The Domestication of the Savage Mind.* Cambridge: Cambridge
            University Press.
Gossen, Gary
    1974   *Chamulas in the World of the Sun: Time and Space in a Maya
            Oral Tradition.* Prospect Heights, IL: Waveland Press, Inc.
Grimes, J.
    1972   "Outlines and Overlays." *Language* 48 : 513–24.
    1975   *The Thread of Discourse.* The Hague: Mouton.
Gumperz, John
    1977   "Sociocultural Knowledge in Conversational Inference." In M.
            Saville-Troike, ed., *Linguistics and Anthropology.* Washington:
            Georgetown University Press.
Gumperz, John, and Dell Hymes, eds.
    1972   *Directions in Sociolinguistics.* New York: Holt, Rinehart & Win-
            ston.
Halliday, M. A. K.
    1967   "Notes on Transitivity and Theme in English, Parts 1 and 2."
            Journal of Linguistics 3 : 37–81, 199–244.
Hallpike, C.
    1977   *Bloodshed and Vengeance in the Papuan Mountains.* London:
            Oxford University Press.
Harding, Susan
    1975   "Women and Words in a Spanish Village." In R. Reiter, ed., *Toward
            an Anthropology of Women.* New York: Monthly Review Press.
Hawkes, Terence
    1977   *Structuralism and Semiotics.* Berkeley: University of California
            Press.
Howe, James
    1977   "Carrying the Village: Cuna Political Metaphors." In J. D. Sapir
            and J. C. Crocker, eds.

Hymes, Dell
    1972   "Models of the Interaction of Language and Social Life." In J.
           Gumperz and D. Hymes, eds.
Irvine, Judith
    1974   "Strategies of Status Manipulation in the Wolof Greeting," In R.
           Bauman and J. Sherzer, eds.
    1979   "Formality and Informality in Communicative Events." *Ameri-
           can Anthropologist* 81: 773–90.
Jakobson, Roman
    1957   "Shifters, Verbal Categories and the Russian Verb." Department
           of Slavic Languages and Literature, Harvard University.
    1960   "Linguistics and Poetics." In T. Sebeok, ed., *Style in Language.*
           Cambridge: MIT Press.
    1968   "Poetry of Grammar and Grammar of Poetry." *Lingua* 21: 597–609.
Jameson, Fredric
    1972   *The Prison-House of Language.* Princeton: Princeton University
           Press.
Jayawardena, C.
    1963   *Conflict and Solidarity in a Guianese Plantation.* London: Ath-
           lone Press.
Jefferson, G.
    1972   "Side Sequences." In D. Sudnow, ed., *Studies in Social Interac-
           tion.* New York: The Free Press.
Kapferer, Bruce
    1976   "Introduction: Transactional Models Reconsidered." In B. Kap-
           ferer, ed., *Transaction and Meaning.* Philadelphia: ISHI.
Keenan, Elinor
    1974   "Norm-Makers, Norm-Breakers: Uses of Speech by Men and
           Women in a Malagasy Community." In R. Bauman and J. Sherzer,
           eds.
    1975   "A Sliding Sense of Obligatoriness: The Polystructure of Malagasy
           Oratory." In M. Bloch, ed.
Keenan, E., B. Schieffelin, and M. Platt
    1978   "Questions of Immediate Concern." In E. Goody, ed., *Questions
           and Politeness.* Cambridge: Cambridge University Press.
Keesing, F., and M. Keesing
    1956   *Elite Communication in Samoa.* Palo Alto: Stanford University
           Press.
Korn, Francis
    1971   "A Question of Preferences: The Iatmul Case." In R. Needham,
           ed., *Rethinking Kinship and Marriage.* London: Tavistock.
Kruyt, A. C.
    1930   "De To Wana of Oost-Celebes." *Tijdschrift voor Indische Taal-,
           Land-, en Volkenkunde* 70: 393–625.

Kuper, A., and A. Richards, eds.
   1971   *Councils in Action*. Cambridge: Cambridge University Press.
Leach, Jerry W., and G. Kildea
   1975   "Trobriand Cricket: An Ingenious Response to Colonialism." Pro-
           duced under the sponsorship of the government of Papua New
           Guinea.
Leacock, E., and R. Lee, eds.
   1982   *Politics and History in Band Societies*. Cambridge: Cambridge
           University Press.
Lederman, Rena
   1979   "On Being in Between: Women and Exchange in Mendi." Paper
           presented at the 1979 Meeting of the American Anthropological
           Association, Cincinnati.
   1981   "Sorcery and Social Change in Mendi." *Social Analysis* 8.
   1982   "Mendi Twem and Sem: The Social Relations of Production and
           Exchange in a Highlands Papua New Guinea Society." Ph.D. diss.,
           Columbia University.
Lee, Richard
   1979   *The !Kung San: Men, Women and Work in a Foraging Society*.
           Cambridge: Cambridge University Press.
Lévi-Strauss, Claude
   1967   "The Sorcerer and His Magic." *Structural Anthropology*. New
           York: Anchor Books.
Levy, Robert
   1973   *The Tahitians*. Chicago: University of Chicago Press.
Lutkehaus, Nancy
   n.d.   "A Constricting Web of Tradition: The Political Use of Language
           on Manam Island, Papua New Guinea." Paper presented at the
           ASAO Symposium on Language and Politics in Oceania, 1980.
MacCormack, Carol
   1980   "Nature, Culture and Gender: A Critique." In C. MacCormack and
           M. Strathern, eds., *Nature, Culture and Gender*. Cambridge: Cam-
           bridge University Press.
McKellin, W.
   1980   "Kinship Ideology and Language Pragmatics among the Mana-
           galase of Papua New Guinea." Ph.D. diss., University of Toronto.
McKinley, Robert
   1979   "Zaman Dan Masa, Eras and Periods: Religious Evolution and
           the Permanence of Epistemological Ages in Malay Culture." In
           A. Becker and A. Yengoyan, eds.
Malinowski, Bronislaw
   1925   "Magic, Science, and Religion." *Magic, Science, and Religion and
           Other Essays*. New York: Dutton.

1935   *Coral Gardens and Their Magic: Soil Tilling and Agricultural Rites in the Trobriand Islands*. Bloomington: Indiana University Press.

Marcus, George

1977   "Succession Disputes and the Position of the Nobility in Modern Tonga." *Oceania* 47: 220 – 41, 284 – 99.

1978a   "Status Rivalry in a Polynesian Steady-State Society." *Ethos* 6: 242 – 69.

1978b   *The Nobility and the Chiefly Tradition in the Modern Kingdom of Tonga*. Memoir No. 42. The Polynesian Society.

Mauss, Marcel

1967   *The Gift*. New York: W. W. Norton & Co.

Mead, Margaret

1930   *Social Organization of Manu'a*. Bernice P. Bishop Museum Bulletin 76. Honolulu.

Meggitt, M. J.

1964   "Male-Female Relationships in the Highlands of Australian New Guinea." In J. Watson, ed., *New Guinea: The Central Highlands*. *American Anthropologist* (Special Issue) 66 (no. 4, pt. 4).

1974   "Pigs Are Our Hearts." *Oceania* 44: 165 – 203.

Meillassoux, Claude

1972   "From Reproduction to Production." *Economy and Society* 1: 93 – 105.

Milner, G. B.

1961   "The Samoan Vocabulary of Respect." *Journal of the Royal Anthropological Institute* 91: 296 – 317.

1962   "Active, Passive, or Perfective in Samoan: A Fresh Appraisal of the Problem." *Journal of the Polynesian Society* 71: 151 – 61.

1966   *Samoan Dictionary*. London: Oxford University Press.

1973   "It Is Aspect (Not Voice) Which Is Marked in Samoan." *Oceanic Linguistics* 12: 621 – 39.

Mitchell-Kernan, Claudia

1972   "Signifying and Marking: Two Afro-American Speech Acts." In J. Gumperz and D. Hymes, eds.

Munn, Nancy

n.d.   "The Symbolism of Perceptual Qualities: A Study in Trobriand Ritual Aesthetics." Paper presented at the 1971 Meeting of the American Anthropological Association, New York City.

Myers, Fred

1979   "Emotions and the Self: A Theory of Personhood and Political Order among Pintupi Aborigines." *Ethos* 7: 343 – 70.

Nadel, S. F.

1957   "Malinowski on Magic and Religion." In R. Firth, ed., *Man and Culture*. London: Routledge & Kegan Paul.

Nader, Laura
    1969   "Styles of Court Procedure: To Make the Balance." in L. Nader, ed., *Law in Culture and Society*. Chicago: Aldine.

Ochs, Elinor
    1979   "Transcription as Theory." In E. Ochs and B. Schieffelin, eds., *Developmental Pragmatics*. New York: Academic Press.

Ortner, S., and H. Whitehead, eds.
    1981   *Sexual Meanings: The Cultural Construction of Gender and Sexuality*. Cambridge: Cambridge University Press.

Paine, Robert, ed.
    1981   *Politically Speaking: Cross-Cultural Studies of Rhetoric*. Philadelphia: ISHI.

Parlier, J.
    1964   "Managalasi Verb Inflecting." *Te Reo* 7: 28–35.

Quine, W. V.
    1960   *Word and Object*. New York: John Wiley & Son and MIT Press.

Rappaport, Roy
    1968   *Pigs for the Ancestors*. New Haven: Yale University Press.
    1971   "Ritual, Sanctity, and Cybernetics." *American Anthropologist* 73: 59–76.

Read, Kenneth
    1959   "Leadership and Consensus in a New Guinea Society." *American Anthropologist* 61: 425–36.

Ricoeur, Paul
    1971   "The Model of the Text: Meaningful Action Considered as a Text." *Social Research* 38.
    1978   "The Metaphorical Process as Cognition, Imagination, and Feeling." In S. Sacks, ed., *On Metaphor*.

Robertson, D. W.
    1974   "Ambunti Patrol Report Number 3." (MS).

Rosaldo, M. Z.
    1973   "I Have Nothing to Hide: The Language of Ilongot Oratory." *Language in Society* 2: 193–223.
    1975   "It's All Uphill: The Creative Metaphors of Ilongot Magical Spells." In M. Sanches and B. Blount, eds., *Sociocultural Dimensions of Language Use*. New York: Academic Press.
    1980   *Knowledge and Passion: Ilongot Conceptions of Self and Social Life*. New York: Cambridge University Press.
    n.d.   "The Things We Do with Words: Ilongot Speech Acts and Speech Act Theory in Philosophy." (MS).

Rosaldo, Renato
    1980   *Ilongot Headhunting, 1883–1974: A Study in History and Society*. Stanford: Stanford University Press.

Ruddle, Kenneth, et al.
    1974   *Palm Sago*. Honolulu: University of Hawaii Press.
Ryan, D'A.
    1959   "Clan Formation in the Mendi Valley." *Oceania* 24.
Sacks, H., E. Schegloff, and G. Jefferson
    1974   "A Simplest Systematics for the Organization of Turn-Taking for
            Conversation." *Language* 50: 696–735.
Sacks, Sheldon, ed.
    1978   *On Metaphor*. Chicago: University of Chicago Press.
Sahlins, Marshall
    1958   Social Stratification in Polynesia. Seattle: University of Washing-
            ton Press.
Salmond, Anne
    1975   "Mana Makes the Man: A Look at Maori Oratory and Political
            Language." In M. Bloch, ed.
Sapir, Edward
    1933   "Language." In *Encyclopedia of the Social Sciences*, 9: 155–69.
            New York: Macmillan.
    1970   *Culture, Language and Personality: Selected Readings*. Edited
            by D. Mandelbaum. Berkeley: University of California Press.
Sapir, J. David
    1977   "The Anatomy of Metaphor." In J. D. Sapir and J. C. Crocker, eds.
Sapir, J. David, and J. C. Crocker, eds.
    1977   *The Social Use of Metaphor*. Philadelphia: University of Penn-
            sylvania Press.
Schegloff, E., G. Jefferson, and H. Sacks
    1977   "The Preference for Self-Correction in the Organization of Repair
            in Conversation." *Language* 53: 361–82.
Searle, John
    1969   *Speech Acts*. Cambridge: Cambridge University Press.
Shore, Bradd
    1982   *Sala'ilua: A Samoan Mystery*. New York: Columbia University
            Press.
Silverstein, Michael
    1976   "Shifters, Linguistic Categories and Cultural Description." In K.
            Basso and H. Selby, eds., *Meaning in Anthropology*. Albuquerque:
            University of New Mexico Press.
Strathern, Andrew
    1971   *The Rope of Moka*. Cambridge: Cambridge University Press.
    1975a   "Why Is Shame on the Skin?" *Ethnology* 14: 347–56.
    1975b   "Veiled Speech in Mount Hagen." In M. Bloch, ed.
    1979a   "'It's His Affair': A Note on the Individual and the Group in New
            Guinea Highlands Societies." *Canberra Anthropology* 2.
    1979b   "Gender, Ideology, and Money in Mount Hagen." *Man* 14.

Strathern, A., and M. Strathern
    1968   "Marsupials and Magic." In E. Leach, ed., *Dialectic in Practical Religion*. Cambridge: Cambridge University Press.
    1971   *Self-Decoration in Mount Hagen*. London: Duckworth.
Strathern, Marilyn
    1972   *Women in Between*. London: Seminar Press.
    1979   "The Self in Self-Decorating." *Oceania* 49: 241 – 57.
Swift, Jonathan
    1970   *Gulliver's Travels*. Edited by Robert Greenberg. New York: W. W. Norton & Co.
Szwed, John
    1966   "Gossip, Drinking, and Social Control: Consensus and Communication in a Newfoundland Parish." *Ethnology* 5: 434 – 41.
Tambiah, S. J.
    1968   "The Magical Power of Words." *Man* 3: 175 – 206.
    1973   "Form and Meaning of Magical Acts: A Point of View." In R. Horton and R. Finnegan, eds., *Modes of Thought*. London: Faber & Faber.
Thompson, E. P.
    1975   *Whigs and Hunters*. London: Allen Lane.
Thurman, R.
    1975   "Chauve Medical Verbs." *Anthropological Linguistics* 17: 342 – 52.
Tsing, Anna Lowenhaupt
    n.d.   "The Voice of History: A Rhetoric of Centers in a Religion of the Periphery" (MS).
Tuitele, M., M. Sapolu, and J. Kneubuhl
    1978   *La Tatou Gagana. Tusi muamua*. Vol. 1. *Our Language*. Pago-Pago Bilingual/Bicultural Education Project of American Samoa.
Turnbull, Colin
    1961   *The Forest People*. New York: Simon & Schuster.
Turner, Terence
    1977   "Narrative Structure and Mythopoesis: A Critique and Reformulation of Structuralist Concepts of Myth, Narrative, and Poetics." *Arethusa* 10 : 103 – 63.
    1978   "The Kayapo of Central Brazil." In A. Sutherland, ed., *Face Values*. London: BBC.
    1979   "The Ge and Bororo Societies as Dialectical Systems: A General Model." In D. Maybury-Lewis, ed., *Dialectical Societies*. Cambridge: Harvard University Press.
    1980   "Anthropology and the Politics of Indigenous Peoples' Struggles." *Cambridge Anthropology* (Winter).
Turner, Victor
    1967   *The Forest of Symbols*. Ithaca: Cornell University Press.
    1974   *Dramas, Fields, and Metaphors*. Ithaca: Cornell University Press.

Wagner, Roy
    1978   *Lethal Speech: Daribi Myth as Symbolic Obviation.* Ithaca: Cornell University Press.
Weiner, Annette B.
    1976   *Women of Value, Men of Renown: New Perspectives in Trobriand Exchange.* Austin: University of Texas Press.
    1978   "The Reproductive Model in Trobriand Society." *Mankind* 11 : 175 – 86.
    1982a   "Plus Precieux que l'or: Relations et Échanges entre Hommes et Femmes dans les Sociétés d'Oceanie." *Annales* 34 : 222 – 45.
    1982b   "Ten Years in the Life of an Island: The Anthropology of Development Policies in the Trobriands." *Biksmaus* 3 : 64 – 75.
    1983a   "A World of Made Is Not a World of Born: Doing Kula in Kiriwina." In E. Leach and J. Leach, eds., *New Perspectives on the Kula.* Cambridge: Cambridge University Press.
    1983b   "Sexuality among the Anthropologists, Reproduction among the Informants." *Social Analysis* 40.
Williams, Raymond
    1977   Marxism and Literature. Oxford: Oxford University Press.
Wilson, Peter
    1974   "The Filcher of Good Names: An Enquiry into Anthropology and Gossip." *Man* 9 : 93 – 102.
Woodburn, James
    1979   "Minimal Politics." In P. Cohen and W. Shack, eds., *Politics and Leadership: A Comparative Perspective.* Oxford: Oxford University Press.
Young, Michael
    1971   *Fighting with Food: Leadership, Values, and Social Control in a Massim Society.* Cambridge: Cambridge University Press.
Young, R.
    1968   "Words under a Bushel." *Practical Anthropology* 15 : 213 – 16.

Index

Abrahams, R., 81
Abrams, M., 50
Acciaioli, G., 67
Adriani, N., 36
Albert, E., 81
Allegory, 17, 108–127
Ambiguity, 14, 18, 50, 60, 64, 88–89, 166, 171–172
Anderson, B., 160
Arena, 5, 11, 14, 16, 24
Aristotle, 199
Arno, A., 22, 26, 83
Audience, 18, 40, 61–62, 76–80
Aufenanger, H., 109
Autonomy, 2, 11–18, 21, 28, 34, 44, 84, 101–107, 123–213
Azande, 167, 176, 181

Bantu, 68
Baruya, 192
Basso, K., 175
Bateson, G., 17, 207–208, 218, 240
Bauman, R., 83, 190, 218, 235–237, 240–241
Beck, B., 127
Becker, A., 190–191
Beidelman, T., 170, 181, 190
Benabena, 109
Bernstein, B., 8
Black, P., 25
Bloch, J., 65–66
Bloch, M., 2, 4, 8, 10–11, 18–19, 24–25, 34, 58, 65–66, 84–90, 97–98, 101, 107, 164, 177, 244, 264
Blom, J.–P., 166
Borker, R., 7, 14, 29
Bourdieu, P., 7
Brash, E., 109
Brennan, P., 109
Brock, L., 106
Brown, Paula, 89
Brown, Penny, 84

Brown, R., 189
Buchbinder, G., 89
Burke, K., 165
Burundi, 81

Cavell, S., 6
Chambri, 20, 173, 192–213
Chung, S., 228
Clark, B., 28
Clastres, P., 9
Cohesion, 115–117
Cohn, B., 81
Coleman, G., 106
Collier, J., 3–4, 26, 35
Comaroff, J., 18
Conley, J., 81
Context, 2, 7–11, 15–28, 35, 40–41, 48, 51, 83, 87–90, 99–106, 111, 115, 138, 179, 187, 194, 217–218, 246, 251–253, 263–265
Cook, K., 228
Crocker, J., 16, 198

Dobu, 190
Dominance, 4, 10, 20–28, 60
Douglas, M., 61, 181
Duncan, S., 223
Dundes, A., 166
Egalitarian, 2, 5, 11–14, 19–21, 25, 28, 31–127, 157, 263
Empson, W., 175, 184
Enga, 109
Evans-Pritchard, E., 166–167, 175, 181, 189
Evens, T., 7

Fajans, J., 67
Ferguson, C., 84
Fernandez, J., 177
Fiji, 25–27
Fiji Indians, 11, 69–84
Finegan, E., 240, 242
Firth, R., 64, 231

Fisher, L., 70
Fono, 24–25, 217–242
Formal(ization), 2, 8 – 11, 18, 27 – 28, 34, 58, 86–90, 97–98, 102–106, 116, 166, 221, 244, 249, 251–259, 264
Fortune, R., 212
Foster, G., 73
Frake, C., 5, 14, 218, 229
Frame, 24, 217, 236–237
Freeman, D., 219, 241–242
Fried, M., 3, 5
Friedrich, P., 184
Function, 2–3, 6, 8–9, 11, 17, 28, 58, 76, 218
Furth, W., 83

Garfinkel, H., 7, 18
Geertz, C., 6, 33, 197, 205
Gell, A., 173
Gender relations, 4, 21–29, 85–107
Genre, 9, 13, 24 – 27, 71, 110 – 112, 131, 139, 218, 247, 265
Gibbs, J., 81
Giddens, A., 7, 10, 29, 34, 61
Gilsenan, M., 165
Givón, T., 228
Godelier, M., 193
Goffman, E., 7, 164, 172, 240–246, 257, 264
Goodenough Island, 190
Goody, E., 80
Goody, J., 81
Gossen, G., 70
Grice, H., 29
Grimes, J., 109, 116–117
Gumperz, J., 7, 166, 169, 190

Ha'a ("oratorical allegory"), 108–127
Hadza, 12
Halliday, M., 115–116
Hallpike, C., 109
Harding, S., 3
Hawkes, T., 9
Heider, K., 67
Hierarchy, 2, 5, 22, 25–28, 34–35, 87–88, 97, 215–265
Hindi, 71, 76–77, 84
Howe, J., 177
Huntsman, J., 81
Hymes, D., 1, 7, 190, 222

Ilongot, 14, 17–18, 26, 60, 88, 131–160
Indirection, 2, 17 – 18, 35, 41 – 42, 54, 58, 64, 69 – 71, 76 – 79, 82, 87 – 89, 108 – 110, 126, 147–148, 153–156
Irvine, J., 9, 26, 59, 82, 98, 102, 105–106, 221

Jacobs, M., 67
Jakobson, R., 9, 15, 26, 29, 227
Jameson, F., 184
Java, 191
Jayawardena, C., 84
Jefferson, G., 223, 230, 240–241

Kalmar, I., 127
Kapferer, B., 6, 7
Kava, 220–221, 224–265
Keenan, E., 9, 81, 88, 177
Keesing, F., 241
Keesing, M., 241
Kildea, G., 179, 190
Kirschner, S., 67
Kiyori ("wrapped words"), 12, 33–68
Kneubuhl, J., 228
Korn, F., 212
Kruyt, A., 36, 41, 67
Kuper, A., 3, 86, 97

Lasswell, H., 3
Lāuga, 24–26, 217–242
Leach, J., 166, 179, 190
Leacock, E., 35
Lee, R., 35
LeRoy, J., 127
Levinson, S., 84
Lévi–Strauss, C., 84
Levy, R., 190
Liget ("energy, passion, anger"), 147–159
Lind, E., 81
Lutkehaus, N., 22

Macaulay, R., 83
Mae Enga, 85, 192
Magic, 26, 161–191
Malinowski, B., 181, 190
Maltz, D., 28
Managalase, 17, 108–127
Manam Island, 22
Mandali ("meeting"), 74, 76, 78

Maori, 192
Matai, 220, 224–225, 234–236
Mauala, F., 240
Mauala, S., 240
Mauss, M., 173, 192
Mbuti, 68
McCormack, C., 65
McFeat, T., 127
McKinley, R., 68
Mead, M., 217, 219, 225
Meggitt, M., 85, 89, 192, 209
Meillassoux, C., 3
Melpa, 166, 173, 176, 189, 191
Mendi, 11, 20–21, 85–107
Mensuat, 193, 195, 197–205, 208, 210, 212
Merina, 4, 9, 89–90
Merrill, M., 106
Metaphor, 15–16, 35–38, 46, 54, 60, 62–64,
    69–70, 78, 108–115, 123, 132, 135, 145–147,
    165, 175–179, 181–183, 208–209
Metonymy, 23, 175–177, 181–183
Millenarianism, 13, 37–38, 51–68
Milner, G., 224, 226, 240
Mitchell–Kernan, C., 166
Munn, N., 181

Nadel, S., 181
Nader, L., 81
Nobles, 243–265
Nuer, 167

O'Barr, W., 81
Ochs, E., 220, 228, 240
Orator, 22, 177, 219–222, 225–227, 233, 236
Oratory (speechmaking), 2, 9, 17–18, 22, 35,
    58, 60, 63, 76–79, 86, 93–95, 101–127, 131–
    160, 163, 217–242, 244, 252, 264–265
Özkök, B., 166

Padarath, R., 74
Paine, R., 34
Pancayat ("arbitration session"), 12, 69–84
Parbacan ("religious speech"), 12, 14, 69–84
Parkin, D., 18
Parlier, J., 127
Performance, 25, 28, 69, 82, 99, 235, 237, 265
Pintupi, 68
Platt, M., 81

Polynesia, 1, 2, 22, 27, 242
Private, 3, 28, 70, 80, 95–96, 169
Public, 3, 15, 17, 19, 24, 26–28, 70–74, 81–86,
    95–97, 101, 108, 163, 167–169, 174, 183, 186,
    190, 264
Purung ("oratory"), 60, 131–160

Quine, W., 189

Rappaport, R., 209–210
Read, K., 14, 87, 90
Richards, A., 3, 86, 97
Ricoeur, P., 41, 190
Rosaldo, R., 160
Rosman, A., 106
Rousseau, J., 5
Rubel, P., 106
Ryan, D'A., 106

Sacks, H., 190, 223, 240, 241
Sahlins, M., 1
Salmond, A., 18, 177
Samarin, W., 127
Samoa, 22, 24, 26, 217–242
Sapir, E., 6, 162
Sapir, J., 15, 175, 190
Sapolu, M., 228
Savelio, S., 240
Schegloff, E., 223, 240–241
Schieffelin, B., 81
Schieffelin, E., 83
Searle, J., 17
Seduction, 59, 175–179
Scfo, I., 240
Shamanism, 37–39, 45, 52, 55–56, 62–68
Sherzer, 190, 218
Shore, B., 217, 219, 228, 240–241
Silverstein, M., 6
Social reproduction, 4, 7, 10–11, 19–23, 27,
    60, 90
Starker, K., 212
Strathern, A., 14–15, 21, 87–89, 103, 167,
    173–177, 189, 191, 209
Strathern, M., 85, 89, 105, 166–167, 173, 191
Swift, J., 161
Szwed, J., 166

Talanoa ("idle talk"), 70, 245–265
Talanoaga, 217–242

Tambiah, S., 181–182
Taude, 109
Thompson, E., 104
Thurman, R., 115
Tino, T., 240
Tonga, 25, 27, 243–265
Trobriands (Kiriwina), 17, 161–191
Tropes, 15–16, 175–180
Tsing, A., 67, 68
Tswana, 23
Tuitele, M., 228
Turnbull, C., 68
Turner, T., 4, 26, 66–67

Turner, V., 193–218

Veni, L., 240

Wagner, R., 127
Wana, 4, 11–13, 33–68
Williams, R., 5, 34
Wilson, P., 166
Wolof, 26
Woodburn, J., 12

Yakan, 229
Young, M., 190
Young, R., 109